For

Virginia and Bob Hickey,
with love and
appreciation of two fine friends.
Margaret Bancroft.

Christmas 1958.

THE *Least Petrel* AT CAPE SAN LÚCAS

LOWER CALIFORNIA: A CRUISE

THE FLIGHT OF THE
LEAST PETREL

WRITTEN ON BOARD
BY
GRIFFING BANCROFT

WITH 46 ILLUSTRATIONS AND A MAP

G. P. PUTNAM'S SONS
NEW YORK AND LONDON
1932

Made in the United States of America

DEDICATED TO
THE PARTNER

CONTENTS

v

CONTENTS

CONTENTS

ILLUSTRATIONS

ILLUSTRATIONS

x

ILLUSTRATIONS

xi

THE FLIGHT OF THE *LEAST PETREL*

THE FLIGHT OF THE *LEAST PETREL*

CHAPTER I

THE MISSION OF THE *Least Petrel*

A MILLION Americans have crossed the line at Tijuana. For years long lines of automobiles, converging at San Ysidro Gate, have mingled with the human freight of great grey busses and special trains. With one accord visitors swarm across the river bridge to swell the milling crowds of Old Town, to overflow eastward to Agua Caliente and the stands of the Jockey Club, or to spread south along the ocean beaches. On a summer Sunday the shores of Rosarito and Descanso Bay are black with parked automobiles. Machines, a crawling ant army, filtering past resorts, road houses, and camps, are drawn by thousands as far as Ensenada. More people still, ten times as many, throng the environs of the Hot Springs and an even greater number remain to play in Old Town. Every city of our country, every township and crossroad, contributes to this horde. As these people return to their homes they broadcast tales and descriptions of Lower California, and so effectively have they done their work that this edge of the Peninsula has become one of the most widely advertised spots in the world.

A million Americans have talked of Mexico, have told of being in Mexico, without, in thought or in fact, having

3

stepped beyond the carnival strip that has been built and dedicated, not to the expressing of a foreign country, but to the fulfilling of Anglo-Saxon desires. The visitors have bought souvenirs and mailed postcards and, above all, have revelled in escape from nationalistic paternalism. They have been satisfied; they are amusement-seekers on a holiday, not sightseers studying a new land. Engrossed with trivialities they have devoted scarcely a thought to what lies beyond the nearest of the brush-covered ridges hemming their horizon, but when they return to their own firesides and give the chosen circle of friends the story of their travels it is Mexico itself they have seen, not a play-box.

The hills to the south are not drop curtains; they do not mark the end. Something lies beyond, and that something is a region of unusual interest. That we, almost without exception, are ignorant of its character is not to its discredit; the reflection is less upon the Southland than upon America. That Lower California is primitive and difficult of access may be a misfortune but certainly is not an excuse for ignoring and discrediting its attractions. On the contrary we owe it to ourselves to become acquainted with our neighbor, especially since the Peninsula in its own right as well as because of juxtaposition repays careful investigation. The territory has a charm compared with which the border sights are crudely artificial and meaningless. The lure of Northwestern Mexico calls and calls again to those who have come under the spell and we, the Partner and I, are among the most enslaved of victims. Our enthusiasm is more than passive; it urges us to protest against the smug complacency which, without the slightest familiarity with the delectable country, discusses and dismisses Baja California.

Our knowledge of the land and its people ripened under peculiarly favorable circumstances. For the past ten years I have been making an intensive study of its ornithology and on nearly all my trips the Partner has been my companion. We have camped in its mountains, she and I, we have packed across the Peninsula and driven most of its length, we have ridden above it in aëroplanes and gone down to its waters in boats, not once but many times. The places to which we have wandered, the routes we have selected, the contacts we have made, have been determined solely by the exigencies of our work. As a result we have obtained, I feel sure, a deeper understanding and a less distorted perspective than would have come from conscious study.

We are about to climax our experiences with a circling cruise. Down one side of the Peninsula and up the other, and the islands in the fabled Sea of Cortéz! No children with Christmas in the offing could have undergone greater paroxysms of anticipation, preparation, discussion. A combination of dreams to which no grown-up is entitled and prosaic considerations rigidly circumscribed by experience. For we have bought the *Least Petrel,* the Partner and I, and Jason is in search of the Golden Fleece.

The story of the trip is written to introduce a country that to us is a personal friend. It is hoped that we may enable others to visualize this little-known corner which in all probability they will never visit. The objective is to give an accurate portrayal, but all the while there hovers in the background another and a more idealistic goal. Shall I confess the secret ambition that the reader will over-reach the ideas I relay, revert to the facts themselves, and arrive at the identical opinions which would have been his had he been with us aboard the *Least Petrel?*

No two persons, making our journey, would obtain identical or even approximately similar impressions; reactions in Lower California, dependent on mood and temperament, are the sport of caprice. Of course I have my own series of beliefs but I feel no desire to urge their general

5

acceptance. There are no doctrines which I advocate nor have I even a wish to influence the reader's judgment. I am not trying to prove that the Territory is good, or bad, that it is a hopeless desert, or a neglected garden, that it is a land of marvels, or contains only commonplaces, that it is a thing of beauty, or of ugliness, that its people are progressive, or backward. I shall tell what we saw and did and thought, but I will not apply the yardstick. My rôle is interpretative, not argumentative, not apologetic.

To show Lower California as we will see it means the telling of the story of our trip, for it is as a narrative that the country comes to us. If I am to draw a picture I will be satisfied only with one so accurate that unqualified reliance may be placed upon it. I demand of myself primarily the painstaking exactness of statement sought for in technical papers. But to give a portrayal that is really true necessitates something more; however conscientiously written a catalogue will not suffice. There must be selection and balance and above all avoidance of the untruths born of suppression or confusion. The finished work must be complete, it must be clear, and it must reflect the spirit of its subject matter.

There are three or four ports which, in former years, I visited in other boats and to which we will not return. To these, because my major purpose is paramount, I will take the *Least Petrel* in order to make the picture complete. Owing to the seasonal demands of our work there will be a few zigzags in our line of travel and these I will eliminate. Preference is given to geographical over chronological sequence because otherwise my photograph would not be clear. I will take liberty with the personnel of the party, dropping names and introducing two fictitious characters. Without the men I have imagined the portrait would not depict the real personality of the country. With these minor exceptions the story will not vary in any detail from the literal facts. Obviously the narrative and the picture cannot both be categorically exact and so, in the matter of minor mechanics, I give preference to the latter.

So much for prosaic considerations. If I am a scientist it is because I cannot be a poet. If I work and study in Lower California I am deferring to some inheritance which demands that I do more with my opportunities than relax and enjoy myself. And if the last few paragraphs too strongly suggest a textbook it is because they reflect my sense of duty rather than my mood. I rebel at having to be so serious when we are about to embark on the greatest picnic of our lives.

CHAPTER II

CAME at last the seventeenth of February, the long-awaited sailing date. Early in the morning, for we could take no chances on official papers, we snatched time from the details of preparation to run down to Tijuana. The day was pleasantly warm and sunny, a precursor of spring and quite in keeping with our spirits. Even the wild flowers by the roadside were whispering that this drive was not one of the preliminaries, that it was the actual start of the voyage.

For sixteen miles the road took us through surroundings typical of Southern California, bungalows in generous grounds, filling stations bordering overflowing highways, brush-covered hills seen flickering through rows of palms or eucalypti, orderly citrus groves smothering country homes. There were the lesser concomitants—a golf course, a dairy, a rural store, a news stand, a railroad, billboards, overhead wires, piped water—a thousand commonplaces of no apparent interest. Yet not one of these but held for us a special significance because, before the day was over, all would have ceased to be parts of our environment.

Through Chula Vista and Palm City and Nestor until we pick up the Tia Juana Valley and follow its dry river-bed to San Ysidro Gate. Out in unbroken sunshine lies a fuzzy hill flecked with brown bushes and tawny stones and crowned with shacks peering from embankments. Down its yellow slopes drops a gangling fence, a tall network of wires supported on spindles, quickly to disappear in the thickets

8

of a willow-bottom but, in passing, to block the little settlement and to stop the commerce of a nation. We manœuvre to the gap over the roadway, we fall into line, bumper to bumper, large men in khaki shunt us to little men in denim and we are across the border.

We are held in position on the flats, past the abandoned race track, over the sand-covered river and up the rise at the customs house. We have but a glimpse of the tourist thoroughfare for we break out of line, keeping north of the pillar, and run through shack-bordered back streets. Several blocks where there is no make-believe, where the workers and the misfits live, take us past the jail to the Municipal Palace. Stark and grey it is, two stories of windows unbroken with doors.

We pass through the portal, the postoffice to one side and the bureau for prostitutes on the other, and enter an unkempt patio. We walk down the eastern wing and pass a series of offices opening into the courtyard. We feel that we are behind the scenes, for in this workshop of the territorial heads of departments there is neither artificial atmosphere nor ostentatious display for the benefit of tourists. The furnishings run to type; they are small and cheap and of darkly stained wood free from ornamentation. The rather numerous office staffs include some women, not many, and the entire force seems devoted to the one pursuit of compiling and assembling carbon-copied documents.

Our first call is at the Department of Agricultura y Fomento where we are received formally but with real friendship. Our papers are handed to us at once; they had been signed and stamped and were ready because we had taken the precaution of filing our applications months in advance. Our relations with this office, which we had maintained for years, had taught us much about Mexican officialdom.

One of the principal difficulties in making such a trip

as ours had now been surmounted. We had the needed coöperation, but it had been secured only by a process which had involved much time and had brought us into contact with many people. At the outset we had had to convince the authorities that we were sincere and that the words "Scientific Research" were not being used as a cloak for exploitation or as a means of personal gain. This has not been easy. The constant bombardment from Americans who resort to almost any expedient to escape admittedly onerous regulations has had no tendency to lull the Mexicans' naturally suspicious mind. I remember that for two years I was looked upon in Sonora as a United States Army spy simply because the family name of my companion happened to be the same as that of a well-known officer.

Patience had brought a widening circle of officials who had confidence that we would deal fairly. Some technical papers published gave us a standing and demonstrated that our purposes were not inimical. The response showed the friendliness of these people as well as their pride and their intense nationalism. They were flattered by the thought that work such as we proposed was to be carried on in Mexico and they were eager to assist any undertaking that would reflect honor on their native land. Once they definitely feel that their country will gain in prestige their coöperation is gratifying and special privileges are granted with more liberality than is done on our side of the line. Characteristically, however, they are not content that their profit shall be wholly intangible. A condition is laid down that a fixed percentage of our hard-earned specimens shall be turned over to the Museo Nacional.

Incidental to the securing of our permits we obtained no little insight into the mechanics of Mexican bureaucracy. The government is far from ideal and yet farther, much farther, from the Machiavellian organization that so often has been pictured. The outstanding condition to be borne in mind is that down there an office is a very personal affair and the various *comandantes* are intensely jealous of their special prerogatives. It is true that we have always approached them from the personal, never from the business side, but just the same it is significant that, over quite a long period of time, we have found them invariably courteous and reliable and not one has asked a private reward for work done or for favors granted.

In addition to being allowed to collect specimens we required permits from the customs house, the inspector of immigration, the health department, and military headquarters. We were received with more formality than had been shown us on our first call, for our acquaintanceship in the other offices was not so intimate, but there was no lessening of the kindly way in which we were treated. In plain rooms, uncarpeted and uncurtained, with only charts and maps relieving the walls, in the presence of serious and well-meaning men not very different from your friends and mine, we received official sanction for our adventure. It is altogether proper that our thanks and appreciation be duly recorded. It is not feasible to make the many personal acknowledgments that are deserved but the name of Sr. Enrique Ferreira cannot be omitted: his whole-souled support alone has made possible my work in Mexico.

Work over we turned to relaxation and to the first sightseeing of the trip. We dropped into Cæsar's, brass rail and all, and ordered a couple of silver fizzes. It was early in the day and the place was not crowded, but we saw a few people we knew, as is usual at Cæsar's. Having nothing better to occupy my time I watched the playing of the slot machines. You drop in a coin, press a lever, and are paid if the spinning dial stops with the color of your choice under the arrow. There were some half dozen machines playable for differing stakes and by various systems and I had the curiosity to figure house percentages. These, of course, showed considerable range, but the smallest amount any owner took was eleven cents out of every dollar invested by the public. Unconscionable greed, yet charity compared with some of the other games.

Many racing books absorb up to and even more than half the bet, roulette gives the dealer five percent, chuck-a-luck seven and a half, and the popular game of twenty-one even more. Stud poker is no longer a fixture and faro has been abandoned, presumably because it offers such a small profit to the house. Craps is one of the favored pastimes and here a peculiar condition exists. Bets laid on the line are virtually even while the player against the field is at a disadvantage of twenty percent and the thoughtless who play other combinations wager dollar for dollar on numbers that should pay them up to two for one.

When it is remembered that Monte Carlo made her millions with but one green on the wheel and by taking less than three percent, the mercenary hoggishness of Tijuana becomes somewhat oppressive. The same spirit is shown at the bars, a ridiculous price being charged for drinks served in very small and very thick glasses. The avowed spirit of all the concessionaires seems to be to collect as much as the public will endure and to give in return as little as possible. I am afraid that my mental attitude, as I leaned against the bar, was not the proper one for my surroundings. I was under the spell of the long trip that lay ahead and I could not see the tinsel of Tijuana's stage setting nor feel the mesmerism of her ballyhoo. The sordid nakedness of the scaffolding showed through the props.

We went outdoors and joined the crowds on the main street. Why is this called Mexico? Surely not because of the acres of one-story wooden shacks whose inspiration, whose very boards, come from north of the line. Nor because of the half mile of low frame buildings that face a paved street lined solidly with automobiles, buildings whose en-

trances are wide enough to destroy privacy and whose
exteriors are a flamboyant mass of colored advertisements.
Surely not because of the traffic officer who successfully
imitates his American prototype nor because of the handful
of subdued soldiers on the hill. Nor can the answer be
found by studying the parade that passes endlessly in either
direction.

Most emphatically these people are not Mexicans; they
are home-loving pleasure-seeking Americans, your neighbors and mine. There are other elements, it is true, as there
would be anywhere. There are those who see here only
a reeking sink of iniquity and those to whom the Casino
is an ideal place for simple, even formal, entertainment.
There are youngsters lured by adventure, there are travellers
eager to see, there are tourists and memento hunters whose
aim is to boast that they have been in Mexico, there are
followers of the races and there are disciples of other forms
of gambling, and there are those who deliberately seek
debauchery. All can satisfy the purposes for which they
come, but only because they have brought their own country
with them.

Let us risk reiteration and make it clear that from the
new West Gate to the far end of the track the manage-
ment is American, the customers are Americans, and the
entertainment is determined by American wants. So when
preacher or editor thunders exorcisms against this cesspool
let it be remembered that it is the code of his own people
against which he is railing and that his sincerity would be
more obvious if upon them he squarely laid the blame.
Certainly neither the Mexicans themselves nor their friends
will assume responsibility, for if America thinks that
Tijuana is contaminating her children she should stop scolding and close her side of the border.

As a matter of fact, except that the tourist does not get
his money's worth, there is little to criticize. It so happens

that the American public sets certain standards and the sponsors of this mercantile undertaking are business men too clever to sanction vulgar displays that might drive away profitable customers. So we find that prostitution is permissible only when confined to back streets, that percentage girls are not popular, that drunkenness must be well controlled, that brawling will not be tolerated, while on the other hand inoffensive drinking and all forms of gambling are highly proper. Degeneracy is absolutely barred, cockpits, dog-baiting, bull-fighting and immoral shows are suppressed, but a fetish is made of horse-racing. On the whole everything is orderly, law-enforcement and policing are excellent, but there is nothing to suggest a foreign country.

The accusations so freely published against the morals of Tijuana are ridiculous and are made by people who do not understand the place. The games are not dishonest, for the public pays in percentage all it will stand and all that the most grasping can ask. Organized vice does not flourish simply because it would not be profitable and because, in this environment, it could not compete with the slums of American cities. Narcotics are not conspicuous, are not as easily obtained here as at home, and certainly are not featured. Private morals are not regarded as the concern of the public and are whatever those who come choose to make them. Chastity is not influenced one way or the other and the visitor, though he may become poorer, is otherwise the same man that he was when at home. Tijuana deals in masses, not in individuals.

Old Town is but a part of the extra-territorial strip that is encroaching down the coast and up the valley. The highway to Ensenada is dotted with road houses and saloons for tourists, clubs that cater to the growing demand for over-night accommodations, and camping sites for those who are drawn to the beaches. The spirit of Tijuana is not weakened as it spreads over the southern outskirts, though eastward at Agua Caliente, where money has been spent with a lavishness that is staggering, conditions are somewhat different. At the Hot Springs the machinery has been geared to a higher ratio.

As an American institution Agua Caliente leaves little to be desired. The hotel itself, the golf course, the swimming pool and the dining rooms in the casino compare favorably with the world's most fashionable watering-places and they are free from the objectionable mercenary atmosphere. On the other hand failure has followed every attempt to introduce the foreign tempo and it is the resultant discord that leaves the most unpleasant impressions. There is to be found an army of servitors dressed in clashing reds and yellows intended to convey Spanish associations, but the clothes are masquerades, not costumes. Nowhere are such garments worn; they reflect no period and no people and are meaningless in portrayal and over-gaudy in themselves. Stroll through the gardens and into the buildings. Where their utilitarianism appeals or their settings satisfy they are frankly American. Where local color is sought their failure has been no less signal than that of the counterfeit waiters. If no false attempts had been made Agua Caliente might have been beautiful, but the Greek mask does not take the place of realism.

Agua Caliente, though it may have failed to live up to its advertisements, has served the purposes of its promoters. It maintains an air, if not of refinement, at least of repression and good manners and it attracts the desired class of patronage in constantly increasing numbers. Its success definitely shows that it supplies what is wanted. But in spite of ambitious claims it is not, nor will it become, the Deauville of America. Contrasting the spirit of the two places it is noticeable that the resort in France draws its clientèle through an appeal to more nearly normal interests. The social life of the beach and of the hotels is paramount;

other diversions are incidental. Agua Caliente offers much to the resident guests, its golf course is superb, its swimming pool marvellous, its gardens and cottages delectable, and yet there is no general acceptance of its advantages, no responsive influx of resident guests. Its customers are transients, the majority merely day-visitors, and the reason is not far to seek. The stigma of liquor and gambling. Those twins are not relegated to the comparative obscurity they merit, they are not accepted as minor matters of course, they have been glorified and extolled and in thought and deed have become the watchwords of the border.

The recording of these ideas is intended to supplement advertising rather than to serve as a criticism. American features have not been dwelt upon; my disregarding them does not imply that they do not deserve praise but simply that, being American, they are not properly a part of Lower California. And yet, apart from Agua Caliente, there is not much to praise, for the rest of the border is an inharmonious medley of gaudy extravagances and tawdry makeshifts. The track, with its concrete grandstand and club house represents reckless expenditure and cries that fact to high heaven. Between the Arch and the Foreign Club are scattered buildings, many not much more than painted barns. Where beauty has been attempted none has been attained, where it has not been attempted the results are hideous. The ensemble is not interpretive, it is not accurate, and, being meaningless, is neither artistic nor picturesque.

Over all hangs the shadow of greed. Government, executive, operator. We did not linger long, the Partner and I. The *Least Petrel* was waiting, Lower California was beckoning; we had torn off the ugly wrapping and were about to examine the treasure.

CHAPTER III

THE *Least Petrel* FLUSHES

THERE is a little yacht club on the shore of San Diego Bay. At all but the lowest tides currents eddy about the veranda supports and the sound of gently moving water comes from beneath the hall. In its simple way the club house reflects the romance of the sea, for on quiet moonlit evenings wavelets lisp stories of adventure passed from the big brothers of the main. Such was this mid-February night. The air was warm and motionless and did not break the glistening sheet of silver across which star-beams traced reflected ribbons of light out into the unknown darkness.

We who so recently had been sightseers in predatory Tijuana were now receiving at an informal leave-taking. At the shore end of the spidery pier was music and dancing for those who had come to wish bon voyage to the various members of our party. This was no gathering of a clique; friendship and interest alone had drawn these people together. Junior Leaguers were present in numbers, as were professional men and business executives. There was an engineer from whom a greasy mass of iron withheld no secrets and there were officers steeped in the lore of the open sea. Mexican officials rubbed shoulders with scientists, collectors, and museum curators. The *Least Petrel* was at home to her friends.

She lay at the end of the club float, her dim hull tracing a shadowy outline against the uncertain lights of the night. Her fifty feet seemed hardly adequate for the task that lay before her, sturdy though she was and broad of beam. Until

17

recently she had been a fishing boat—but why go into the lady's past? The gear of her trade had been stripped from her deck and had been replaced with a flat roofed cabin that looked for all the world like a frontiersman's shack. She was a queer looking craft, a veritable sea-going houseboat. She had already brought many a supercilious smile to the faces of the fisher folk and we knew that in days to come speed-boat racers would wave patronizingly as they overtook her and yachtsmen, if they deigned to notice her at all, would wonder what pleasures could be had in quarters so limited or with arrangements so primitive.

And yet we introduced the *Least Petrel* with no apologies. Indeed, as we conducted the tours of inspection, our sentiments were wholly of pride. We were as susceptible to praise and as impatient of criticism as any fond parent. Slow? Well, eight knots an hour is hardly speed nor do we believe that two hundred miles a day would appeal to a Lindbergh, but a happy fortnight passes quickly and three thousand miles is a long way from home. Comforts? Perhaps the thoughts of our visitors turned to the homes they had left or to the near-by club craft tugging at anchor. My contrasts were with the peon huts and makeshift boats and burro trains to which, more than once, we had been driven by the urge to wander in primitive Mexico.

The Partner was game. Neither veiled patronizing nor downright sympathy abated by one iota her excitement and enthusiasm. She tried to make it clear to her friends, though I suspect with indifferent success, that ours was not a yachting cruise but purely a marine camping trip. To relays of visitors she showed the "dormitory"—a room six feet by seven in which four men were to work and sleep. She opened the door of our "bridal suite" with its superimposed twin beds and its floor area of two square yards. The galley was her pride, a real doll kitchen resplendent with new aluminum ware and so tiny that she had been limited in her selection of cook to applicants barely five feet in height.

The men who came aboard were more interested in the "cabin" with its desk and gun rack, its radio and its combined dining and work table. They wondered how the nine of us could ever assemble and they pictured us sitting theatre-like in compact rows. They inspected the hold, which contained practically everything we would require for the ensuing five months. They peered into the glory-hole and intimated that there was at least one of the crew who would have to diet before he could hope to squeeze down the steps. And they examined the pilot house in which Captain, packed among instruments and charts and wheels, was taking leave of his family.

The mass reaction of our guests was dazed incredulity. They were practical people, prosaic, and not carried away by the chimeras of rainbow chasing. Not more than three of the women, at the most, could understand why the Partner would do such a thing, would give up the comforts, to them the necessities, of everyday existence and exchange conventional social life for impossible months of horror. Most of the men, I'm afraid, looked upon my hobby as evidence of mental weakness and felt a superior pity for anyone who would so waste his time. Hardly a soul who really expected that we would ever return. Somewhere or somehow only disaster lay ahead and the less a person knew of things nautical the more certain was he that the *Least Petrel* would founder in distant, unknown waters.

I doubt if any of us has a clear recollection of those two hectic hours. The Partner, I remember, appeared on the dance floor in one of her shorts costumes, an outfit that amused her friends, would shock Mexico, and was destined to afford a maximum of comfort for the entire trip. For my part I was proud of the *Least Petrel* and so happy in her ownership that I expressed myself in no uncertain terms. What would she have meant to Jason or to Lief the Lucky? Had Columbus sailed in her he could have been in Spain again in thirty days, and then what would have been her position in history? As she stands, or rather floats, she could have decided the Battle of Salamis either way, and with a bit of dolling could have accounted for the combined opposing fleets. Who are we to cherish her the less because she has been denied opportunity?

Ten o'clock is coming and all foolish banter must cease. The engine is idling, the facetious search for stowaways is ended, hawsers are being cast off, and we travellers are climbing aboard, running out on our guests. Twenty years of hoping and scheming, of planning and of waiting for the breaks, have finally borne fruit. The *Least Petrel* is spreading her wings, she is moving, her flight has begun.

CHAPTER IV

LOS CORONADOS ISLANDS

As we shoved clear of the dock we found ourselves in a globe of lights—above us and below and on every side, large and small, moving and still, blue and white and yellow and red and green. They threw weird shadows over the fleet of anchored yachts, they made ghosts of the crowd on the wharf, they danced to the music floating from the club's twinkling windows and they rode overhead on the ends of searchlight beams, dancing from cloud to cloud. They dotted and dashed from yardarms and they marked the ever-receding pendulum swing of the ferry. They passed on moving ships, from trains and automobiles, they confused the skyline, and they performed kaleidoscopic marvels with our erratic perspective.

On any other night they would have been nothing but the ordinary lights of the harbor and even now, I suspect, that's all they were to Captain. Phlegmatic he stood at the wheel, passing this to port and that to starboard with the indifference one of us might have felt in driving his car down town. A well set up man in his early forties, broad and stocky and strong, with chiselled features and weather-beaten face, ex-fisherman, ex-whaler, ex-tugboat mate, he had for thirty years sailed and steamed the seven seas in every type of craft, and for him I had sympathy. Our great adventure was everyday routine, our romance another job.

When detail began to emerge from chaos I found myself sitting with the Partner on the hatch of the glory-hole. From the galley I could hear Juan rattling his dishes and

Charley, in the engine room, checking the oil feed. The others were aft in their cabin preparing for the night, but for me the element of time did not exist. We seemed to be moving with greyhound speed, to be racing inexorably down the channel.

We flashed past green and dull red buoy lights, the hum of industry to starboard and to port the stateliness of man-o'-war row. An incandescent liner, orient bound, loomed among the darting shore-boats and against the glamour of aërial night practice on North Island. Perhaps we were nothing but another old fisherman chugging down the bay, but I don't want to believe that and I won't. Our magic carpet was passing through a fairyland which marked the end of everything modern and beyond which lay untold centuries of the past.

It was to be borne upon us that we were dropping away from desiderata greater even than physical comforts and mechanical wonders. We had passed Ballast Point and were entering the dimmer waters between Point Loma and the jetty when, unexpectedly, we were hailed from a yacht. As she drew abeam we flooded her with our electric torches. Her decks swarmed with the merrymakers we had last seen on the club float. They laughed and they cheered as they circled across our bows. Then came reaction. The homeward turning of their craft broke our last contact with concentrated civilization.

We were alone on the ocean. All other boats had melted into the surrounding void. Point Loma's light was falling astern and the mournful sighing of the whistling buoy was coming from our beam. Father Neptune's slumber was not disturbed by insignificant us, so our furrow pointed unwavering to the first anchorage. The pyrotechnic display in San Diego Bay had lessened to a distant curtain, small and soft and diffused by haze. To port were still the lights of Coronado Beach and, beyond, isolated dots from the border resorts. Forward the night was broken by brighter openings or darker masses that are now what they were in the days of Cæsar or Homer or Adam. Man is an unnoted visitor; no longer either conqueror or vandal.

We were alone on the ocean—absolutely, not comparatively. All traffic had turned at the end of the kelp beds and now there remained not so much as one of the occasional lobstermen making the night run to Ensenada. No fish or bird broke our solitude nor, for half a circle, any light of earthly source. We were being introduced to the isolation which, in the days to come, would be complete. We were adventurers who still had but a step to take to be back in reality but who, were that step not taken soon, would have forgone the opportunity.

An hour and we were in the shadow of South Island. The blurred peaks that any clear day can be seen from the higher levels of San Diego resolve themselves, on close approach, into a group of two larger and two smaller islands and a number of isolated rocks. They rise abruptly from the water in a series of cliffs and ledges and, on all sides, sink precipitously to tremendous depths. There are no beaches, not even gravel bars, to aid them in their stand against the pounding surf. There are neither trees nor, except for mice, mammal life, nor minerals of value on these dreary monuments of economic waste; they are without water or resources and although many futile attempts have been made to utilize them, are uninhabited and abandoned. So, as we ended our short run by dropping anchor in the cove, there was neither welcome nor protest against our intrusion.

We were up in the morning and had started the day before the sun was high enough to peer into the anchorage. Our first move was to run over to North Island. The early hours are those most apt to be free from troublesome wind and conditions on Los Coronados demand that every advantage be taken of breaks in the weather. So we left the sheltered cove and once more were on the open ocean. Its surface was glassy but not quite level, for a long ground-swell was rolling from the south, lifting and dropping the floating seaweed and rocking lullabies to occasional sleeping water-birds.

We chugged along the panorama of solitude for half an hour, until we were almost upon the rocks of North Island. The slopes of that wedge run under water for a long way before they level off and we were uncomfortably near the rocks before I could find any bottom with the lead. As soon as it touched we dropped the anchor, which ran out all our chain and most of our hawser. Captain tested the job and was dubiously uncertain, but Charley shut off the engine, the skiff was launched, and we were prepared for our first day's work.

Captain rowed us ashore, three at a time. Delicacy was required as we approached the rocks, for the vertical motion of the water was greater than was apparent and timing the swell was puzzling. But conditions were propitious and Captain was skillful; he held us near but not quite against a perpendicular ledge until one after another we made the jump and six of us were on the island. Besides the Partner and myself there was my assistant Tony—J. Elton Green —Mr. Frederick S. Rogers, archæologist and photographer, and two collectors representing eastern museums. We were on familiar territory and needed to waste no time in finding bearings, so we climbed over the tidal rocks to the foot of the zigzag trail.

North Island has an official height of four hundred and sixty-two feet but on this first day, with everyone soft and unused to walking, it seemed several miles to the top. We crawled upward on dirt lying at a one to one slope, held in place only by a scant growth of iceplant and scattered, stunted sage. There were traces of last season's

24

nests where a great colony of Western Gulls had raised young along either side of the path, but we were now far too early in the year to find breeding birds. Near the crest, where we eventually arrived after much panting and puffing, the soil becomes softer and here formerly were the burrows of a large colony of Cassin Auklets. One of our objectives was to ascertain whether or not the birds were holding their own on the island. The only nesting holes we found were old and so we were reluctantly forced to the conclusion that the auklets have disappeared from Los Coronados.

Once the summit was attained our physical discomforts were over; an easy trail ran in either direction along the top of the ridge. We were not too proud to rest, and the view would have been well worth the pause even had we been hurried. The west side of the island has not fared well in its struggle with the elements and has been battered and worn into an almost perpendicular cliff broken with potholes and a number of irregular slides. Almost at our feet, so far below that I have seen people throw themselves flat at sheer terror from looking down, stretched the white line of breakers eating away, with a patience that does not reckon centuries, at the base of this interloper. We could hear the combers roar and grind and we knew that, as long as we cared to watch, we would see them strike with little effect, slowly subside to position, then strike and strike again in everlasting repetition.

To the east, but not so immediately underneath, lay the *Least Petrel* in a sea that from this height seemed frozen. Behind were two small islands, each of which, singularly bears the name of Middle Island. They are much alike, steep pinnacles of rock with just enough soil to support scattered growths of brush. Over them loomed South Island and six miles beyond was the Point of Rocks and Lower California's coast.

We moved north along the path on the saddle and found ourselves at the point of a bluff which broke on three sides abruptly to the surf. It was a piece of cruel landscape, battered and eroded and unstable. There were blow-holes where sand-carrying wind had bested the less resistant rocks, there were scars marking the downfall of huge blocks, there were treacherous ledges and there were ridges that would not endure—a quivering, naked precipice suffering with open sores from the petty and remorseless torture of its enemies.

Retracing our steps and following the crest trail we passed edges where a falling body will roll down either slope unchecked till it splashes into the water. Near its southern end the contours of the island soften perceptibly and it is here, later in the season, that great colonies of sea-birds will congregate to breed. These last weeks of winter, however, showed only Brown Pelicans taking active interest in nesting and they had done little more than appropriate sites. These they would guard and hold against all comers until the time arrived to build and lay.

We found more signs of auklets but still none that were recent. We had to content ourselves with this superficial survey, for we could spare this archipelago but one day and time was pressing. We went aboard the *Least Petrel* again and moved her to the more northerly Middle Island. A great boulder of rock this, but near its centre is a crater-like basin, some hundred yards across, filled with soft earth. Here grows brush that is home to sparrow and finch and among its roots are the burrows of Socorro Petrels. To these holes the owners, and the claim-jumping Black Petrels as well, will return when summer is well under way.

On our Middle Island, by climbing over the rocks to the southern tip, we found a hundred foot cave, one whose gravel bottom, well above the tide line, is eagerly sought by nesting Murrelets. There is a very similar hollow on the other Middle Island, one which, being under water, has been seized upon by a herd of sea lions. A phenomenon of special interest and, in times of storm, of grandeur, is the blow-hole. It is a V-shaped tunnel into which breakers crowd and, under pressure, squirt jets of foaming water as much as fifty feet into the air.

Soon after noon we reached the anchorage of the preceding night and now had opportunity to admire a beautiful little refuge. For half its circumference it is surrounded by sheer walls of unscalable rock polished by wind and sea. To the south the ridge is less hostile; there is even a trail that winds its way upwards over to Pirate Cave. The cove itself is a fairy pond so well sheltered that one can study marine growths and fish on its white, sanded bottom. It is relieved by an abutting pinnacle that once held the aërie of a guarding pair of Bald Eagles.

We made our way to the top of South Island along a rather easy trail that has been constructed for the convenience of visiting excursionists. We hunted in the grass and among the bushes for snakes, but, meeting with no success, devoted the rest of our time to collecting a small series of Song Sparrows. These birds illustrate one of the technical objectives of the expedition. They are endemic on Los Coronados Islands and have apparently bred there, without the introduction of mainland blood, over a very long period of time. During this geographical isolation either they, or the parent stock from which they sprang, have developed minute differentiations and it is from the study of these otherwise inconsequential variations that we attempt to read the history of the evolution of the birds.

South Island is six hundred and seventy-five feet high and about two miles long. Its eastern side averages steeper slopes than its western, but neither is as abrupt as those of North Island. The geology of the group presents many interesting questions concerning which there is no little difference of opinion among authorities. Biological evidence tends strongly to support the theory that Los Coronados Islands are affiliated much more closely with the Channel Group than with the adjacent mainland. In any event they are volcanic uplifts and their existence dates back over an indefinite period of time. Their avifaunal life is their most interesting feature, though they are a favored resort of deep-sea fishermen and day-time excursionists. Scenically they have little to offer and commercially nothing. Nevertheless they have a fascination and an appeal and everyone in our party regretted that we could not spare them more time. The fact that not one of us came aboard until after dark is eloquent of our regard.

CHAPTER V

AT some vague hour of the night there was the thump, thump of the cold engine starting, the vibration when it began to race, the rattle of heavy chains in the bow, and much conversation as new hands learned to weigh anchor. I tumbled out of my bunk for a last look at the cove in moonlight, at the unshaded blacks and eerie shadows and harsh shapes. A moment and we were in open water, in the lee of a mass that loomed black and forbidding above and carved a void in the star spotted sky. The staccato of the Diesel and the hiss of the wake echoed from shadows that threw back our voices in unnatural whispers.

I was in the pilot house keeping an unneeded lookout with Captain when we passed the point of the island and laid our course for Todos Santos. After that there was nothing to hold my attention, no boats to speak or dangers to avert, so I paid toll to the day's hard walking and turned in to sleep. I woke when the hook went down in Ensenada Bay.

We were flying American and Mexican flags as well as our club insignia and a yellow square inviting the quarantine officer to come aboard. Pending his arrival no one could go ashore so I called to Juan to start breakfast and asked the Partner to come topside and look at the town. Ensenada faces a little bay, an alluring half moon sweep that was dotted with small craft at anchor. Steep hills behind push the town almost to the shore and the setting promises intrigue and romance. But disappointments begin on the

29

waterfront. The beach shows too much wreckage that has not been repaired, too many accumulations that have not been salvaged, too frequent evidences of lethargy and discouragement. The stub of a pier, the skeleton of a boat, the vacant flour mill in the background, the incongruous frame buildings, all are redolent of old ambitions and frustrated hopes. The stage was set for great events; inertia has wasted the waiting years.

A skiff put out from shore bringing inspectors of customs and health and immigration. Three young men came aboard. Two were in white duck and wore official caps; the grey business suit of the other was conspicuous with holstered gun and a belt of loaded cartridges. The officials were ushered into the cabin and at once began to delve into our papers. These proved to be amply sufficient; from now on, however annoying the tediousness, examinations of documents were to be but matters of form. No inspections were made nor were we ever asked to account for anything in our heavy cargo.

Having entered it became necessary to clear, so I gathered the loose sheets and took them ashore to a broker. While he was working everyone in our party, except Juan, made a tour of the town, some to see new sights, some to renew old acquaintances.

The entrance to Ensenada, prosaic by water, by land is spectacular. The Tijuana highway comes swinging down from mountain grades and crosses the little valley that lies below the lighthouse. It works its way along a bench between the ocean and high half-vertical hills and it follows the narrowing passage until blocked by a massive cinder. A level trail scarcely wider than an automobile has been blasted from the face of the cliff and clings precariously between sea and sky as it circles the lava rock. At one end of the horizontal groove is a barren countryside without house or fence or tree; at the other is the tiny city.

ENSENADA

Ensenada is prematurely old. The town is spread in plain view at a somewhat lower level than the road and gives as a first impression a mass of unpainted frame buildings, a rectangular field three or four blocks in width by ten or twelve in length. None of the glamour of antiquity meets the eye; age is suggested rather by a need of paint and the absence of new construction. The few buildings that have character, the three-story frame directly across the plaza, for instance, tell of architecture of forty years ago and of lumber that has been exposed half a century. The wooden relics of other days prevail throughout, they overshadow the built-up section and spread to the fringes, to the sentinel box that marks the edge of town. The octroi is now deserted; Ensenada is challenging Tijuana for a share of the spoils and no longer throws obstacles in the path of the visitor.

I often wonder what became of the old man who was the last custodian of the shack. He stopped us one night, just after dark, and finding our tonneau packed with supplies gave us an homily on buying in San Diego instead of patronizing local stores. I handed him my documents, passports, and special permits. I doubt if he could read, for he held the sheets before his face and studied them with unmoving eyes, as one looks at a photograph rather than at a letter. He talked uninterruptedly for forty minutes, with us impatient to be on our way. And to what purpose? Our purchases had been made, he could not send us back nor override my authorization and refuse to let us pass. His was the old-time attitude toward the traveller and, being vested with a bit of authority, he was childishly determined to make a display.

The town begins with the triangular plaza dedicated to Hidalgo. An imposing statue of the liberator is flanked with wooden buildings and backed with remnants of the boom of the eighties. To understand Ensenada one need pick up her history from the days when a little pueblo

31

simultaneously became a territorial capital and the scene of a desperately serious attempt at English colonization, and then one must follow her misfortunes as the growing importance of Mexicali deprived her of political prominence and as economic conditions ruined and drove away her foreign settlers. The wave left in its wake high ceilings and bay windows and British cottages, unnecessary governmental quarters as well as too pretentious country places. In view of its present necessities Ensenada for a long time has been overbuilt, except in regard to lodgings, and the consequence, of course, is that old structures have been utilized and little has been done to add or replace. The people have adapted themselves to buildings far more than they have adapted buildings to needs.

From the brokerage we wandered across the plaza and up the main street to find that if Ensenada has a past she also has a present. A train of twenty-odd burros was coming towards us, each little beast loaded to his ears with firewood piled high on his back. The woodcutters were picturesque, but axes, water-casks, and canvas strips disclosed lives of hardship. The drovers talked to their charges, herded them, and even led a few, and finally brought them to rest where yesterday meets today—in front of a Standard Oil filling station.

We passed the Green Mill, several saloons, and a number of shops handling drugs, foods, and souvenirs. There were always autos on the street, much as at home, and there were the inevitable tourists on sidewalks and in stores. There were friendly officials who, from jefe to guard, always had a smiling welcome and a bit of interesting news. There was Sawday in the general store and Hussong in his saloon and Goldbaum the broker, whose knowledge of the Vizcaíno Desert dwarfs that of any other man. There was the Chinaman, whose meals had seemed sumptuous on our return from many a camping trip, and there was Wilson.

A MILLION AMERICANS HAVE CROSSED THE LINE AT TIJUANA

ENSENADA

THE NORTHWEST LITTORAL

ENSENADA

He and I have a common reminiscence that always amuses us, a holdover from bygone days and something that could never happen again. I had come up from the south after three days of driving a crippled car over impossible roads, and I was tired. I reached Wilson's garage after dark and it looked like home to me. I had scarcely begun to tell my troubles and to ask if my machine could be fixed so that I would be able to reach San Diego, before I became aware of an almost inaudible voice muttering over my shoulder. I wasn't interested in what this slovenly peon had to say and I told him so. He was persistent, so I turned my back. Still the murmur, until I snapped that I couldn't hear him and didn't want to. The monotone kept up even after I'd disclaimed any knowledge of Spanish, so I faced him and told him to shut up and get out. He shrugged his shoulders with a sort of hopeless look and shuffled away.

When I turned back to Wilson the mechanic was crawling out from under the car and taking from his mouth the cotton waste he had stuffed there to keep himself from laughing.

"Did you see that traffic wart at the intersection?" he asked.

"Wart?"

"Well, it's really just a stone."

"Man. I've seen a million stones in the road, all sizes and colors and shapes."

"Don't you even know who that man is who was talking to you?"

"I don't know and I don't care." I was tired.

"Well, he's a Mexican cop who was trying to arrest you for cutting the wart. I see he's given it up as a bad job."

Ensenada is more sophisticated now. It knows Americans better, their ways and shortcomings. It is offering attrac-

tions to tourists, supplying their demands and becoming
up to date. It is taking the step that is costing it the last
of its native charm, though, if truth be told, it is long
since it was a purely Mexican town. Its one-time commercial importance brought many outside contacts from
ships and sailors and its dream of glory broke other barriers
and ended provincial purity. Now that it has learned to be
dependent on the coming of northern wanderers it has
ceased to dislike the gringo and is studying artifices to keep
him entertained.

A past and a present. Bungalow courts, garages, and La
Mariposita; cafés, American bars, and the spinning wheel.
Streets where, if Northerners go, they do not stop. Stores
with no display windows, often with no signs, bars without mirrors or rails, hole-in-the-wall shops. Tourists in
knickers and soldiers in shoddy, yachtsmen in linen
and peons in manta, Mexicans in touring cars and Iowans
in Model T's, over-dressed week-enders, short-skirted natives, mantillas over bobbed-hair, Johnny Walker and
tequila.

Lazy, sleepy Ensenada. What will good roads and easy
access do to you? Today you offer recreation to the stranger
and a glimpse of Mexico to the friend. The tourist is
content—he thinks he is seeing Mexico. And the old-timer
also is content, for in the back room behind the bar or in
the closed office of the counting house the Ensenada that
was and the politics and prejudices that are come bubbling
to the surface. In your heart not at all Ensenada, and in
your customs very little when you are not on parade, have
you as yet fallen under the blight of the invasion. Today
you are simple and care-free, giving little nor asking much
—one wonders what you will be tomorrow.

CHAPTER VI

THE NORTHWEST CORNER

THERE has been established by biologists an area known as the San Diegan Faunal District. It runs coastwise south from Point Conception and spreads eastward until it is stopped by the mountains. Within that region nearly all forms of life are homogeneous and, to a large extent, differ from those of bordering zones. This simply means that the combined influences of rainfall, temperature, soil, geography, and altitude mark boundaries within which highly specialized individuals may spread and beyond which they will not prosper.

As is quite logical, the southern line of this area does not coincide with the international boundary. The Mexican extension of the San Diegan Faunal District can be traced to the farther limits of the watershed of San Vicente River and until that drainage is passed there are no material differences between the physical geographies of the two sides of the border. Disappointment is in store for the traveller who expects to find new conditions and environments within the first hundred miles.

If the reader who is familiar with Southern California could visualize that country as it was seventy-five years ago he would have a fairly accurate picture of the northwestern corner of the Lower California of today. Except for man-made improvements, cities and roads, farms and orchards and irrigating systems, railways and electricity, there are no outstanding differences. The streams are the same and the hills, the fields, and the climates. Below San Vicente a change does come, but it is an abrupt and sweeping demarcation whose approach has not been foreshadowed.

The littoral of the Mexican extension of the San Diegan District is nearly everywhere identified with sage. There are many species of cacti struggling for survival and competing for the favorable environments. Cholla is more widely distributed than the flat-leaved, and most numerous of all, though the least conspicuous, are the various echinocacti. On high benches along the shore, especially where the soil is sandy and fogs of regular occurrence, agave display their coarse flowers at the ends of ten-foot stalks. Of trees there are only sycamores; occasionally a few of these find free water in the gravel of river-beds. Grass is scanty and short lived. It comes with the first rains of winter and seres almost before spring has started. Seasonally a profusion of wild flowers color the open spaces, but their tenure of life can be computed in weeks.

A few miles inland oaks and cottonwoods begin to appear in the valleys, sumach and holly in the ravines, and willows and elders in the stream bottoms. On the mesas and hills the soil is poor, heavy with rock and thinly underlaid with hardpan. Farther east comes the granite belt. Some giant with lavish hand must have strewn the countryside with the huge grey boulders that crop out from the surrounding chaparral. Mile upon mile they spread to tinge the stubborn hills and decorate the skylines. As the mountains are approached rainfall steadily increases and before the eastern edges of the district are reached there develops a profusion of arboreal growth wherever granite is being leached into the meadows.

Drainage is through a series of valleys that run at right angles to the coast and parallel each other at intervals of a few miles. On their lower levels they carry surface water only during and directly after the heavier rains, but at all times there is a very considerable subterranean seepage.

The valleys themselves have been deepened and widened out of all proportion to the volume of the flow and the resulting flats, rich with the spoil of the hills, hold what little agriculture there is. A Russian colony farms on the Guadalupe and there are a few small orchards and vineyards in La Grulla. Santo Tomás has quite a bit of farming and San Vicente a little, but the aggregate for the district is pitifully small.

Rural life, where it has not been affected by the American invasion, centres about the haciendas, the fifty thousand acre grants. The home buildings are nearly always in one of the river bottoms. Often there is an adobe so old that it is timbered with hand-hewn beams, but it is apt to have for company other buildings which do not harmonize. Few of the gardens have been kept up and the outbuildings and barnyards seem to reflect the discouragement of the people. Often there still live the imported cacti and giant palms of the original grantees but these are caught in a medley of undergrowth and the need of attention and weeding in the grounds is as conspicuous as the shortage of paint and repairs on the houses.

At best this is a hard country from which to wrest a competence by raising stock. The soil is poor and will produce only in response to rain which, in turn, is uncertain and erratic. Natural disadvantages are augmented by the character of the people, their impracticable laws and their lack of capital. The result is poverty, the type that entails frugality rather than suffering. It does seem as though the ownership of an estate that cannot be ridden around in a day would insure at least plenty of good food and comfortable clothing. It seldom does in Lower California.

The men and women who live in this first hundred miles have been greatly affected by the pressure of American influences. A surprisingly large percentage have visited or worked north of the border and have become familiar with our inventions. The contact has had little modifying effect on living conditions but it has brought sophistication to the Mexicans. Within the time covered by my own trips into the country I have seen the rubbing away of the spirit of the old frontier and the remnants of early-California ideals. There was a time when Mexico came to the border and the country held more of an appeal.

The ranch owners of today are descendants of the first grantees. In general there has been no probating of estates nor division of property and the consequent communal life has become the dominating factor in rural social conditions. This has not resulted, as has so often been the case in other parts of the world, in steeping the people in conservatism. It is noticeable that the younger women wear knee-length skirts and bob their hair and that at least one modern invention is to be found on the outside and another within nearly every home ranch. In the yard there may be a harrow or a windmill or, more probably, a battered automobile, and in the living room a sewing machine or a phonograph. Old and young, the people seek in San Diego their amusements and recreations. On the whole their wants are simple and their philosophy seems to be to accept what they have rather than to struggle to improve themselves. As a corollary they are not combative and they do exhibit a greater tolerance than is found in correspondingly primitive sections of our country.

The extent to which these Mexicans are frontiersmen is illustrated by an incident connected with a horse trade I made some years ago. Harry Mansur was to deliver to me ten young mares from Hacienda Descanso. These were three and four year old animals, range horses that except for the brand had never felt the touch of a human hand or even been corralled. Mansur undertook to herd them alone to a point twenty miles from San Ysidro across a well built-up part of San Diego County. When ready to start he found that his cow-pony had become lame, but that did not balk him; he put his saddle on one of the outlaws and drove in the other nine. Only where the highest traditions of horsemanship have been preserved would such a feat be possible.

In the southern half of the first hundred miles the topography of the lowlands has been affected by high interior mountains. Watersheds have become increasingly larger and consequently less numerous and we find that three river systems divide the terrain between Ensenada and Vizcaíno Desert. La Grulla feeds into the estuary at the base of Punta Banda, having, before crossing the plain, come from the most beautiful cañon in Lower California. There are sycamores and massed willows in the winding gorge, and water, sometimes knee deep, runs over the road. Through the resultant vegetation tantalizing glimpses are to be had of chiselled rock or wild hills or even cultivated land. The charm of the composition and the contrasts can never be forgotten.

With increasing altitude La Grulla widens. It opens into valleys dotted with oak, growing, here and there, in thick groves and having for backgrounds sumach or sage and, later, lilac or manzanita. It undergoes many changes as it travels from pine forests and melting snows above the timberline and finds its way across wooded foothills. It is perhaps best known from the gun club that bears its name and occupies no inconsiderable portion of its length, but it is host, too, to several ranches and small farms. The human element, however, is pitifully small and the synonym of The Crane is Wilderness.

Santo Tomás lies twenty miles to the south. In its upper parts it is sister to La Grulla but long before it reaches the ocean it is a level ribbon of alluvial silt. At the mission the width of the potential garden can be measured by the mile and, to a limited extent, has been occupied by vine-

yardists and growers of produce. A great valley given over
to fields of wild mustard and arrow-weed and broken, here
and there, with a patch of onions, an acre of beans, a stand
of corn, or a bit of vineyard, is but one of Mexico's many
neglected opportunities.

San Vicente is a second Santo Tomás but its possibilities
are less, as is its present development. And then, as we
who are on the *Least Petrel* watch San Isidro Point emerge
from the haze, take shape, and finally draw abeam, there
comes the knowledge that we are definitely leaving behind
us the familiar Southern California conditions. Deserts lie
ahead, and for them not much is to be hoped, but of the
first hundred miles—well, one cannot but contrast them
with the other side of the line, with San Diego and Los
Angeles and a three million population. I know the comparison is not fair, that artificial influences have been at
work, that one is not wholly due to American enterprise
nor the other entirely to be blamed on Mexican economics
—and yet.

CHAPTER VII

I MIGHT as well record for the Partner, and my statement admits of no exceptions, that I have never taken her any place to which she did not want to go, in which she did not wish to remain, and to which she did not hope to return. Such, of course, was the case with Ensenada. Nevertheless noon of the nineteenth found us opposite the lighthouse on Fiscal Mole, churning our way across Todos Santos Bay and bucking the light chop that had come up during the morning.

We were headed straight into the wind and it was cold. The *Least Petrel* was amusing herself ducking her bow into seas and tossing spray over her deck, so, all things considered, the lee of the cabin was popular with those who did not care to remain inside. The position had compensations, however, for the vista of the receding shoreline was more attractive than that of the approaching islands.

On either side, some ten miles apart, a long ridge detached itself from the mountain mass and struck boldly out to sea. The slopes were steep and angular and, in general, crowded the shore to drop perpendicularly as black seawalls fringed white with surf. The lines also extended inland and formed the sides of an amphitheatre strangely out of place in these mountainous surroundings. For us, with a blur of color, distance softened the harsh details of the hills and perspective developed contours and shades which transformed rugged spurs into sweeping lines of beauty.

We were fortunate, this midday, in catching the fleeting lights at a moment of effective combination, at a favorable instant in the play of shifting tints that, narrowly confined, ran the gamut from bleak to colorful.

The deep crescent of Todos Santos Bay is covered with water over only its western half. There is included within the low contour lines the arc of the double beach that pushes from La Grulla almost to Ensenada and outlines in shining white the Estero de Punta Banda. There is the almost level plain that begins at the tidal line and, stretching broadly on either hand, shoves back the mountains to respectful distances. Once upon a time, so naturally do land and water blend, the bay itself may have pounded against the foot of the rugged screen that tumbles from the sky or perhaps La Grulla was a glacier and gouged this bed from the heart of the hills. A hundred square miles is occupied by the base of the great U which surely is a celestial stage waiting for the Gods to inaugurate a drama.

We watched the view recede and take new shapes, forgetting the cold and the wind and bucking boat until, from the pilot house, came a call for men to drop the anchor. We were in the lee of Todos Santos, comfortable and sheltered. Contrasted with Los Coronados these islands are low and flat, the more northerly nowhere rising more than sixty feet above the water. The other, however—they are separated by a navigable channel—has several ridges and its highest point, a dome near the southern end, reaches a height of over three hundred feet. The floor of the islands is thickly covered with stunted brush interspersed with cholla and flat-leaved cacti and, in lessening amount, this growth climbs the hills. Other than in the bare spaces where rocks break through, roots hold the soil in place to form a protective bulwark against the onslaughts of the elements.

The islands, an old story to some, were a treat to Peter and Gregory. Peter, of course, was first to be ready. He came bustling out of the cabin carrying a shotgun and weighted down with the paraphernalia of collecting, his hamper filled with cotton, paper rolls, and cornmeal, his pockets bulging with cartridges. He was a short man, dark and stocky and very strong, and he moved with quick decision, half assertiveness, half nervous energy. Quite a different type was Gregory, blonde, somewhat too tall for his weight, every gesture indicating the æsthete. Both were devoted to their profession and were keen for whatever good fortune might await on Todos Santos. There were no shadows to give premonition of sinister days to come.

The naturalists had been the first to go ashore and even before they were lost to view in the little valleys we could hear the bombardment of their firearms, every shot indicating some bird hitherto unknown to them. Tony and I did no collecting, contenting ourselves with a tour of inspection while the Partner rested, or, as she claimed, attended to housekeeping duties. We crossed the southerly island, the one beside which we were anchored, and came to the seaward side above the coastal cliffs. As we proceeded along the shore-line towards the isthmus a seascape of savage beauty revealed itself at our feet.

The wind had freshened to half a gale and great waves were rolling in from the ocean. These met a countercharge of outlying rocks against which they split and crashed, spouting cascades of foam and forming clouds of spoon-drift. The combers rushed upon ledges, to falter and break; they found their way into pools which they changed to swirling caldrons. Ever relentless wind, goading, and roars and cries and shrieks and whistles.

We skirted bluff and tor until we came to the half dome at the southern tip of the island. Against the face of the cliff on a shelf almost overhanging the water was the nesting site of the Duck Hawks. Most of Lower California's islands support one or more pairs of these peregrines, birds almost identical with the famous hunters of European falconry. It is their habit to perch on conspicuous pinnacles from which they tyrannize over nocturnal birds and levy heavy tribute on grebes and terns and the smaller gulls. Petrels, auklets, and murrelets, breeding in burrows or natural holes, exchange guardianships of their nests only after dark or before daylight and otherwise so comport themselves as apparently to be safe from the diurnal Nemesis. But the falcons are vicious and fast, they strike with an accuracy that is uncanny, and once their prey is at a disadvantage it has no chance. In spite of this prowess, however, one cannot but marvel at the success with which the peregrines defeat a system that, on its face, nullifies all their advantages. The readiness with which they do so was attested by the gruesome heap of skeletons and feathers lying at the foot of the cliff.

Three or four miles across the whitecaps stood Punta Banda, too large, too imposing, to pay heed to the breakers that were pounding at her feet. She, too, is guarded by an armada of outlying rocks. Some, large enough to be called islets, support nests of Osprey and on one is the huge home of a pair of Bald Eagles. Banda herself is hostile and her approach is vicious, especially when a bit of sea is running, but at least she does not conceal her dislikes and neither in the wave-washed ledges nor in the pyramidal slopes of her ambitious spires is there a suggestion of treachery.

As we turned toward the boat the wind was falling, promising a pleasant run for the morrow. The lee of the island is the more gentle side and where marked with walls and knife edges they, too, are on a quieter scale than those of the weather slope. The inner beach was host to a swarm of migrant shore birds hunting by dodging in and out among the waves. Few gave heed to us, walking above, but not so trusting were the Black Oyster-catchers. These large plover, migrants from the north with feathers of jet and bills of carmine, raised a vociferous protest at our intrusion. Flying in pairs, close together and barely off the water, screaming with every wingbeat, they circled far out and back again to stand on a boulder, perhaps, and whistle until they repeated their antics. Had we really been on their nesting grounds they could not have been more disturbed.

We reached the *Least Petrel* long after the return of the naturalists. Their specimens were spread over the dining table and they were preparing skins as fast as their nimble fingers could move. To give them an opportunity to finish their work we decided to lay over for the night. The wind went down with the sun, the roar of the surf dropped to a murmur, the anchor light was set, Ensenada, La Grulla, San Miguel, Punta Banda, and the islands, one by one, slipped into the night, and the *Least Petrel* rocked her weary passengers to sleep.

CHAPTER VIII

SIERRA SAN PEDRO MÁRTIR

THERE was light from a moon in the western sky as we slipped out of Todos Santos Bay through the channel between Punta Banda and the islands. At first the motion of the swell was tiresome, but as soon as we were on our course to San Martín we had a following sea that was not at all unpleasant. Hourly the ocean became calmer and when the land breeze died there was hardly a stir from offshore to take its place. We relaxed to enjoy a run that, negatively, developed into one of the pleasant incidents of the trip. We were still tired from the strains of intensive preparations and gladly abandoned ourselves to inaction and to rest.

I tried standing a watch at the wheel but was promptly and permanently relieved from steering any compass course. My eyesight was not equal to the task of simultaneously reading the needle and keeping a safe lookout. So a disgruntled Tony took my place and I proceeded to wander about the decks on amusement bound. The Partner was in her stateroom, armed with diary and pencil, and was not to be disturbed. Captain was asleep and poor Charley Schnack, suffering from seasickness, craved no conversation. Peter and Gregory were in the dormitory, one asleep and the other busy on his notes. So I set up a gasolene box on the after deck and threw over a fish line.

There wasn't much hope of catching anything, the boat was moving too fast. Who cared? I watched the artificial minnow darting near the surface of the water and at intervals conscientiously pulled it in to remove possible shreds

46

of kelp. My mind was never off the shore-line and I soon found myself watching for the more familiar landmarks. Those directly on the coast could be determined readily and with finality but mountain hunting in the interior developed many of the elements of real sport. I was soon joined by the Partner and later by Tony and then San Pedro Mártir became our big game.

Somewhere in the distance it lay stretched to its full length; the trick was to identify it. We could do so with ease when its hazy-blue crest formed our skyline for fifty miles. But when foothills intervened and even La Providencia slipped from sight, only close watching could detect the first reappearance of a fragment from behind some slope or the peeping of a rim from above a ridge. Our greatest interest centred in the cone-shaped pinnacle that reached above us to the height of nearly two miles. This was the hub of our orbit. After today it would not be visible for many months to come. When next we look upon it we shall be on the waters of the gulf and between us and La Providencia will be an inferno of baking rocks piled into soaring cliffs. The western approach of this sierra extends a friendly welcome to those who know its eastern side.

San Pedro Mártir is credited with an altitude of some eleven thousand feet. The figure is misleading because there is included the famous pinnacle that adds nearly half a mile to the height. The main ridge, however, attains nine thousand feet, sufficient to make San Pedro a large mountain and to give it a predominating influence over the northern part of the Peninsula. The range is isolated on two of its sides, on one falling to sea-level, the other to the comparatively low desert. To the north it is connected directly with Sierra Juárez and with the Cuyamaca Mountains of San Diego County. The southern decadence of the mighty Sierra Nevada melts into the Vizcaíno Desert and drops to two thousand feet.

The approach from the west is over hills ever increasing in size and height and showing a gradual but constant transition from coastal conditions. Sage gives way to brush until hundreds of square miles become solidly banked with lilac. During these last days of winter, hillsides, bursting into bloom, are acquiring the lavender mantle which impregnates the air with its peculiarly pleasing aroma and gives a vivid touch of color to the landscape.

Nearer the summit lilac is replaced with manzanita. That dwarfed hardwood, shoulder high, seizes every foot not preëmpted by trees or rocks. It swarms over exposed faces where it alone can endure the hardships, spreading until it forms an almost impenetrable collar around the higher levels. Anyone trying to crawl through will soon come to believe that there is personal hostility in the smooth red trunks and the unyielding branches. He will do as I have done many a time—hunt for the nearest granite slab that will give a moment's rest.

San Pedro is a block of granite. Its sheer sides, whether walls or ridges, expose the stone in varying stages of decomposition. The trail crosses miles of pellets whose fertility results in a chaparral that can be penetrated only where passage has been cut. Pack-trains may wind endlessly through slides of small boulders or perhaps climb along a face of rock in place and yet so steep that the ponies must indeed be careful. It is on the summital ridge, however, that the mass of unused building material reaches its climax.

There granite boulders are strewn with wanton lavishness. Rounded and weathered and grey, frequently exceeding the size of a suburban dwelling, they crowd the length and width of the rolling upland. Imbedded, the rock waves suggest a titanic storm frozen to immobility. Isolated, the fragments conspicuously piled upon each other or flung at random among the pines are the giant headstones of the spirits of the mountain. They are surrounded by beds of

POINT LOMA

A CORNER OF SAN TELMO

ON THE HIGHER LEVELS OF SIERRA SAN PEDRO MÁRTIR

needles and circles of cones and, as underbrush is virtually absent, they complete the picture of a well-kept, spacious park.

Nevertheless the covering of the ridge of the sierra is a true forest. Here is the Peninsula's only stand of yellow pine; some of the trees attain magnificent proportions. Silver firs are plentiful above the eight thousand foot contour and willows cluster along the borders of the streams. The terrain is broken by upland meadows, ancient, perhaps intermittent, lake beds covered with dense grass. At La Grulla, for instance, and at Santo Tomás and Santa Rosa the clearings are several miles in length. They support no trees except along the edges which are ringed with a heavy band of conifers.

At one end of the mountain lie the ruins of the Misión Santa Catarina de Yuma, at the other the stone foundations which once supported the walls of Misión San Pedro Mártir. At San Antonio trout are so abundant that fishing ceases to be sport. There are deer and sheep and quail in these highlands, but the numbers are so small that little incentive is offered to hunters.

There is no resident human population, for in winter the mountain is impenetrably blanketed with snow. Only in summer do people appear, bringing cattle for pasturage. Occasionally the alpine solitude may be disturbed by a wandering prospector or hunter or naturalist. Otherwise this most favored portion of the territory, unrivalled either in altitude or rainfall, is abandoned to the cougar and the condor. Enough of its waters could be impounded to support a great community at the base and no really serious obstacles, either of engineering or of finance, stand in the way of such an addition to the wealth of the world. But all this is below the border and there are many reasons why the Mexicans will neither do the work nor allow it to be done.

It is easy to criticize what might be considered a dog

in the manger attitude and yet there is much to be said on the negative side, especially since this is but one of countless similar situations. To make the project attractive to outside capital there is needed assurances that would run counter to fundamental law more seriously than the government cares to be committed. In the end what would be gained? Foreigners would make the investment and not only take the profits but also colonize the land. That might be a fine thing for Mexico but would it be for the Mexicans? They have not forgotten the history of Texas.

It was with keen regret that we watched the fading of Sierra San Pedro Mártir. We had been sorely tempted to pack into it this spring and though the deck of the *Least Petrel* was our final choice more than one of us felt the call of the pine cones and the oaks and the lilac. The Partner especially, for she had been raised in the mountains. I have never honored her more than I did that morning, as she willingly turned her back on loved association to face the unknown hardships of desert land and water.

CHAPTER IX

CAPTAIN's system of navigation was simple. Far off-shore or after dark he ran by dead reckoning, checking the readings of his log as opportunity offered and construing in his own favor any discrepancies between the position he calculated and the spot where he thought himself to be. At other times he glanced at the nearest cape and knew just where he was. His familiarity with the coast line, its soundings and dangers and anchorages, was a source of constant wonder. On the other hand he had little interest in and consequently almost no knowledge of what lay beyond the breakers. I believe the man really dislikes land and is happy only when he has hundreds of fathoms under his keel.

So it was, as we ran down the coast, that, with mariner-like precision, he marked the progression of headlands. They were such everyday matters of course to him that none of our enthusiasm, no amount of heckling in the pilot house, could lift him above the level of a conductor calling names of streets. There wasn't much fun trying to pester him, besides he had been asleep since breakfast, and so hadn't joined in hunting San Pedro Mártir. Even mid-morning, with San Isidro in the offing and most of us on our toes for a glimpse of Vizcaíno Desert, brought to him merely another cape to be passed, another landmark by which to check his course.

However, no Captain was to dampen our ardor, the Partner's or mine, and so, when we found ourselves becoming impatient at the imperceptible development of blurred haze into a recognizable peak, when San Pedro hid herself too long or Vizcaíno seemed unchangeable, when the fish refused to bite and there was no work to be done, our minds left the boat and wandered inland, to El Camino Real. At times we could almost see the roadway and all day we were able to point out to each other the precise cañons through which it twisted or the hillsides over which it climbed. We had travelled it often, and scarcely a mile but held the memory of some incident or the unforgotten picture of some association.

El Camino Real is the title of the road that once connected the missions. Its northern terminus is in Central California, beyond the waters of San Francisco Bay. Southward it extends below the Victoria Mountains in the Cape Region of San Lúcas. A long road, and for half its length it still remains the only arterial highway. Time was when the missions were the sole resource of the traveller. He rode, for no one journeyed afoot and carriages could not be used, from one source of hospitality to the next and, whenever possible, did so between daylight and dark. The chronicle of this post-road of adventurer and official is the early history of the two Californias.

How differently, on the opposite sides of the border, has the pathway been dealt with by Fate! The southern section is so much the older that a dozen missions had been founded on the Peninsula a full half century before the first adobe brick was laid in California. Yet the series of the Franciscans, the missions of California, have been accorded their due respect, have been protected as historic spots, and, in some instances, even restored for occupancy. In Lower California, save only those whose masonry is proof against weather and vandal alike, no semblance of form remains and the abandoned sites are at the mercy of any squatter who can make use of them. Relative sacrifice, hardship, and antiquity have not received the honor earned.

EL CAMINO REAL

When we were passing Punta Banda, at daybreak, El Camino Real was running straight away from us, eastward up La Grulla's cañon. The road eventually turned south and then kept abreast, up hill and down, until its course brought it to a great valley. Where the wagon tracks cross the river stands all that remains of the mission Santo Tomás. The site is marked by a palm, venerable and tall, the only animate survivor of the eighteenth century. Could that plant but tell what it has seen! Its tiny leaves sprouted beside long walls of grey adobe, the first sound to reach it was the rhythm of a chant, its first glimpse of mankind was of Indians coming to baptism.

When it became tall enough to look over the roofs there was a scene of industry to survey, for the fathers trained the congregations in knowledge other than ecclesiastical and institutions were predicated on self-support. The palm saw the mission grow to its glory, decline, die, and disintegrate. Was it a roof that first collapsed for want of care, or was it a wall that softened in the rain, and caved? Was it the more sudden work of earthquake or looters? Whatever the sequence, for the last many years, for the span of a human life, the towering head has seen only crumbling decay, demolition with never a touch of restoration.

Today there flows a tiny stream brought in ditches, perhaps in the padres' viaducts, to a garden of trellised grapes. A family, prosperous they are for this country, has a home on the old site and if they have not protected the ruin they at least have furnished companionship and they are not destructive. The two best preserved walls, roofed with layers of palm leaves, stable cows and a buckboard. The remaining scattered bits of ruins struggle against encroaching weeds and are slowly succumbing to neglect, as Santo Tomás passes through her last agonies.

El Camino Real parallels us as we follow the coast southeasterly. An hour's run from Punta Santo Tomás brings the *Least Petrel* to San José Point, its great bed of kelp holding us miles offshore. Two hours later we are opposite San Isidro and all the while there have paraded before us a series of cliffs that fall from mesa and hilly highland. We catch a glimpse of rolling foothills, brown and bushy spurs of the mighty range behind. We see them where, too proud to yield gracefully, they have come down to the sea and made their stand. Their tokens of defeat are the wounds they expose, the stubs of crude amputation.

El Camino Real crosses these hills ten, fifteen miles inland, crawling into coulees and over upland levels, finally picking up a tributary of San Vicente and slipping down, mile after mile of sandy creek bottom or granite sageland, until willows appear and lead to the great dry river. Upstream a short distance, through a stand of saplings, over the knoll where a scant half dozen houses have won recognition as a town, past an outlying ranch house, and to the spot chosen by Juaquin Valero to build his mission.

Poor San Vicente! Across a stony knob lies sprawled a skeleton unshielded from sun and abandoned to decay. There is indecency in the nakedness of these ruins. No home is beside them, no road or trail leads to the remains, there is not even enough sage to cover respectably the few tiers of adobe that trace foundation lines. Yellow and dead and deserted San Vicente faces the valley and the river; she has lost the struggle, wind and rain have battered down garden and chapel, and her memory has not sufficed to win even the simple cross that sentiment raises above the common soul who expires on the roadside.

Relentless as time, without beginning or end, El Camino Real is our constant shadow as we watch, from its inception, the unfolding panorama of Vizcaíno. Ever those tall bluffs that stand on the water's edge, those peaks that tantalize from unknown distance, those great mesas rivalling the mountain tops, those haunts of antelope and bighorn,

54

those weird transfigurations of an unfinished country. We know the air is drier because the haze is lessening, and as the browns turn to greys we see the changing vegetation and sense the coming desert. An hour passes, another comes, and still the high flung cliffs and a hinterland ever harsher, ever less complete.

The sun is at its zenith when we first see Colnett, where the bench above the cliffs opens, where the great mesa swings stubbornly into the ocean and marks one of Lower California's most famous capes. Of three tiers is it built, of stone cut straight to the water edge, of an ebon layer, counterfeit coal, and of a sand blanket held down by the roots of agave and sage. There is a full circle—one half is an outstretched arm bent at the elbow to protect, one half is a sheltered bay leading to a cobble beach, to the dike of San Telmo River.

We had not slipped free from the shadow left grieving at San Vicente. El Camino has followed, mile by mile, up the river into Sierra Cresta Blanca, through the pass to a great level valley, south with the drainage, down a box cañon so narrow as almost to close above, so deep as almost to be darkened. Then, as though passing through a door, the road squeezes from those towering walls of rocks, out of the defile and into Vizcaíno Desert. It debouches at San Antonio del Mar, it passes over stretches of sand, it winds through strange cacti until it overtakes us at Colnett Bay.

Up from the marshes it climbs to a bench so soft, so impalpable, that wheels sink deep and tracks are but perpendicular meeting places of tiny slides. Straight it goes, between agave piled as stumps on either side or standing as stalks in rows that draw together as perspective pinches at the horizon, and on, a drop into a cañon and forthwith an ascent straight up, a run over firmer ground through cholla and chaparral associations, and then Santo Domingo.

Upstream where the willow-bottoms end, where the cañon

opens behind the massive Peña Colorado, in whose caves
the Padres Garcia and Hidalgo first lived and said mass,
surrounded by this desert's most ideal conditions, a brown
rounded hill overlooks the river. A noble pedestal, rich
with history, and its statue is a pig-pen! A brood sow and
her litter, grubbing in filth, were fenced and kept at the
foot of the old pulpit when last we had looked through the
doorway of the chapel of Misión Santo Domingo. Many
walls remain in part, and there are other stys where entrances
have been blocked or breaks filled in with brush. Not only
does trough replace altar rail but vandalism gave the final
touch of indignity when the mission's last glory, her great
bronze bells, were stolen by thieves who had not the courage
even to complete their crime. Fearing the consequences,
when well out to sea the cowards ruthlessly jettisoned the
treasures.

From Santo Domingo the road crosses the river, skirts
Red Rock and turns south. It goes on, into the far away
where we cannot follow, but we have had a glimpse of
one link in the chain. Camino Real, yours has been a strange
fate. Southern California and Vizcaíno Bay. In the wastes
how nearly time has completed your cycle; how nearly
you are again the trail over which the first black cowl led
the first coat-of-mail.

CHAPTER X

In a previous chapter we traced the San Diegan Faunal District to its arterial outpost, to the southern drainage of the San Vicente River and the small range of hills dignified with the name of Sierra Cresta Blanca. The importance of these mountains, if you choose to call them such, lies in the fact that, while their northern slope is San Diegan in character, on the south they open into the Vizcaíno Desert.

They enter the sea at Point San Isidro. We came abreast during the latter part of the morning and had our first glimpse of the desert associations that cover by far the greater part of Lower California. It may be that the wide stretch extending to Cape San Lúcas and circling back to Mexicali is not, strictly speaking, a desert. Authorities are somewhat contradictory on the meaning of the word and even their most satisfying definitions seem to leave large portions of Lower California on the border line. In our Southwest, however, custom has given a definite interpretation and assigns the status of desert to regions which do, in fact, support substantial growths.

The local distinction between a desert and a wilderness follows very closely upon the preponderant development of thorns on vegetation. This artificial cleavage line is not a coincidence, a direct relationship between spines and aridity being readily traceable. Plants growing under circumstances which render difficult the replacement of lost portions must practice self-preservation and they do so by becoming unattractive to browsing animals. Evolution began to cover

57

them with thorns and once the process had commenced
survival carried it through to completion. Feeding enemies
will naturally concentrate on unprotected trunks and foliage
and so will eliminate both the species and the individuals
who do not protect themselves. If we consider as desert
any area in which substantially all edible vegetation is
armored, then Vizcaíno is properly designated.

Basically the soil is fertile. It is true that there are large
areas where volcanic rock has not yet disintegrated and
over much of the surface the soil is shallow or else is
impregnated with alkali, but these barrens are more than
balanced by deposits of rich silt and by plains and mesas
of great agricultural potentiality. The larger part of Lower
California would become a garden could it be irrigated,
but there are almost no waters available for impounding
and rain is hopelessly inadequate. Not only is the aggregate
far too little but such as does fall is distributed with
ruinous waste. For one thing storms are apt to come in the
form of cloud-bursts. Five inches may be precipitated in a
single afternoon with clouds emptying themselves so rapidly
that distribution is confined to a few thousand acres.

I have been mud-bound for days at a time by roads that
were impassable to an automobile, and that, too, with dust
but a few miles away in every direction. This country,
lying as it does between two large bodies of water and
having a relatively low crest, is the playground of storms.
Their channels are vagrant, for San Pedro Mártir, having
slipped behind, no longer controls the weather and rain
strikes here and there at random. Enormous amounts of
water are lost and, conversely, any given spot may go years
without receiving a drop. Local vegetation is necessarily
limited to forms which have developed a superlative degree
of drought resistance.

If you drive through this country you will cross great
plateaus cut with interminable valleys and arroyos. You

will climb lava-studded grades and follow drainage courses hub deep in silt. You will pass through cactus growths of jungle-like proportions. You will enter watersheds, as at El Rosario, that, meticulously perfect in detail, serve no apparent need, and you will traverse mesas or plains that seem to be without drainage. You will have been in a region too diversified to classify, one that alternately is decaying and unfinished, and you will probably emerge vastly impressed, but dissatisfied with your knowledge and confused in your mind.

If you camp on Vizcaíno and extend the hand of fellowship your acquaintance will become a friend and traits, subtly withheld from the stranger, will generously be revealed. Hills no longer are inanimate; they change in color, shape, and character to suit your every mood. If you rest in the midst of a jungle it metamorphoses itself to a park, it reveals little openings and clearings, and passages through which it may be penetrated. Miniature displays, perfect in conception and artistic in composition, will arrange themselves with the tiny growths to the fore and increasingly large cacti in the background. A terraced picture, but never artificial. In season flowery atoms will smile at you from behind sage roots and invite your further confidence.

Vizcaíno cannot be read casually; it yields its secrets only to experienced patience and concentrated work. It harbors many birds, for instance, but not for the careless passer-by. Desert-like they are unbelievably shy; they learned generations ago that safety depends upon keeping enemies at a distance. Yet there are means by which they can be approached and studied, their nests discovered, their instincts analyzed, and their life problems investigated. There are reptiles and insects and mammals whose histories rival the plot of any novel. Lava hills are hostile, silt and sand bottoms are monotonous, and path-finding in the mazes calls for unending pains, but a reward comes to those who love the desert. They are answering its call with full assurance that in doing so they will stumble upon many an unsuspected setting of enduring charm.

An examination of the flora can be made with less exertion. The marsh reeds of San Telmo and the willows of the oases are interlopers; fresh water vegetation is not endemic. On the other hand there is the cirio, the fifty foot ocotillo that is found nowhere in the world but on Vizcaíno. The diameter of the truncated cone often tapers from three feet at the base to a few inches near the top. The trunk is free from branches until the tip is reached but there it often opens into a multi-fingered candelabra. How hawks and ravens do love to place their nests in the palms of those hands! The setting is more than appropriate, for the cirio suggests an artificial framework rather than a living tree.

Nature's generosity to the cirio places enemies in a dilemma for points of attack. Woodpeckers and flickers, the carpinteros of the Mexicans, find the wood too tough for drilling. The bark is covered with a greenish fuzz which, inspection reveals, is massed with barbed thongs, stubby and curved and set to give a maximum of protection. An attempt at either nibbling or climbing is not apt to be repeated. The gargantuans do not compete with each other, for even where their occurrence is most congested they are generously spaced. Over great stretches they are to be found every few hundred feet and, on the other hand, so irregular is their distribution, there are widespread associations where the trees are rare. Even so, from the outpost of San Pedro Mártir to the limits of the Lost Plains they are seldom altogether absent from the vista of sage and cactus.

Rivalling the cirio in height and greatly exceeding it in size and number is the sahuaro or cardón. This is the familiar Giant Cactus of our own southwest, the cluster of corrugated cylinders that, sometimes at formal angles but more often in eruption, spouts from a basal stalk. On the Vizcaíno Desert it is to be found both in dense forest formation and standing as solitary guardian of surrounding underbrush.

Pitahaya, cholla, garambullo, yucca, and echinocactus— the list would fill a book. Tiny balls of grey that coax to be caressed but are prepared to spit fire into a friendly hand, venomous snake-like arms that crawl along the ground seeking a place in the sun, sage that crowds briars and cacti and softly tinted babies into a medley, half-spheres of pure spite and head high posts of devilish dispositions—and then a clearing fringed with grass and flowers, cut with rodent and burro trails, curtained with painted mountain shapes; such is the pictured memory of Vizcaíno.

We have glanced at the desert from the seat of an automobile and we have strolled about afoot. There is still another point of view, one in which perspective compensates for loss of detail. From the deck of the *Least Petrel* we watched the desert parade. It begins at San Antonio del Mar, where ranching, mining, drilling, and distilling have successively been attempted. San Telmo is a pueblo so old that the mark of the adzes is to be seen on its timber. Adobe, palm, and irrigation ditch, it is almost the only habitation from San José, nestling against the great sierra, to Cape Colnett, the famous half crescent where the projecting mesa drops chiselled edges into the ocean. Next Santo Domingo, supported by the river delta, and then San Quintín, with its bay and salt works and scars of abandoned English colonization. Socorro consists of two houses near the beach but El Rosario thrives about its dusty plaza because there is surface water near the river mouth. George Brown, veteran exploiter of the Peninsula, is taking great blocks of stone at Onyx, where is the only school house in the world built entirely of that rock. San Fernando and

Santa Catarina are oases whose water, conducted in little earthen ditches, supports unspoiled peasant farmers who retain all the courtesies of a bygone age. And so on, past Calamajué with its bleak walls and Agua Prieta with its rusting machinery until Vizcaíno disappears in the great Lost Plains.

Man has come to this desert and has been absorbed. A primitive road, little used, which runs through virgin brush and dips in and out of lonely coulees, joins together all his settlements. These may embrace two or three families or a village of a few hundred people, never more. What, then, of the other score of thousands of square miles? You may, in your wanderings, chance upon dim tracks running to the highway or leading down to the coast, a path which can come only from some ranch house. If you follow the trail back to the neighborless home you will find merely a hut of appalling simplicity. The human element is negligible on Vizcaíno.

Many are the places printed on maps. Travelling, you would be disconcerted, or amused, by the fact that most of the namesakes of the saints are represented by an anomaly such as an adobe ruin, a well, or even a bare junction of roads. Shall we say that from Sierra Cresta Blanca to the Lost Plains, from the Pacific Ocean to the Gulf of California there are a hundred people away from the beaten path? It would be an exaggeration. Shall we say that if you covered the outlying areas day after day as rapidly as you could walk you would, on an average, meet some trivial sign of human occupancy once every twenty-four hours? It would not be true. Vizcaíno is as God left it. Man's mark is a pebble fallen in the sea.

CHAPTER XI

FROM Punta Banda to San Martín Island the chart shows eighty-five miles. We made the run in little more than ten hours, having both wind and sea astern, but even so reached port too late to do more than go ashore and look around. We dropped anchor in Hassler's Cove, an interesting little bay protected by a natural breakwater of large boulders. We swarmed over the rocky beach, a small caravan of explorers searching in a desultory way for possible objects of interest below high water. We went no farther than the lagoon where we made some effort to tabulate the population of shore-birds. This favored resting place of the migrants is partly tidal and we found its shores dotted with sandpipers, plovers, and the larger waders. Herons, standing knee deep and well offshore, appeared to have assumed the rôle of sentries but in reality were only fishing. On our approach they became alarmed and silently flapped away.

The evening marked the end of the third day. Our accomplishments so far, if not noteworthy, at least were not disappointing and we all felt that if the trip maintained the average of its beginning no one would have cause for complaint. We had examined a number of places and our museum collections were well started with specimens chosen in anticipation of laboratory work to be done on our return. A study skin, by the way, is a bird or small mammal so stuffed that it resembles the dead animal a hunter retrieves rather than the living one which served as target.

The purpose of assembling these skins was to enable

us to compare groups of birds. If all those of a given species from one area possess a physical trait that is found in none of those from some other section, then segregation is proven and, if the fact were previously unknown, there has developed a bird to be described and named. This is the means by which ornithology determines distribution, the work of one man being added to that of another until the aggregate covers the globe. Collecting skins, however, was by no means the principal objective of our trip. It was, nevertheless, the one which required the most time and consequently there often was difficulty in preventing its importance from becoming exaggerated.

The goal of avifaunal study is an understanding of the bird; his anatomy and his distribution are relatively unimportant accidental happenings in comparison with life itself. As disclosed by his instincts and other mental inheritances, the conduct and development of his young, his nesting habits, adaptation, individual psychological variations, mental limitations and above all by the processes to which he must conform in order to survive and breed, the operation of the machine transcends its construction. Data for such information can be acquired only in the field because our systems of recording are crude and our investigators untrained, and yet without correlation of observable facts, their correct interpretation, and their reconciliation with each other, the foundation of ornithology cannot have been reached.

Perhaps I can best illustrate the purposes of field work by referring to the present-day school of behaviorists. The theoretical psychologist reasons out what the mental reactions of birds should be and he closes his syllogisms with certain convincing conclusions that carry theory to fact and thereby largely disregard instinct. We, on the other hand, deal only in observed realities and have it driven home to us on every hand that instinct is the preponderant determinant of conduct, human or animal. Instead of endeavoring to ascertain what should be, our one interest is the interpretation of what we actually witness. Or should I confess that I embarked upon this adventure because of insatiable curiosity regarding what and why?

On at least this part of the trip islands offered not only more comfortable anchorages than the mainland but also better opportunities for concentrated observation. So a day on San Martín, which was all we could afford, promised to be exceedingly well spent. In the evening we divided the work and laid our plans and early next morning started on our climb to the top of the island. The first sharp ascent from the landing brought us to a lava-strewn bench. It was densely covered with volcanic fragments that attained perhaps a cubic yard in size. They made walking difficult and tiresome, for they were jumbled at all sorts of angles and, too, were separated from each other by substantial crevices. Further impeding progress and causing many an awkward slip, with resultant bruise to shin or elbow, was a sticky, crawling form of iceplant. It covered rocks and hid cracks and we grew to dislike it so thoroughly that, I'm afraid, we allowed our prejudice to include the island as well.

The Partner and I were soon deserted by Tony and the other naturalists, who found Rock Wrens more interesting than scenery. The birds were pert little devils at that, hopping about us as we moved, singing and bobbing, often approaching to within arm's length to tell us that our presence was not desired. When we rested it was usually to find ourselves within an area which some pair of wrens looked upon as their private property. They were polite but quite insistent that we should move and tried every trick in their repertoire to induce us to stop trespassing.

We made the climb slowly. It was hard work; the hill was steep and there was no escape from the treacherous footing. We first crossed the stretch of fairly level ground that serves as a pedestal for San Martín's two peaks. The island is a mile-wide volcanic oval surrounded with a sea wall whose regular contour is broken only by the lagoon and the ledge of boulders that shelters Hassler's Cove. San Martín is not prepossessing. A little brush and cactus without arboreal growth, a dreary brown mass with no strong features to relieve monotony, it commands attention chiefly because it is unique.

As we neared the summit of the taller peak a flock of Great Blue Herons flushed from under our feet. We crowded on to the apparent apex and peered over the edge, to look down upon a scattering of old nests, long thin twigs in yard-wide bundles that showed signs of recent repair. They were in an extinct crater, a perfect miniature a hundred yards across and fully fifty feet deep. Studying the ancient caldron, it did not require much imagination to see pools bubbling with molten rock or vents pouring out steam and smoke. How many centuries, or eons, I wonder, since this inverted cone, so well preserved in its shelter from wind and water, had been a thing of life?

When we sat down to rest we turned our backs upon it, facing eastward. Five hundred feet below was the ocean and across a few miles of water that was motionless to us were spread the plains of San Quíntin. Conspicuous in the foreground were the famed Five Hills, mounds larger than San Martín and so convincingly its sisters that only my having been to them overland assured me that they, too, were not islands. Far in the background, running north and south to the limits of our vision, were the foothills that here begin their climb to San Pedro Mártir and the backbone of the Peninsula.

Just behind Five Hills were the bay and town of San Quíntin. That is, if half a dozen old wooden buildings facing a staked line of beach sand constitute a town. One's impressions of San Quíntin are dependent on wind. Given a quiet day it is a picture of struggle and loss, of a city surveyed into lots and blocks, of a boom that came and broke, of a family that lingers on, of a possible passer-by who stops, of a rambling hotel with many floors and rooms, with little furniture and no paint. One night, in the dining room, I had supper by the light of a kerosene lamp. I could see a bare floor and shadowy pillars but, such was the inappropriate size of the salon, I was sitting in space with four walls lost in gloom.

A wind howls. It grows in intensity but remains constant in perseverance. All day it blows and all the next day, until breathing becomes difficult and concentration impossible. Then comes the feeling that San Quíntin hasn't much to offer and is about as miserable a place as there is in the world. The bay is subject to the same vagaries and has had almost the same history. In good weather it offers the best anchorage north of Cape San Eugenio and not many years ago was a regular port of call for coastal freighters. Its entrance has shallowed until now even the *Least Petrel* would have to feel her way with care and duck hunters or fishermen are almost the only men who break its solitude.

The Plains of San Quíntin do not at all resemble those at the base of Todos Santos Bay. The former are so nearly level and so low that, having recently emerged, they are not yet leached of their salt. They support a bit of brush with small herds of cattle and wild burros and one very modest ranch. Salt is collected from deposits just north of town.

Our interests, as we sat on the rocks of San Martín, began to wander farther afield until we were searching the landscape for marks by which to identify El Rosario Valley. Even at a distance of fifty miles I am sure I recognized the sandstone cliff that rivals the Half Dome of Yosemite. Some force of nature, ice or water, took half a mountain sheer, leaving the other half in place and marking the

67

cleavage with a precipice of—I dare not estimate how many feet. It seems to come from the sky and its vertical drop is interrupted only by the talus that slopes on an angling plane to the river-bed.

Follow the sand toward the sea and you pass successively through a forest of giant cactus, home to flickers and owls, into miles of arrowroot, range of quail and verdin, and through all but impenetrable patches of willow, which means water and habitation. Irrigation ditches run everywhere and green fields and trees appear, cultivated plots, houses, and at last a village. Surrounding an unnecessarily large plaza are single storied adobes one of which has an overhanging porch roof and a garden. People live in all the houses, even in those containing the Chinaman's store and Mesa's saloon. There is a creditable school, token of the sincerity of Mexico's attempt to overtake progress, and there are three or four side streets of a few houses each. The description sounds dreary and that is just, for El Rosario, even to its friends, is not attractive. The un-sprinkled plaza is too large and with nothing, no structure, not even vegetation, to hold the silt in place, is dusty and dirty. It is, and until Americans come it will remain, a settlement whose spirit of hospitality is touching, pathetic even, in view of how little its inhabitants have to offer.

On the south is a rolling country, to the north a mesa that towers to a height of some twelve hundred feet. Somewhere El Camino Real scales that wall, working back and up with a ravine, for behind the village are the ruins of Misión El Rosario. The United States were British Colonies when the buildings rose on the most fertile spot of Vizcaíno Desert, and enough of the long walls remains to attest their one-time importance. The villagers, by accident or design, have kept apart from the mission grounds and have made no attempt to utilize its remains. There is no litter within the enclosure, no grass, nor anything but emptiness.

It bespeaks age, respect without reverence, authority fallen to influence, a soul that barely lingers.

On a mound where walls have decayed to bricks and bricks to dust is a cross-beam held by two homemade posts. Here are suspended the mission bells of El Rosario, a cluster of huge bronze bowls cast in Spain for its king and sanctified in Spain by its church. They call the faithful few of today, they whose summons were once answered by thousands, and the devout follow the musical peals to a little dugout that has been salvaged or rebuilt but is still closed with the ancient doors of carved wood. So survives the mission that is now a church, it administers to a tiny congregation without ordained leadership, and it fulfills a modicum of the ambition of the inspired men who pioneered El Rosario.

CHAPTER XII

SEBASTIÁN VIZCAÍNO BAY

WE were a weary boatload that evening; walking on San Martín comes under the head of hard labor. Of course no one had given in to the iceplant and rocks, but each of us, when his allotted work had been done, was glad that there was a *Least Petrel*. We went aboard with the thoroughly comfortable feeling of going home. I knew the Partner had tired, for she changed from her shorts into regular clothes and put in the evening reading a novel. Peter and Tony and Gregory had birds to skin and boxes to pack, Juan worked till past ten on his dishes and on bread he was baking, and I tried a little writing, but threw my notes away because they were pure drivel. Charley and Captain turned in as soon as supper was over; they were due to make a midnight start.

We had decided that the best way to speed up the trip was to do more travelling at night. That entailed careful planning and timing, for since there are no aids to navigation and no lights on which dependence may be placed we must, after dark, be on the high seas or at least in safe waters. It would not do to start too early tonight, for instance, and take a chance on piling up on San Gerónimo. Twelve o'clock was the earliest hour that gave a sufficient margin of safety and, I presume, we left at that time. All I know is that I rolled over in my blankets when the engine started and was asleep again before we were out of the cove. When I finally woke breakfast was ready and San Gerónimo less than an hour ahead. This certainly is an easy way to travel.

We ate leisurely, to the accompaniment of the usual table banter, assembled the gear to be taken ashore, and then gathered in the bow to watch the island approach. San Gerónimo lies about five miles from the mainland and is low and small, its length being somewhat less than one mile. It is about six hundred yards across and is nowhere much more than a hundred feet above the water. It is quite different from anything we as yet had seen, its yellow color being conspicuous from almost any distance and its barrenness apparent while still miles away.

The anchorage at the southeast end was good, with a sand bottom and, in this weather, a lee protecting us from the swell. To reach this shelter we skirted the southern tip of the island and found that our close approach did not increase the attractiveness of San Gerónimo. It is a great rock banded with an exposed sea-wall ten to twenty feet high and blanketed with a covering of mixed ash, sand, and guano. There are three abortive peaks on an otherwise fairly level surface that has just a suggestion of vegetation. A surrounding brood of outlying rocks reaches and even permeates the kelp beds, and the shoreline leaves a memory of ugly ledges, submerged or awash according to vagaries of wave and tide.

We lost no time in landing. Captain rowed us ashore in the usual two installments and we jumped out onto the shingle beach that lies in the pocket under the peak. It was a couple of hours later that the Partner and Tony and I followed the others to the top of the island. The first thing we did, taking advantage of conditions, was to make a cursory examination of life along the beaches and on the rocks at the foot of the cliff. There were the migratory shore-birds of course—we saw none of special importance —and gulls, pelicans, and other to-be-expected sea-birds. Not much of a reward, perhaps, for coming to such a distant island, but such is collectors' luck.

There was no difficulty, however, in finding other things of interest and so, without entirely neglecting birds, we began to investigate marine life. It was present in an abundance that gave us a foretaste of the approaching tropical waters, and we studied seaweeds and grasses, small mollusks and limpets, abalones where the depths were greatest and swarms of tiny beings we could not classify. Particularly did we enjoy the tidal pools in which, if we exercised patience, we could detect many a shy form moving in and out among the mosses.

All this was play, not work, and we took it in that spirit. Which was just as well, perhaps, because when we eventually did reach the volcanic crust of the upper portions we found that San Gerónimo had few inducements to offer at this time of the year. However, I did collect a beautiful set of three Osprey eggs from near the top of the ridge. The Fish Hawk prefers to build on the tip of an inaccessible pinnacle but, in antithesis to many other birds, he does not forego nesting when a desirable site is unavailable. If driven by necessity he will use trees or oil-derricks, accept ledges or giant cacti or, on islands, even build on the ground itself. His nest is a bulky cylinder of coarse sticks padded on top with seaweed and so placed that danger may be discerned from nearly every direction. The nest I found on Gerónimo was on the skyline of a spur and could be reached without difficult climbing. Though not an ideal site by any means it did give a three-way view and after all the Osprey is a bit of a philosopher, he does the best he can and lets it go at that. At the same time he offers unusually lucid illustrations of bird psychology. His very failures show, by their frustrated attempts and by their half successful accomplishments as well, the things that he really wants to do.

Both before and after our picnic luncheon we explored the barren island, reading the signs of last year's nestings and anticipating the hordes that will come with the later days of spring. Of old nests and broken eggshells and desiccated carcasses we found an abundance, for San Gerónimo is really a great rookery. It has everything— desirable size, soft soil, convenient contours, abundant sea-food and, above all, freedom from predatory mammals. We enjoyed our bit of sleuthing, for it was a beautiful day and, compared with the other islands we had tramped, walking here was easy.

The only trouble was with the burrows of the auklets. The little pests had honeycombed the soft crust and every few strides someone's foot would break through with an awkward jolt and bring him to a sudden stop. Of course the burrows were those that had been used last year and were empty now. Cassin Auklets are strictly pelagic except when breeding.

The annoyance of an occasional stumble was too trifling to interfere with our pleasure and those of us who could do so lingered on to the last minute. The three technicians had been aboard for hours, preparing specimens, before the Partner and I could reconcile ourselves to leaving. There was so much to learn. Gulls, disliking our presence on future nesting grounds, circled us uneasily, cormorants, awkward and helpless ashore, took to water where, if necessary, they could dive, ospreys, looking for unwary fish that were not too heavy and not too far below the surface, harried the quieter waters, plover, hunting, dodged about in the ebb and flow of waves—all had something to teach if we had the wit to learn. Behind every thought and act lay a reason, accidental or basic, individualistic or groupal, instinctive or acquired, and though our powers of interpretation are woefully limited every hour of observation does add to an understanding of the things that birds do and the desires that motivate them.

All aboard. We're leaving early on an over-night run;

we must be past Sacramento Reef before dark. A short distance south of San Gerónimo the sea washes and breaks over the foulest bit of water it has ever been my lot to see. Three square miles without a rock that is dry or a surface that is honest is this seething caldron of hell that has levied its toll on coastwise shipping. Large boats and small, it has ground them without mercy and spewed them over its helpmate, the storm waves. It flaunts its first and greatest trophy, a giant rod torn from a passenger boat of pioneer days that has left here only her memory and her name. The paddle-wheel shaft of the steamer *Sacramento* is gripped by demon teeth that through the years have held one end aloft in threat, growling at all the world, beware.

As we passed Sacramento Reef to starboard the gruesome shaft of the turbulent graveyard pointed to the sinking sun. Of a hundred glorious sunsets there can be no justice in choosing one to remember and describe—yet there was that night, when the soft bosom of Vizcaíno rose slowly to draw to herself the passionate embrace of a descending globe of fire and framed a nuptial bed with the glories of paradise. Color and temperament. No less in magnificence was the peace of the pearly blue above the cloud line than was the malignity of the snarling, hissing reef. No whiter were the fluffs of nimbus that hovered in benediction than were the foamy lines of hate that crashed on the mausoleum. Was the ocean green? Were its waters blue? They changed as crimson turned to orange and carmine into pink. Shafts of living flame swept across the sky or rushed to deck the sun and open into a diadem such as no queen has ever worn.

And then the fading, for such a wonder cannot endure. Slowly was the toga drawn aside and the banked clouds adorned themselves with cast-off shreds of a rainbow. Of what avail to note a color? A fleeting instant and it was gone, to be replaced with a tint that surpassed perfection. Even the reef quieted under the spell of celestial pyrotechnics as the disk of pulsating blood, emerging from its last veil, stood revealed, naked and glorious. Then did the courtiers swerve from laughter to tears, then did the lesser lights succumb, and then the stronger, until ghoulish evanescent twilight seized her flash of triumph.

The *Least Petrel* alone was unappreciative. She plugged on, a point east of south, maintaining an even pace for her thirteen-hour run. Sun and salt air are conducive to sleep and, as there was little work that could be done while the boat was under way, it was not long until we had extinguished all but the running lights. Captain took the wheel up to midnight, after which he was relieved by one man after another until Elide Islet hove in sight.

This little island is a guano-covered rock forty feet high It is about a quarter of a mile long and perhaps the same distance offshore and of interest chiefly because it marks the entrance to Santa Rosalía Bay. This port must not be confused with the mining town of Santa Rosalía on the Gulf. The duplication of names on the Peninsula is wanton and senseless and has caused any number of mistakes, some humorous, but some that verge on tragic.

We hurried so as to finish breakfast before the hook went down, being anxious to get ashore. We could spare but a few hours here and this was to be our only direct contact with the littoral of Vizcaíno Desert. We scrambled over the cobble beach and began our search for nests of Desert Thrashers. These rare birds until recently were known only from this bay and their eggs are still undescribed. Though they are unusually early breeders we had another disappointment in store. We saw any number of old nests and some that were being built but we found none occupied.

The littoral has come under the influence of salt air blown in by the trades and is a sandy strip whose vegetation is largely brush, heavy and high when the soil permits, but gnarled and stunted where it has to fight for a foothold in the dunes. We tramped those associations steadily for three hours and at the end felt we had become well acquainted. They give impressions very different from those of the desert itself, their flora and their fauna are distinct, and they suggest northern rather than southern wastes.

The extent of the typical littoral strip is indeterminate. On Santa Rosalía Bay it is unadulterated and at other widely scattered points along the coast it also appears in pure form, but often it is mixed with the true desert until, at best, we can but approximate where one ends and the other begins.

On Santa Rosalía Bay are marks of habitation, for there is a ranch some twelve miles in the interior and to this coast, perhaps once a year, men come for cargoes to be lightered to the shore. People have even lived here—the privations that pioneers will endure are among the marvels of humanity—for I found the rotting timbers of a caved-in well among scattered relics of abandoned housekeeping. Only by indirection is the loneliness of this bay relieved and an unknown, unseen neighbor makes his presence felt —to such extremes does one go for companionship beside the waters of Vizcaíno.

We left Santa Rosalía Bay near its southern end and just cleared Cape Santa Rosarita and its outlying bed of kelp. This promontory is as much a landmark to us as was San Isidro, for beyond it begins a country unlike anything we have seen and comparable only to the plains of San Quíntin. From the far away Point of Rocks on California's border had come the series of bluffs that formed an unbroken procession of mountain stubs and transverse ridges and eroded edges of mesas. For hundreds of miles the anomalous mixture of volcanic uplifts and broadly painted strata had followed the coast, but at Santa Rosarita Point they ended abruptly.

SEBASTIAN VIZCAINO BAY

The rugged coast vanishes, the hills disappear, and in their stead comes a great plain level with the ocean. In places it reaches the breakers but more often a protecting line of sand dunes has been thrown up to mark the contact. Picture a level ocean bottom extending ten miles or forty miles out to sea and dot it, here and there, with widely spaced volcanic islands. Let the floor emerge and dry, scour it with sand blasted in the teeth of the trades, plant at random a very little scrubby sage. The result will be the eastern shores of Vizcaíno Bay and the great stretch that sweeps behind Point San Eugenio, jumps San Ignacio Lagoon, and hems half the Peninsula.

That this plain has but recently risen is shown by the sprinkling of shells that could not have maintained their present condition for any geological length of time. We know that the shore is still rising, for it is a common experience of the men who navigate this coast that the bars of all the lagoons have shallowed and that entrances which once could be made no longer are attempted. Strange to say, this is not the first emergence of the plain, for on its bed are to be found countless fossil shells in which can be read the history of alternate rise and fall.

So passed the afternoon, with Lagoon Head taking form as a volcanic peak, drawing abeam and passing astern, as we, fascinated, watched the mountains turn inland and draw further and further away. The plain grew wider and assumed gigantic proportions, developing meanwhile a color tone and a bizarre beauty marked by harsh contrasts with vagrant buttes and distant ranges. The panorama of grey sand and yellow hostile hills bleaching in the sun shifted detail as our perspective moved, but in character they changed not at all. Another day was waning as we slipped deeper into Vizcaíno Bay, into an environment where time and space, having no limits, cease to exist.

CHAPTER XIII

EVEN the expected can surprise. We were running south across a great arm of the ocean. A following sea was beginning to assume uncomfortable proportions and there was a bit of wind, too, with clouds banking along the horizon. Vizcaíno Bay was bare, not a sail, not a bird, and in the haze we could see no land unless, by chance, that indistinct line to port marked the edge of the desert plain. The afternoon was waning, the sun was no longer keeping us warm, and promise was of a cold, uncomfortable night.

And then the breakers, which at first we did not recognize for what they were. But waves do not curl and froth when there is neither near-by shore nor protruding rocks. By the time the combers had become unmistakable we saw that our course would leave them to port by a margin that seemed dangerously small. It was becoming apparent, too, that the waves were not being retarded by any tiny or isolated shoal, but that the line of whitecaps was lengthening, that it extended shoreward as far as the eye could follow. Captain was indifferent and we, having confidence, were persuading ourselves that there was no hazard in paralleling the ugly furrows, when to starboard appeared another field of disturbance.

Farther out to sea, more incongruous and more threatening, ran a second line of whitecaps. We passed between, full speed ahead, and for one long hour threaded our way with destruction close beside on either hand. We did so with safety, if not indifference, for today the breakers served as channel markers. But let the weather play one of its tricks. let the sky become so dark that deep and shallow water are one color, let the sea become so quiet that it ceases to break or so rough that the two lines blend into one, and perhaps another little vessel will add its carcass to those that strew Lower California's beaches. It was a long sixty minutes of tension before the sand dunes came to us, but half an hour more brought us safely to anchor in Scammon's Lagoon.

The day's work was over and we were too comfortably situated to worry about the wind. It was freshening to storm proportions and late in the evening steadied into a half gale and as such blew all night and for thirty-six hours afterwards. We did not wait it out but early the next morning moved the *Least Petrel* a few miles up the northern channel, anchored near the first of the two bird islands, and went ashore to start our regular routine.

Bird Island is a crescent of sand flanked with a marsh of reeds. The dune is a mile or so in length and but a few hundred feet across, curved almost to a semicircle and with its apex facing westward, directly into the trades. The marsh is on the lee and spreads over many hundreds of acres of land that is flooded by one tide and exposed at the next. The solid field of single-stalked grass is broken only where it is permeated with the drainage ditches that feed into each other until they build an effective arterial system.

As may be imagined the wind was creating quite a disturbance on the unprotected crescent. The air was a dense cloud of sand that stung the face and more than halfway choked and wore one down because it could not be disregarded. A hundred and fifty, perhaps two hundred days in the year is the rind of fine grains peeled from this protruding bar, gathered into a wedge of smoke, and flung for half a mile broadcast over the marsh. What wasted effort! For at high tide the currents slide over the fen, slip between the growing stalks they nourish, and flake by flake retrieve the spoils. Booty laden they steal back to windward of the bank and there restore the sustenance without which the island could not survive a season.

Bird Island is interesting because of its history and, on quiet days, attractive because of its guests. Herons and egrets of seven species breed here, the marsh offering them at once food and safety from marauding coyotes. But it is not man alone who is barred from the Garden of Eden. The scheme of Nature demands that life shall not exist unless earned by suffering and struggle and so we find a colony of gulls, hungry and remorseless, ever alert for the momentary exposure of an egg or a chick.

We spent a day on Bird Island, not half enough, there was so much to do. We were especially interested in a Marsh Sparrow that is apparently endemic here and has not yet been named. The gulls of Scammon's are also unnamed and there was some fact new to science to be learned from nearly every resident we saw. There were interesting traces of the presence of men, signs of abandoned camps and scattered shells of the three hundred pound turtles that abound in the lagoon. There was other spoor left by the fishermen— mullet, turtles and even whales, at one time or another, have brought many wanderers to Scammon's, but not one has ever remained to make this a permanent home.

Our second day in the lagoon was divided among the half dozen small islands on which we landed during the course of a run that took us twenty miles back from the entrance. The most interesting of our stops was on a half moon of clam shells. Here was a barrier half a mile long, averaging a hundred yards across, and, like Bird Island, bending back from the prevailing wind. But on Clam Island there was not a grain of sand nor a blade of vegetation. In fact there was literally nothing but shells. They were uniform in size, of about a three inch diameter, and in a state

A HIGHLAND HOME

DESERT SPRINGS

A FLIGHT OF TERNS IN SCAMMON'S

of preservation that suggested recent life. They were piled
in a series of ridges that stood twelve to fifteen feet high
and either followed the contour of the circle or else pushed
out at right angles to form little peninsulas. This island was
unnatural, it was eerie, for on it there was virtually not a
fragment, not a shell that was either imperfect or worn.

There is another islet, round and flat, on which, of all
things, lies the trunk of a large tree. Where it grew and
how it reached this resting place is a mystery. A pair of
ospreys, feeling that a few feet above the ground are better
than none, have built a nest on the log and have raised
young there, year after year, at least ever since the first visit
of the men who now navigate Scammon's. The nest, low as it
is, can still be seen before the island itself becomes visible
and is commonly used as a bearing from which to locate
channels. It will probably be so used for many a decade to
come, for such a nest is a perpetuating institution. It continues indefinitely without regard to the lives of the founders because, when either of a pair dies, the survivor takes
another mate and the new couple, reverting to the status of
the old, retain the homestead.

A small island, so thickly overgrown with cholla that
walking is difficult, supports what is perhaps the most concentrated mouse population in Mexico, and a sandstone outcropping near the centre of the lagoon has been settled upon
by two species of plover. There is an insular hill—I estimated its length as ten miles—which nearly closes the channel and, biologically, is part of the surrounding mainland.
A number of eyots are given over to oyster-catchers and
complete the picture of the lagoon as an incipient Venice.

Farther north, in the earlier days of the trip, we had met
the Black Oyster-catcher, a bird without a white feather
and one almost never found away from a black background.
His habitat is the dark stretch of water-washed rocky islets
and coastline from California to Alaska. In Scammon's

we have another species, the Frazar Oyster-catcher, whose breast and belly are pure white, and we have also in Scammon's only environments of light grey that become dazzling in the sun. Clearly each bird is less conspicuous in his own surroundings than in those of the other and the dividing line between the two races coincides with the geological change. It is probable that we have here an example of protective coloration brought about by evolution; indeed, if biology were not so replete with exceptions we might consider the point as interesting and convincing proof.

The end of the second day in Scammon's found us twenty miles from the entrance and about halfway to the head of the lagoon. This is a large body of water and, never having been surveyed, is anything but easy to navigate. Since the channels are to be followed only by watching the lanes of blue and green water, when night overtook us we were compelled to anchor. Our last view in the evening was of a solitary raven on a tidal bar. He was the lucky finder of a clam, quite a treasure in this desolation. The trouble was he couldn't open it so he carried it to a height of fifty feet and dropped it. Fine idea, but the mud bank was too soft and the scavenger's careful inspection showed him that the bivalve was still unbroken. We saw the bird repeat the process a dozen times, with what luck I don't know, but I hope that his perseverance was finally rewarded.

The wind died out during the night and morning broke clear and calm. That was a relief. We decided not to go any deeper into the lagoon; it was beginning to narrow and become less interesting. We would have enjoyed visiting the salt deposit from which an unlimited amount of the mineral can be shovelled in usable condition, but it was several miles away and not worth the time and effort.

Our run down the lagoon is something never to be forgotten. We followed the southern shore, often a sandstone bluff reaching ten or fifteen feet above us. Sometimes there were dunes and occasionally little patches of beach with a bit of salt water grass. Land to north and in front was lost under the curve of the horizon so perforce we turned again to port and looked across a plain whose surface was so level that it, too, followed the curvature of the earth. There was vegetation on the flat, a chaparral here, a cholla there, enough to make the landscape even more forlorn than had it been sterile. In the distance, so clear was the air this morning, could be seen the tops of mountains to the east and to the south the inappropriate links of the range that forms Cape San Eugenio.

A butte, steep and isolated. Ten miles away, or twenty or thirty, its slopes are yellow with barrenness and corrugated with erosion. It glitters in the uncompromising sunlight and, with no place in the composition of the scene, it yet attracts the eye beyond all its deserts, an unfinished blatant daub on the landscape, an epitome of everything the world should not be. Scammon's is depressing and just as we were beginning to believe that we were in the most neglected place in the world three men appeared on the beach, waving frantically.

Such signals of distress are not to be disregarded. Captain brought the castaways aboard and we listened to their tale of woe. It seems that their home, a little ranch, was in the mountains four days away by pack-train. They had come down to the coast, as they did every year, to lay in a supply of sea-food, and when they reached their shack a few days before it was to find that they had been robbed. As they probably owned almost nothing and had left little of that in Scammon's the situation did not strike me as serious, but it was. The thieves had done a hundred percent job, taking not only everything that was in the building, but also the house itself. All they had left were the post holes.

Poor devils. They were in desperate straits for water, their keg nearly empty and their firewood gone together with the still from which they had planned to evaporate sea water. They were bitter against the foreign fishermen who had perpetrated this outrage and who can blame them? We gave them food and water which we could poorly afford but which would enable them to reach home, and put them back on the beach. Pathetic, of course, but it was funny. I wish I could repeat the dramatic way in which the old man described his feelings as it gradually dawned upon him that the house for which he was looking had actually disappeared.

The rest of the day passed uneventfully. It would not do to cross the bar until just before dark, so we felt our way along the shore, stopping and landing wherever and whenever anyone felt so inclined, and generally conducting ourselves in a shamefully lazy manner. Anti-climax was getting in its deadly work. Even the eight-mile run between the lines of breakers had lost its thrill and when we were again on Vizcaíno Bay, plowing monotonously into the night, no one aboard was interested in anything.

CHAPTER XIV

THE SAN BENITO ISLANDS

THREE in number, outposts in the open Pacific, they lie beyond Cedros and a hundred miles west of Scammon's. So we crossed Vizcaíno Bay, an overnight run by log and compass. Dawn found me in the pilot house watching the horizon widen as twilight strengthened and extended visibility. Presently from sea and mist emerged a group of insular pinnacles.

"The San Benitos?" I ventured.

"Cedros," answered Captain. That didn't make sense. At an eight-knot speed we should have been thirty miles farther on our course.

"Currents," said Captain, "currents and engine trouble." I doubted one and was sure the other came from throttling the fuel feed; Captain was too canny to be caught in the dark anywhere near danger.

Cedros is one of the larger islands, being twenty miles long and averaging five across, and its size was a deterrent to our landing. No short visit could do it justice. Its flora and fauna are of outstanding interest but they have been so extensively studied that only by weeks of collecting could we hope here to add appreciably to biological knowledge. We felt that time could be spent to better advantage on smaller islands and in places less thoroughly explored. So we reluctantly decided to content ourselves with what we could see from the boat.

Marking the western limits of Vizcaíno Bay the island lay north and south directly across our course. From the water it is a corrugated wedge of yellow ochre, isolated, forbidding, scorching. At a distance its walls rise abruptly and reach their four thousand feet as almost vertical bulging ribs. The curved arc of the top adds to the impression that the island is a lump of raw material, misplaced and forgotten. Like a half risen sun, like a full rigged ship hull down on the horizon, Cedros is detached, in and yet not of the seascape, a carved relief that surely must be a blazing butte more appropriately resting on an unseen desert plain.

The details of the island we fortunately did not have to take on faith. In her girlhood days the Partner had spent a month as a guest at Brown's mining camp and there were few places to which she had not ridden or rambled. Her interest was especially awakened in the cedars from which the island takes its name, in the heavy growth that ranges along the summit and draws sustenance from condensed ocean moisture. The trees parallel those on top of Guadalupe Island, though upon the adjacent Peninsula this cedar is unknown. By the time the higher levels of the trades reach Sierra de la Giganta they have passed across a wide stretch of hot coastal plains and slopes. The desiccating bed absorbs too much water to enable the air to support anything more exacting than Yucca Palms or Elephant Trees. On Cedros, however, the untouched west wind brings cloudbanks straight to the sweltering lands and convulsively drops its burden at the shock of the contact.

The Partner knew, too, of the water holes and the lesser vegetation and of the deer and smaller mammals and of the wealth of bird life. Compared with the mainland of Lower California, excepting its oases, portions of Cedros might be regarded as fertile. There are oaks and other heavier growths and there are ravines choked with brush. But if for the moment one forgets environment and contrasts Cedros with a prairie country or even with Southern California as a whole there is no mistaking it for anything but a lesser desert. It is uninhabited, except for a small fish cannery on the southern tip, and although many attempts have been made to profit by its mineral wealth the net result is only abandoned mines and prospect holes. As it stands today Cedros is nothing more than an intermittent camp for fishermen and turtle hunters.

We were not long in rounding the pinnacles which I had mistaken for islands. The gruesome eastern walls of Cedros did not hold our attention however, for we were trying to pierce the haze that lay across our bows. Captain insisted that in the darker shadings he could identify the Benitos and even to our inexperienced eyes the blur in which the most honest of us at first could distinguish nothing soon began to assume definite form. Slowly but surely two islands became unmistakable and by mid-morning we were abeam the more easterly.

Our course brought us close inshore with the island to starboard. It is a mile and a half pile of volcanic ash and lava surrounded by a sea-wall of irregular contour. There are indentations running back to tiny beaches of sand or pebble and there are projecting ridges that thrust outward until they slip under water and become ugly reefs. The upper portion of the island is marked with peaks the tallest of which reaches four hundred feet. Irregularly spaced are many little valleys and plains that wind in and out among the harsher slopes and support intermittent fields of sage and stunted brush. The sand and guano that has become mixed with the ash does not suffice to relieve the island of its sombre tinge of black. East San Benito is dark and forbidding, but it promises many a pleasant hour to those who can penetrate its reserve.

Though there is neither fresh water nor human occupancy on any of the Benitos life burst from the shoreline to herald our approach. Nowhere, not even in the Gulf, have I seen sea lions in such hordes. They littered the water, diving and racing through the foam they churned, fearful either of approaching us too closely or of being caught in shallows which might prove unsafe. Every now and then appeared a head breaking through the surface to watch, motionless and reproachful, with little more than the face exposed. Meanwhile the herd was growing as added beasts crawled from sun-baths on the beaches or flopped down rocky slopes which a man could scarcely climb, and all the while the day was made hideous by these caricatures of dogs, by the shrill yaps of the females and young and by the guttural roars of the great thousand or twelve-hundred pound bulls.

In the background were birds. They were not disappointingly few in number but neither were they present in an abundance at all comparable with more congested spots. We were able to identify the larger species, especially the osprey. A dozen of the fish-hawks were flying with slow, full wing beats along lines that appeared to run behind cliff tops and yet weirdly brought the birds across the faces of sea-walls. The apparent movement of the island was real to the point of ghostliness. A flock of pelicans came flopping from their nests in one of the cañons as we rounded the point on the southern end. Awkward things they certainly were, getting under way and flying out over the water. To me the birds themselves and their every movement proclaim them antediluvian heritages that have neither counterpart nor place in our modern world.

It was a short run to an anchorage where two islands gave modified protection. Middle Benito is small and low, its greatest height being barely eighty feet. It is so openly exposed to breaking seas that at no time during our stay were we able to effect a landing upon it. Judged from the boat it is an emerged reef that has accumulated enough soil or guano to support a scant vegetation. West San Benito, on the other hand, is several times larger than its eastern mate and is correspondingly more rugged. Its peaks are half as high again as those of its sister, are steeper, and the profiles are more broken. There is proportionately less level land on the main island, the valleys are smaller and the cañons narrower. The two resemble each other, however, much more closely than the differences in their geological histories would suggest.

We were eager to land, to start work which promised more than anything yet undertaken. We did well that first afternoon, adding the Thayer Gull to the ornithology of Lower California and finding a few surviving McGregor House Finches. These linnets and the question of whether or not they were extinct had largely been responsible for our coming to the Benitos. We estimated later that on the two islands there probably remain twenty-five individuals and that the race seems to be holding its own. But any species whose continuance hangs on such a slender thread seems doomed, for one bit of hard luck and there is no recovery. We found San Benito Marsh Sparrows to be abundant and Tony achieved a triumph by bringing in the first set of their eggs that had ever been taken. He and I ranged over the hills and made a nice addition to my series of osprey eggs while Charley hunted for and found mottled specimens of presumably intergraded oyster-catchers.

But the honors of the Benitos fell to Fred Rogers, and Lady Luck, in electing to bestow her favors upon him, won universal commendation. A fine old gentleman he is, admired by everyone aboard, and with the added attribute of courage. We naturalists knew at least that we would everywhere find birds to study and unanswered problems to solve one way or the other, but he had joined us with no real evidence that there ever had been ancient life on our line of travel. Exploring a virgin field he risked returning empty handed from a trip whose hardships were not to be lightly regarded. His recompense came that afternoon, for at dinner he told us that, even if the rest of his work were a blank, he had been repaid for the entire voyage.

Rogers' first move had been to search for signs of early camp sites. Primitive man was closely limited in his choice of locations and in his means of earning a living but the experienced archæologist has many guides to lead him to former habitations. One is the preference for rolling knolls which are safe and comfortable, and another is the relatively indestructible traces of occupancy. Shells are the most conspicuous relics, for the early inhabitants of West Benito were almost dependent on sea-food and brought quantities of clams and mussels and abalones to their homes to be prepared and consumed. So Rogers travelled from one likely looking hill to another in search of heaps of broken shells.

He found quite a number of former camp sites and his next task was to search the grounds for introduced flints. Sometimes there is certainty, sometimes difficulty, in distinguishing between bits of rocks which have been deposited naturally and those which have been brought by human agencies from outside sources. Identification of foreign pieces, rich in disclosures of the wanderings of the owners, involves work to be done in the museum, not in the field. The examination of artifacts is made *in situ* in order to select specimens, but reading them is beyond the acumen of such beginners as ourselves. We could see knives when they were shown us, and flakes and scrapers and fracture lines, but I, at least, of my own initiative could not have been sure that they were anything more than bits of rock which had happened to break into their present shapes. The hammer stone, however, was another matter. Even a tyro could see that the elongated cobble had been used to pound something hard, for both ends were matted with dents that could have been made in no other way. I am sure that microscopic tests will reveal bits of flint imbedded in the pestle.

THE SAN BENITO ISLANDS

Although it would not be safe to draw sweeping conclusions from this preliminary survey there are several interesting things that had been proven by Rogers. The former existence of human life on this island is established and as corollaries there must have been sources of fresh water and there were also means of navigating the ocean. The artifacts of the Channel Islanders of Southern California demonstrate those Indians to have had a much higher culture and one differing from that of the San Benitos and it is probable that the latter is also distinct from that of the early inhabitants of the mainland. It is by no means impossible that Rogers has discovered a race new to anthropology and it is certain that he has traced wanderings previously unsuspected. So to him goes the palm for the day, perhaps for the trip.

The next morning he and I went to East San Benito, an hour's run with dory and outboard. Rather to our surprise we found evidences that the two islands belong to distinct geological ages and, what was more unexpected, that on this, the smaller, there are no traces of prehistoric men. Why one island should have been frequented and the other neglected is a puzzle for which we could suggest no answer. Rogers hunted diligently all day and I looked through a series of osprey nests for egg types which I particularly wanted. I also made a further study of linnets and sparrows and thoroughly enjoyed the hours of easy exploration. It was still February by the calendar, but spring was in full bloom in the archipelago.

Our great thrill came when we reached the deep coves along the eastern side of the island. Drawn up on every sand beach, sunning themselves and basking in the warmth of perfect weather, were family groups of Elephant Seals. At least in recent times there have been no northern records of these brutes other than from Guadalupe Island, two hundred miles away, and we could hardly believe our eyes as we counted forty-two. That this was part of the Guadalupe herd there can be no doubt, and I am still wondering what system of navigation brought them to this pin point after an absence that may have run into generations.

At our approach sea lions fled before us, almost filling the surf. They were frightened and they were angry and they made no effort to suppress their feelings. Those we surprised made ludicrous efforts to hurry, flopping from the beaches or risking necks sliding the slippery rocks. They swarmed a hundred yards offshore, swimming back and forth at that safe distance and splitting our ears with their disgruntled bellowings. Out from camps held in common with the Elephant Seals they came, and in panic they poured between the larger brutes. The indifference of the latter was superb. Many did not so much as move and the most attention that any paid to the wild riot was to raise a head out of curiosity, look about for the cause of the excitement, and calmly drop back to sleep.

We climbed down to the first beach where the beasts lay and found a typical family consisting of a bull, four or five cows, and half a dozen suckling young. They took no notice of us, even when we were within ten or twelve feet, the distance at which caution bade us stop. It is impossible to exaggerate their indifference; it was absolute. Man is so accustomed to have all animals fear him that an exhibition of any other feeling seems uncanny. We have all heard of animals which, with or without provocation, will attack a human being or are otherwise dangerous to approach and so we half expected these monsters to send us scampering up the cliff. Their utter lack of interest as to where we stood or what we did fairly staggered us.

No less astonishing was the indifference displayed by the mothers toward our handling their offspring and the fearlessness of the babies themselves. The youngsters regularly crawled twenty or thirty feet back from the water though adults barely dragged themselves out of the waves. This position enabled us easily to pass between the parents and the cubs, something, I believe, no other wild animal would permit unless impelled by overwhelming fear. In the interest of accuracy I should note one exception. There was a cow, her baby ten yards up the beach from where she lay, who resented intrusion on our part. The hundred pound tot was hungry and cried all the time it was not being suckled, a most peculiar call that can best be described as a cross between the bleat of a goat and the yelp of a dog.

The mother came at us open mouthed and we had no false pride about moving. Her means of locomotion were quite different from those of a seal. She raised herself half erect and, using her flippers as a fulcrum, plunged straight forward with no suggestion of a twist. Her body was dragged as a dead weight upon her belly. Her progress was slow but her desire to drop her huge carcass upon one of us was quite clear.

The bulls are enormous creatures, fifteen to eighteen feet long with a weight that runs into tons. The sixteen inch elongation of the probosis which they inflate at will and which they curl back over the face when excited is responsible for the name given to the species. We tossed pebbles upon them, puzzling and angering them, but they were too stupid to connect us with the annoyance. They bent their heads backward, mouths wide open and huge tusks exposed, weaving their necks from side to side and challenging the unknown to single combat. That it is by constant battle that they maintain their harems is shown by the wide area of overlapping, nasty scars that covered every neck and shoulder.

Our clearest and most pleasant memory of the Elephant Seal is of a family in repose. Neither mounted specimens nor captives in a zoo picture the spirit of these animals fulfilling their destinies in the environments to which by nature they are adapted. They had come to Benitos for their vacation and every private apartment in the resort was occupied. On pleasure bent they slept away the sunny hours, face down upon the beach. They played with sand, tossing it upon themselves until their backs were covered. The tips of their rudimentary forelegs are developed to resemble a hand and they pick up and throw gravel much as we would do from the same position. In perfect peace, with never a fear or worry, they yet have a facial expression that verges on pathos.

Their eyes are weak, ludicrously large and set far apart, suggesting that they hunt their prey at great depths. They are carnivora, but so slow are all their movements that I cannot imagine them capturing any but the most sluggish of quarries. Hardly an eye that was not diseased. One wonders if a curse to which they will succumb has been laid upon this race of giants.

CHAPTER XV

OUR last day on the Benitos began propitiously. The Partner, Tony, Peter, and Gregory of course must see the Elephant Seals and Rogers took them over, acting as guide and photographer. They were away all morning, leaving me to my writing, and the party very nearly was marooned. A sharp wind, coming up about noon, had rolled in seas that made the launching of the dory a matter of judgment and patience. The Partner came aboard full of stories about the gargantuans and the half hour spent in trying to get off the island.

The afternoon was devoted to mopping up unfinished work. The naturalists had specimens to prepare and the Partner and I wanted a few more hours on West San Benito. She had by this time assumed charge of the reptile collecting, spiritually and inspirationally. We all enjoyed bringing to her the snakes and lizards she would not touch, and we shared her enjoyment in the valuable acquisitions accumulating in her formaldehyde bottles. As we couldn't present the lady with candy or flowers we satisfied our masculine instincts with offerings of these animals.

I took a twenty-two rifle ashore, also a box of shot cartridges. We walked across the more level stretches hoping, but in vain, to find a sparrow nest, the while I picked up an occasional unwary lizard and she filled her arms with hyacinths and other wild flowers that did not know winter was still with us. We explored the hillsides, especially the slopes of soft ash that were peppered with bird burrows.

It was much too early in the season for occupants but we could read of those who would come. Auklet signs of course were abundant, but on this island the little divers were outnumbered by petrels and shearwaters. Acre upon acre we passed where openings were so close together that it seemed impossible the holes did not cut into each other. Life offers these pelagic birds so nearly nothing that they actually become an inspiring example of Nature's insistence that the species shall survive.

The days upon the San Benitos had been happy as well as profitable. The out-of-door life and the constant walking were building health and developing muscle, and isolation from the world had so far given only favorable reactions. It is a matter of temperament, I suppose, that makes some miss morning papers and mail and intercourse with circles of associates while others revel in the freedom that comes with the certainty of no outside interruption. The Benitos were our property, they had given all the privacy that could have come with a fee, and they had yielded us the right to possess ourselves of anything we coveted. It was not a couple of barren cinder piles we were leaving but two real friends who had had much to tell and who had withheld nothing.

By the time the Partner and I returned to the *Least Petrel* the west wind had become strong and was rather gusty. As there remained much to be done we postponed sailing until eight o'clock and those of us who were able to do so seized upon the interval for rest. When it came time to leave Peter began to question the ability of Captain to follow the course in the dark.

"I'm not taking any chances," Captain assured him. "I know every foot of these waters as you know your way down town and there are plenty of headlands here to give bearings."

Peter did not press the matter, but he was not satisfied.

TONY INVESTIGATES

YUCCA IN THE LITTORAL OF VIZCAÍNO

IN THE CIRIO BELT

He made no oral protest as we started, though his relief was obvious at our safely passing East Benito. We were making good time, running before wind and sea, and when we reached open water the great swells began fairly to shove us on our way. We were almost back-tracking now, crossing towards the mainland and planning to skirt the northern side and eastern end of Natividad Island.

Cedros, we knew, lay ahead and we were seeing, or imagining, its darker outlines against the field of stars, when suddenly the engine began to race, then sputtered, and stopped. We had our report in a moment—the governor spring was broken and could not be repaired in less than an hour or two. In the meanwhile we had turned broadside to the wind and the *Least Petrel* began to roll heavily in the trough of the waves as we drifted to westward.

We were uncomfortable but it was all in the day's work. As there was no danger we didn't give the little accident much thought until we began to notice the effect it was having upon Peter. The last person aboard of whom one would have suspected such a thing became nervous, then frightened, and finally panicky. If the boat, on the down roll, took a severe slap he was sure she would not right herself. When she failed to turn turtle he watched for combers that would swamp her and meanwhile she was drifting on the rocks of Cedros where she would be smashed before the engine could be started. Eventually we did get under way. We were appreciably closer to the island, but that was all.

Captain paralleled it, running due south, headed for the passage along the north side of Natividad, but every foot of the way Peter kept his eye on the dark line of rocks toward which the wind was blowing and measured our drift against the progress we were making toward the cape. Once past San Augustín we turned sharply southeast and once more ran before the wind. The boat had steadied and not even to Peter was there any menace toward which we were

97

being forced. His nerves were shot, however, and Natividad became his bugbear.

Captain knew exactly where the *Least Petrel* lay, and, which was more important, precisely how far away was the island, but Peter did not. We were headed directly at Cape San Eugenio but at the proper time Captain turned south into Dewey Channel. He paralleled the coast of Lower California for a couple of hours, passing Breaker Point and Kelp Point to swing into his anchorage. It was neat navigating to be sure and permitted of no guesswork, but there was not any risk involved. The course was familiar to Captain and every minute he had it placed, but all poor Peter could do was to stare into the night, prey to his fear and always uncertain whether he saw land or not.

I turned in when we passed Cape San Augustín but sleep was long in coming. I was worried over the results in the months to come to this break in morale. I tried to see the night's run as Peter had seen it, and there was a very small boat on a rough and very large ocean. Storm waves breaking over sunken ledges, winds and currents shoving relentlessly all day long and through the night, these are no opponents for man to challenge. When stark black adds to the terrors of the unknown who dare trust simple wiles when the only hope is to outwit what he cannot oppose? And to face this alone, in empty seas studded only with enemies and far beyond the ken of anyone or thing on whom to call for help—yes it must be the element of distance on which Peter had broken.

A night express racing into a blizzard. Give imagination free reign, lose confidence in the power of gravity to hold the cars on the track, distrust the engineer in catching every block signal, picture an obstruction fallen across the roadway, in every respect save that the countryside is filled with people here is a richer culture in which to breed the germs of fear. Peter's mind does not work as it did tonight if he takes an automobile ride, if he goes hunting with a companion, if he is exposed to bacteria in a theatre, in any of his everyday pursuits, and I know he has travelled much upon the water. If my surmise be correct, if he has succumbed to emptiness, the prospect opens possibilities I dread to consider. If in one short week this country has broken the nerve of our strongest man what will it do to him in four months time? Will he experience fear and yet remain a man or will he break still further when he reaches the greater loneliness in the Gulf?

Since nothing can be done the wisest course is to stop fretting and wait for whatever the future may reveal. Let us think of something else, of Cape San Eugenio, for instance, toward which, at the moment, we are headed. It marks a most important turning point in our study of the Peninsula, for below it we come in contact with conditions differing from anything we have yet encountered. I had occasion, in earlier chapters, to explain the San Diegan Faunal District and draw its boundaries and to describe the area lying to the south, spreading clear across Lower California, and named the Vizcaíno Desert. We are now entering a third, technically termed the Northern Sub-faunal District of the Cape Region.

From San Diego the coast runs roughly south-southeast to San Gerónimo Island and then turns southeast to Scammon's. Cape San Eugenio is due west from the mouth of that lagoon and there the coast swings southeast again as far as Cape San Lúcas. Cape San Eugenio also limits Vizcaíno Bay, so altogether it develops into an interesting landmark. It affects, or at least delimits, climatic conditions, for here abruptly begin the mangroves that require subtropical warmth. We meet such birds as the Mangrove Warbler, Elegant Tern and Heerman Gull breeding close to but not north of the Cape and fishermen echo ornithologists in presaging the coming of the Gulf.

Even the weather finds this a turning point. Spring storms ordinarily do not range below Vizcaíno Bay nor are summer gales apt to extend above Natividad. The stage is set for another scene and my mind is at peace, speculating on what will be revealed when the curtain of night is raised.

CHAPTER XVI

WE woke to find ourselves in a quiet bay. It was a sheltered body of water two or three miles in diameter and nearly circular in shape. Bordering it and following the curve of its outline was a beach of fine white sand that added the touch of comfort to our feeling of security. Along the tangent from Kelp Point to Cabo Tórtola the skyline was jagged with great swells rolling in from the ocean. A storm was under way, but a series of protruding rocks, partly closing the channel, halted the march of the waves. They could not reach to annoy us in our welcome little haven. This is the Turtle Bay of the fishermen and as such it is known along the waterfronts of San Diego and San Pedro. Officially it was and remains Port San Bartolomé and I cannot see wherein a change of name is warranted. For one thing, strangely, there are no turtles here. Under the shelter of the southern headland is an arm of San Bartolomé to which turtle hunters, so I've been told, were wont to bring their catches in preparation for shipment to the States. The bight became known as Turtle Bay and under that designation appears upon the charts. The extension of the local name to include Port San Bartolomé itself is the general practice of the boatmen but is inexact and tends to unnecessary confusion.

In former days when their vessels were small and effective cruising ranges for fishermen were short, San Bartolomé was the frontier of the little known waters below. It is now a way port for the hundred footers whose equipment of refrigerating plants enables them to bring frozen cargoes from Cocos Island or even the far-away Galápagos. But all the romance of the little way station has not been lost. Turtle Bay, for they will not call it otherwise, is the starting or finishing point of many an old-time tale of the seas, and no fisherman but enjoys the telling of his experiences there, of the catches he made and of the men he has met.

The surroundings of Port San Bartolomé, as we saw them before going ashore, were the barrens we had expected and to which we were becoming accustomed. We were in a plain that stretched away until, at greater or lesser distances, it was closed by an overlapping circle of isolated mounds and small ranges of hills. On either flank pressed extensions of the headlands of the harbor entrance and between them lay level country that was broken only by an occasional rise. This was not the flat expanse we had seen at Scammon's, for here was soil rather than sand. The surface had been submerged in one or more of the undulating vagaries of the Peninsula, but it showed none of the characteristics of subaqueous origin.

At the time of our visit there was under construction a small fish cannery on Kelp Point. We made a call, Captain, the Partner, and I, and were received by a very lonely couple who did not miss by much the fate of having been shipwrecked on a desert island. They were waiting for machinery—development in Mexico seems always to be waiting for something—and we who had looked forward to hearing of what had been going on in the world found the rôles reversed. The little frame house which the Quamas have built on the hill at the foot of the pier is even more desolate than would have been a camp. On the outside there is nothing but the four walls; not so much as a blade of grass relieves the stark nakedness. The reason, of course, is that the only water that can be secured comes from the tanks of the irregular supply ship. A survey of the grounds, of the machine shed, of the floor of the wharf reveals that to the most trivial item everything has been brought down by boat. The environments made us appreciate as nothing else could have done what it means to live in a land that cannot contribute the slightest resource of its own.

Quamas treated us most hospitably, filling our tanks with fuel oil and water, caring for mail to be forwarded when opportunity offered, and giving us much detailed information about the country. One of his men sold us lobsters, and now you urban housewives listen to this—eighteen for a dollar! We were more than glad to get them. Our food, though particularly good, was so limited in variety that a certain sameness was inevitable. A trivial detail, this, especially as exercise was giving enormous appetites to us all. But out of it a new worry was developing, one which possibly a change of diet would check. Gregory was showing every symptom of becoming whiney.

We moved the *Least Petrel* up the bay and after an early lunch went ashore on exploration bound. The Partner and I walked for several hours towards the hills, over soil that was almost bare. It was eroded, more by wind than by water, it was rough with hummocks that often were held in place by the roots of a despairing sage, it was soft underfoot and baked dry. We made our way toward the mesa and eventually reached a tiny ravine where we found a bit more vegetation. There were growths here we had not seen on the plain. The number of species was no less surprising than the scarcity of individuals. It seemed almost as though we were in a museum collection where nothing was meant to be duplicated.

We swung back nearer the foothills and climbed a ridge. We could clearly see where our bay had once spread to double its present size and where another inlet had formerly come down from beyond San Bartolomé Point or possibly across from Vizcaíno Bay. About us were a number of scattered peaks and to our left a small range of isolated hills. They all were volcanic uplifts reaching a fairly uniform height of a thousand feet. That they were replicas of the ridge on which we stood was evident. Theirs were cruelly eroded slopes salved by no vegetation, unless in some accidental ravine, and they were wholly unprotected from the glaring sun. Nowhere in the vista was there relief from wave after wave of utter desolation.

Our return to the *Least Petrel* took us over swales, mesas, and arroyos, but brought no change in surroundings. Ever barren soil and aridity and heat, hellish in the cañons when details were forced upon us, hellish on the summits which revealed unnumbered miles without reprieve. Nowhere along the western slopes of the Californias is another such scene, another such kiln of sterility. We had by now established the nature of the peninsula that thrusts a thousand square miles of desert into the ocean, the triangular wedge culminating in Cape San Eugenio. The base we saw from Scammon's Lagoon is the one-time sea bottom that sweeps from the ocean at Vizcaíno Bay back to the ocean again at San Ignacio Lagoon. The apex is the ancient island on which we had tramped, the volcanic uplift that was rendering the world no service in the brief interval between its coming into being and its destruction by the elements. A half decayed, stillborn monstrosity.

We had a gorgeous dinner that evening. Will I ever forget either those boiled lobsters or that Brown Betty? I remember every man celebrated by shaving—a duty we were under contract with the Partner to perform not less than twice a week. Gregory blossomed with a new lease on life and Peter's lapse, which had been universally ignored, was apparently being atoned for by special congeniality. The Partner, of course, reacted to the praises of the food as also, presumably, did Juan, though I am quite sure he would have been equally cheerful if we had joined in damning it.

Charley had his engine patched, Captain had taken a well earned rest, and morale ran high.

Rogers had scored another triumph. How it was possible none of us could imagine, but this peninsula, perhaps when an island, had once supported a considerable primitive population. Their numbers and the length of their occupancy were in part revealed by the camps Fred found and in part by those which were described to him by Quamas. The culture was more highly developed than anything yet discovered, or even suspected to exist, in Lower California, and, as far as could be determined that night, the artifacts were of people whose coming into and going from the world have left no other record. Not only had Rogers made a find of outstanding importance but he had blocked out a field which will repay months of careful exploitation. We naturalists must look to our laurels.

As a matter of fact our reports were almost negative and of value principally for that reason. My personal census complete, covering five hours and including every resident land-bird I saw, even those in the distance, totalled three Grey Sage Sparrows, one San José Say Phœbe, four Santa Margarita Gnatcatchers and a pair of Northern Rock Wrens. The other collectors averaged about the same. Tony, who had ranged farther afield and into a higher country, saw even fewer birds but was consoled by an unexpected find. A sandstone cliff in eroding had exposed the fossil skeleton of some large mammal. It was so far above ground that he could not examine it closely and we had no facilities for excavating. Some day we intend to return, properly equipped.

The isolation of its bird life peculiarly fits San Eugenio Peninsula to be an ideal region in which to review and clarify certain basic economic laws. In its surroundings complications are reduced to a minimum and counteracting influences become manifest. It is a small scale working model with every piece in plain view.

Let us start with the simple statement that birds here are few because food is scarce. We do not have to infer that truism—we can see it. We can dissect all the contributing causes to a check in population, extremes of weather, lack of proper nesting sites, disease, parasites, and predatory enemies, and eliminate them as determinants. We can do so with certainty because every one of them is so fully exposed to examination that we can ascertain its influence, not by inference, but by the direct evidence of our own observation. Every factor is in the foreground; nothing is concealed or obscured.

The number of individuals present represents the maximum the country will support. Again the proof is before our eyes; we simply need weigh the flora against the fauna as each appears, here and there. We can see that there must be fluctuations, that the food supply is variable and that there will be pendulum swings of adjustment. If too many birds be present the surplus will starve; if too few the deficit will be corrected by local breeders or by an influx from the mainland, or both. Subject to temporary corrections the saturation point will always be maintained. We are looking at the bushes where the nests will be and the hills from which the outsiders could come.

If by some means the food supply of this region were doubled the lot of the birds now living would, for the time being, be greatly bettered. In the end, in one season or at the most two, the saturation point would again be reached and the only change that would have taken place would be an increase in the number of individuals struggling against starvation. I am well aware that in this line of reasoning there is nothing not generally understood and accepted by naturalists and economists. But the human mind seems to draw a distinction between matters it believes and things that it knows. Cape San Eugenio transfers the axioms from one category to the other. If mankind is timid in trusting his own reasoning power more than one step beyond experience, then this bleak land can carry certainty a bit deeper into theory. It gives courage to feel sure at least of the conclusions drawn directly from what it demonstrates.

We can see, with reservations, that the theory I have outlined is of universal application and that it will apply to humans and to animals alike. We can see the final tentacles of many of man's problems bared on this sun-baked dissecting table. I am not trying to persuade myself that I learned anything new, but I did obtain a confidence I have never had before that the biological laws governing the bird I study also govern myself.

Scientists may appreciate, but the world does not. Take, for instance, the case of the wheat-growers of the Middle West who are agitating for legislative assistance. Their saturation point is overproduction. Anything that is done to improve their condition may bring temporary happiness, as in the case of the birds. In one season, or two, or three the benefits that may be given will merely result in turning more men to growing wheat and in the end there will simply be a greater number struggling against overproduction. Unless there be established some check against the number of birds on one hand or the number of farmers on the other, the results will be inevitable and will flow from the workings of the same law. Could anyone, I wonder, stand beside me on the shores of San Bartolomé Bay and question that?

It may be that Peter's mind is not the only one to have been affected, that this is no place for speculations on extraneous matters, especially those having no claim to originality, that Cape San Eugenio is not the environment in which to dispose of farm relief legislation. Yet there was that long walk of the afternoon. There is the difference between learning theories from study and seeing them proven before your eyes. In a word, if I have been prattling banalities, if the Cape has nothing to teach, if the world accepts these truisms, why all this agitation for farm relief with its train of impossible hopes, ponderous pledges, and broken promises? Mental outlooks such as I obtained here have, to me, been one of the greatest features of the trip.

The next morning we crossed the bay to anchor near the southern beach. A salicornia-like hedge, between the water and the plains, held a promise of Marsh Sparrows. We devoted the forenoon to hunting them and succeeded in getting together a satisfactory series. We had by now specimens taken from Todos Santos Islands, Scammon's Lagoon, San Benito Islands, and San Bartolomé Bay and, by comparing them with each other, could see that we had four varieties of birds. The differences are small and revolve about darker or lighter shadings but they are constant and may enable us to work out puzzling distributional questions and migration routes.

We had callers after lunch. Arvis and Pennington, farmers whom we had known in the pueblo San Ignacio, are fishermen half of every year. Arvis gave us a sackful of undersized lobsters. Crawfish in these waters are taken alive by means of funnel-mouthed traps baited with dead fish. The market is in California where game laws do not allow lobsters to be sold until they have attained a specified size. Theoretically those too small are to be freed and to have a chance to breed and grow. In practice they are usually eaten by the fishermen or disposed of illegally. Fortunately we did not have to struggle with our consciences; in Mexican waters we were within the law.

In the afternoon, while the others skinned and Rogers hunted for new camp sites, the Partner and I explored the beach. We strayed into the semi-permanent camp of a Japanese colony of abalone gatherers. The abalone is a large semi-spherical monovalve whose shell attains a length of ten inches. It fastens itself to rocks and boulders below the limit of low tide and is taken, commercially, only by men in diving suits who pry it loose with steel bars. The meat is preserved by any one of several methods, usually either by drying or canning.

The dozen buildings in the camp were simple, but of imported lumber. The boats and the diving tackle, for open sea use, were very primitive. We found all the workers at home, for they could do nothing while the storm was blowing, and we spent a very enjoyable hour with them. They were polite and cordial and there was nothing they would not do or tell but, as they understood no English and as their pidgin Spanish was incomprehensible to us, conversation was difficult. There is about the Japanese an air of energy and efficiency that contrasts strongly with native Mexicans. Perhaps it is because the Asiatics are the more northern race, perhaps because only men ambitious to better themselves come to the New World, but whatever the reason their surroundings give the impression that their work is being done. Their standards of living do not suggest any greater success, though of course that may be accounted for by thrift and saving. Even in their contact with strangers they put more enthusiasm into their politeness.

We met one man in particluar whom we remember, he was so cordial and did struggle so hard to explain his doings. Down on the beach alone, a mile below camp, he was carrying a five-gallon gasolene can across a stretch of cobbles exposed by the tide. We watched him, puzzled as to what he was attempting, so he came to us and let us look into his pail. It was half full of the most disgusting squirmy and slimy things one can imagine. They were small octopi and I suppose were a relief to a steady diet of abalone and lobster, but our education didn't go that far.

Of course we had to know how he caught them and he

showed us, with much pride and many smiles. He carried with him a small bag of rock salt. Coming to a likely looking aperture, picked out at random or by expert knowledge, your guess is as good as mine, he dropped in a pinch of salt and rammed it home with a twig. This was too rich for Mr. Octopus. A protesting tentacle appeared from between the rocks, it was deftly seized and another choice morsel was dropped in the can. A gruesome occupation for the most genial soul we met on our travels.

CHAPTER XVII

THE BEACH AT THURLOE HEAD

ALL aboard for the South. We had a good thirty-three hour run ahead and, as Captain wanted to pick up Cape San Lázaro by daylight of the second day, we were starting an hour before sundown. We worked our way toward the mouth of the bay and when we lost the protection of Kelp Point found ourselves in a sea that was steadily growing rougher. The swell left by the storm was heavier than we had anticipated and our first clear view of the horizon to seaward showed a skyline serrated by huge combers. We weighed an uncomfortable night against the rumored attractions of Thurloe Bay and unanimously agreed to put back to port. Far be it from us to play the part of heroes.

In the morning the *Least Petrel* crossed the bay and anchored off the Japanese camp. The Partner and I, with Captain, were to go clamming and Charley was to lead the expedition. This engineer of ours is the best all around out-of-doors man with whom I have ever travelled and whatever promises succulent food is his specialty. The first thing after breakfast he dropped into the hold to reappear with sacks and shovels and prys for which he alone knew the use, and we were off.

We crossed the mile wide neck that separates San Bartolomé from Thurloe Bay. It was a sandy stretch holding a meagre growth of the brush of the littoral and was liberally sprinkled with deposits of shell. As we approached the ocean we found ourselves entering low sand dunes and here, in thicker bushes, I flushed a Desert Thrasher. It had no nest so I pursued the bird. It teased me for half a mile, keeping just out of gun range and eventually disappearing in heavy cover. When I turned to go back I found myself facing a pair of lovely looking pirates.

This was surprising; I thought I had accounted for everyone for a hundred miles around. It turned out that the men who had been following me were harmless and friendly and had acted from mere curiosity; they were guards who had been left to watch the *Emma G.* She was piled up on Thurloe Beach and when I reached her she was lying sidewise to the sea, her keel awash at this low tide. She had been a fishing boat, a trifle smaller than the *Least Petrel,* and her fate was a commentary on the dangers of navigating this coast.

At night headlands look too much alike to be distinguishable and so the custom on an inshore run is to start from a known point and note the capes in sequence as they are passed. A few nights ago the *Emma G.* had come bowling up the coast and her captain in some way had duplicated his count. Believing that he had rounded Cape Tortuga and was actually inside San Bartolomé Bay he was thinking only of anchoring when he struck, full speed ahead.

The *Emma G.* was so well sheltered that her pounding had done her no serious injury. If she were dragged off it is probable that she could continue on her course, unaided. There was little hope for her, however. Salvage so far from a base would be very expensive and the wreckers would be so long in reaching her that the little boat probably would have gone to pieces prior to their arrival. The owner will doubtless abandon her to underwriters who will not risk losing more than the face of the policy. It does seem a disproportionate magnification of an error of one in his count.

From the hull I walked down the beach. There is here an indentation in the coast line, a curve that affords an anchorage protected from the north and known as Thurloe

Bay. It has a wide gracefully sweeping border of white sand, one of those sheltered, gently sloping beaches so popular with swimmers. Here I found the others of my party. Charley and Captain were wet to their knees and the Partner to her waist, but they had a sack nearly full of very large clams. The art of finding these mollusks is simple. Between high and low water marks are easily recognized little blow-holes which must have something to do with feeding or breathing, for at the bottom of each vent is a clam. Two feet deep they pass their life cycles in a monotony that causes one to wonder at the instinct of self-preservation.

We made our way back to the *Least Petrel,* shouldering every pound we could carry. Waste? We did not have half enough. The amount of food the nine of us could consume before it spoiled was a source of constant wonder. A larder that seemed stocked for an indefinite time would melt away over-night from the combined attack of good cooking and day-long walking. There was little need to pamper our appetites; neither a clam nor a lobster was thrown overboard and yet they all were gone before we reached Magdalena.

The younger men were not aboard when we returned. They had heard of a living stream a few miles to the south and were putting in the day investigating. They had a long tramp for their pains but did find some recompense in their first sight of a wild antelope. The water, as was to be expected, did not materialize. Strange it is how often, when one hunts for these flowing springs, he either does not go far enough up the cañon or else he works the wrong watershed. What a garden Lower California would be if rumored water could irrigate!

Rogers and Juan had spent the morning on Thurloe Head. Near the point was a series of terraced sea-walls, superimposed in three tiers, each representing a distinct geological period and each marked with camps of differing eras. Rogers' needs included human remains, so he set the Basque to digging in an auspicious spot while he himself made further explorations. Our cook was a man of many prejudices. One of them, it now developed, opposed disinterring the remains of peaceful dead. He did uncover a skeleton, a treasure trove that probably would have established the identity of a prehistoric race. One glance was enough for Juan. He shovelled back the dirt as fast he could and, on Fred's return, told most convincingly of failure to find anything. It was just as well, for the peace of the party, that Rogers did not discover the lapse.

This was the sixteenth day of our trip and, in distance, we had now completed the first quarter of the cruise. We were half-way to our turning point at Cape San Lúcas. But we were to make only one more stop in the Pacific; time and weather had combined against us and we were even now overdue in the Gulf. So when late afternoon found us again at the harbor mouth we laid our course southeast for Magdalena, sacrificing many points of interest in the two hundred miles immediately below Thurloe Bay.

San Roque and Asunción Islands, each about three quarters of a mile long, are among the greatest of rookeries. South of the sandstone beds of Asunción there are no breeding auklets, but the delimination is abrupt, for this is one of the largest of their colonies. I had last been ashore there late one June and it seemed to me that I had never seen so many contiguous burrows. Every few steps, from one end of the island to the other, my foot broke through the crust and hardly a nest that was unoccupied. Not by adults, however. During incubation and the earlier days of the chick one or the other of the old birds is always to be found, but as the smoke-colored ball of hair-like down attains size he develops an appetite that taxes the combined efforts of father and mother and drives them to harry the sea day and night.

A dozen races of sea-birds crowd for nesting space on

these meeting places of north and south. Perhaps the most conspicuous are the big Brandt Cormorants, known to many as the Shag. They nest in compact circles of several hundred birds each. Scattered over the island were fifteen or twenty colonies, conspicuous black patches dotting a surface of otherwise unrelieved grey. As we approached the one we planned to investigate we found that we were to have rivals. Gulls, sensing what was coming, gathered from far and near and, lighting, surrounded the oval, keeping only beyond the reach of angry beaks. When the sitting birds could no longer withstand their fear of us they flushed and then the hungry horde rushed in for the feast. We were running too, such of us as were not thrown by auklet holes, and we managed, by separating our forces, to protect the eggs from the marauders.

We collected the specimens we needed—there was no object in not being generous to ourselves—we took our photographs and made our notes, but in the end we had to leave without having exhausted the patience of the gulls. Long before the timid cormorants had ventured a return from the water to which they had fled every nest was empty, every egg was gone. The episode is not quite the tragedy it seems, however, for in a week or so the cormorants will have laid again and in the end neither their happiness nor their productivity will have been permanently affected.

An explanation of the purposes of our collecting seems appropriate here. Eggshells are the oldest manifestations of heredity. Long after evolutionary processes have brought about anatomical modifications and the development of new color and feather patterns the shape and tints of eggs remain unchanged. The reason is not far to seek. Neither the pigmentation of eggs nor their markings, neither their shape nor their specific gravity nor the thicknesses of their shells have the slightest bearing on the question of the survival of the race or of individuals. The statement may admit of a few possible exceptions as, for instance, among the limicolæ; I am not as yet prepared to say. But in general other than in size eggs do not follow structural modifications as new species are transformed into new genera simply because there is no reason why the non-utilitarian characteristics should change. The sole determining factor is heredity; environment plays no part.

The analysis of shells is susceptible of a much greater degree of refinement than is possible with the anatomical determinations now in vogue. Larger series of eggs than of skins as a rule are available as a basis for data and furthermore measurements of shells can be made with a greater degree of precision than is possible with characteristics purely of the birds themselves. As a result inheritances that in no other way can be traced, divergences and relationships hidden from systematism, can, through oölogy, be added to our knowledge of ornithology.

As a concrete example consider the Cassin Auklets of Asunción. Scientists have been unable to separate them from the Cassin Auklets of Alaska, the other extreme of the range of the species. Yet eggs show that the two geographical groups represent decidedly different birds with wide and age-old divergencies of inheritance. Suppose I had before me a series of fifty eggs each from eight spaced stations along the Pacific Coast. Properly analyzed it would be possible to map from them the areas within which an interchange of mating takes place and those which are definitely isolated. There is no other known method by which this information can be obtained.

Eggs show, for instance, that the American Eared Grebes diffuse their blood and remain homogeneous throughout their range while the Northern Pied-billed Grebe has, as it spreads from the Atlantic to the Pacific coasts, at least two distinct forms not otherwise recognized. Instances could be

multiplied indefinitely; my own work, still in a most ele-
mentary stage, has already led directly to the description
and naming of half a dozen new birds. The latent value
of oölogy is real and represents the greatest unworked field
in avifaunal biology.

The reason that science has not accorded its deserved
position to the study and analysis of eggs is due primarily
to the lack of technical knowledge on the part of observers
and the difficulties inherent in properly correlating the find-
ings of fact by independent groups of students. Obviously
to do justice to the work is beyond the power of any one
man, and yet without standard units, without an understanding of the mathematics involved, without the necessary manual dexterity in physics, without the needed skill
of interpretation, in short, without specifically and simultaneously becoming experts, the work of one analyst cannot be dovetailed into that of another.

My ultimate objective in collecting eggs and in studying
them is the desire to take the first steps towards giving
oölogy the proper foundation to make it a scientific adjunct
of major importance. Research is a fascinating pursuit;
more than any other one thing it brought our party and
the *Least Petrel* into these southern waters. The pleasure
of being out-of-doors is augmented by the sport of hunting, but the goal of helping, even a little, to reconstruct
the biological tree, makes the trip worth while and eases
the hardships when they become discouraging.

We had passed Asunción Island during the night and
shortly before daylight were abreast of Abreojos Point.
Here the coast begins its great curve to the east, but we
no longer are to follow. Instead, we cut straight across
for Cape San Lázaro, a hundred and thirty-seven nautical
miles away. We are avoiding Ballena Bay, which comes
in just below Abreojos Point and into which, in turn,
feeds San Ignacio Lagoon.

This is the largest of Lower California's lagoons, unless
Magdalena Bay be considered one of them. It differs from
Scammon's in a number of important details. For one thing
it is much wider and, on the whole, is surrounded by higher
land. Near the mouth its shores as well as those of its
islands are fringed with mangroves which, in turn, bring in
the Mangrove Warbler, the White Ibis, and three or four
other southerners not found north of San Eugenio. Nevertheless San Ignacio resembles its northern counterpart. It
is as bare and as deserted as Scammon's and it, too, is
visited only by the turtle hunter or the wandering fisherman in search of mullet.

Near the western end of the lagoon is a double island,
Isla Ballena, to which the Partner and I once wandered
by pack-train from the pueblo. The beach of the islands,
where not of sand, is a layer of cobbles. The stones are
small, about half the size of one's fist, fairly uniform in
size, and they form an even blanket. Immediately under
the first tier is a sheet of clams, of small brown shells an
inch across. We removed the gravel from an area a square
yard and exposed a tiled bed. The mollusks do not lie upon
each other but they do touch on every side without gaps
or unoccupied spaces in the compact strata. We gathered
our forage simply by scraping the clams together in a heap
and scooping them into a pail.

Fishermen working nearby had acted as guides and had
rowed us to the islands. They, too, had packed in from
the interior and they had a camp on the shore. Theirs was
the only habitation in all this great region and even so was
scarcely an improvement on the open desert. The nearest
water, so brackish that a human could not drink it, was a
ten-hour ride away. The regular duty of one of the men,
on alternate days, was to drive the pack animals to and
from the tanks. It happened that on our return from the
island an old friend of our camp men had just come from

the basin and that fact nearly wrecked our trip. Everyone was set for a grand day and night fiesta; I still look back upon getting my own men untangled and on their way as one of my achievements.

The *Least Petrel* was far offshore when she passed San Ignacio Lagoon. Daylight disclosed no land in sight. We were in the lane of ocean travel between Panama and California but the run was not as lonely as some which we had made, for we sighted four ships during the day. There was still quite a bit of sea and I was not wholly at ease about Gregory and Peter. However, if they had troubles they kept them to themselves and on the whole the day passed pleasantly.

We had counted on birds to relieve the monotony of the run but there were few in sight at any time. Neither did we catch fish. The relation between birds and fish is close. The basis of ocean life, in so far as most of the larger predaceans are concerned, is the small fry, the sardine, to give it its popular name. It occurs in large schools which are relentlessly pursued by mackerel, tuna, barracuda, and the other deep sea hunters. If the little things get too close to shore they are attacked by the various species of bass, and if they seek safety near the surface they draw flocks of birds, of gulls and tern and pelicans, of man-o'-war birds and cormorants and shearwaters.

This two plane attack is of such regular occurrence that fishermen count upon the diving birds to betray the presence of the tuna. One wonders how any of the little things escape, when or how the pursuit comes to an end, but in some way a surplus of breeders does survive, for it is not the direct loss of their prey that is emptying this sea of tuna and bonita, but over-fishing, both for bait and for the market, by the fleets from San Diego and San Pedro.

We had known, of course, that food fish were disappearing from the coast of Lower California, but it required such a run as we were making and a comparison with former days to drive the lesson home. Within the last decade a thousand miles of coast have been worked with an ever increasing number of men and boats and tonnage until what was an almost certain source of wealth now yields at best a precarious livelihood.

At noon we were passing San Juanico Point, eighty miles to port. Just below is San Gregorio Lagoon, one of the places to which I have always hoped to go. If the day had been calm and if we could have appeared off the bar during one of the higher tides we might have risked an entrance. There is supposed to be running water here, of which I am skeptical, and a rich farming country, which inspection would probably reduce to one of the oases with which we are familiar. I suppose I should stop fussing at the weather and treasure the fact that there is still a spot in Lower California which might hold a surprise.

Toward nightfall Captain insisted that he could see San Lázaro and accordingly he set his course a bit closer inshore. On the run we had just made dead reckoning is not wholly dependable, for there is a variable inshore current that sometimes reaches two or three knots an hour. Captain had gauged it correctly today, however, although it was a gamble in which we all were interested. The eagerness with which we watched for the reappearance of land was very amusing to Juan. "I've seen people act like that after twelve weeks," he said, "but never after twelve hours."

Night fell before San Lázaro was on the beam but, as we had our landmarks, there was no uneasiness. Supper over we sat at the table and even played bridge, but it had been a hard day and so one by one we yielded to drowsiness and, leaving the boat in Captain's care, turned gratefully to our bunks.

CHAPTER XVIII

MAGDALENA

I WAS on the stern of the *Least Petrel,* sitting upon a gasolene box and leaning against the cabin wall. An audience of one, I waited on dramatic effects that could be witnessed from no upholstered chair in theatre loge, that could be crowded under no vaulted ceiling or be staged in no assemblage of men. I was looking towards Magdalena but I could see only two yellow lanterns, for the black drop-curtain was still spread across the stage.

There was starlight, enough to reveal a long row of hills, there were shadowed nocturnal birds, and there were anchor lights gleaming from mastheads of fishermen and dancing towards me across the bay. Floating out of the night was the mournful yowl of a coyote and the lapping of waves on the nearby shore. So I waited, I who had never seen Magdalena, and wondered what would be revealed when the unfolding came. There was promise of the secrets that inspire stagecraft, but the playwright would have given me some inkling and I had none. He would have displayed one scene and then another, but my curtain had fallen on an ocean that was real and would rise on a hamlet that was living. When Nature turns to drama fortunate is he who can attend.

No writer can climax the placing of his reader in an unknown, unlighted spot to be seen for the first time when dawn aids twilight. No artist with all the wonders of this age to command can approximate the heralding of a day.

His lights do not come from everywhere, nor do they envelop, they do not progress with smooth perfection nor do they enhance instantaneously and with infinite care every minute detail. Theirs not the soft shadings, the never-ending transmutations, the subtle blendings. Man comes in halting stages, the steps of a toddling child; Aurora bursts in a single movement, the sprinter winning a race.

It must be that the play is now about to start, for a star is gone that I am sure I marked a moment past. Now some magic hand is plucking the twinkling lights, drawing down, whenever my eye is turned, those whose destinies have been fulfilled, and shoving in their stead along the fringe of the horizon low clouds that, grey below, on their upper edges are tinged with the pink of the coral. The hills are showing silhouetted teeth as the curtain is drawn on a port enshrouded in romance and steeped in history.

Not Minerva this, but the flowering of an embryo. In dim shadow are naked savages gathering shellfish on the beach. They are gone; others come, proud owners of fire. And now a galleon of Spain in which Ulloa passes, and then Cabrillo, and then Vizcaíno himself come boldly into the bay. A century elapses, a hundred years, and then almost a generation more, before another of European blood tells of Magdalena, but in the mists I see Francis Drake on the *Golden Hind* and de Gali homeward bound from Manila and Cavendish, after the rape of the *Santa Ana,* passing, possibly entering, I cannot tell. I see Indians left to themselves for four generations and listen to folklore of the great white birds that came on the wings of the wind.

Is it dawn at last? Padre Guillen is riding a mule, perhaps dreaming of the founding of Misión San Luís Gonzaga, but three more generations precede the days of the Boston Yankees and the traders, freebooters, smugglers that followed the wake of the good ship *Dromio.* I see them swarming in and out of this bay writing one of the blackest tragedies to be recorded against the race of man. The grandest of fur bearers was the sea otter, and to have saved him to the world, in this favored environment there need have been left but a seed or the sanctuary of but one, the least of the islands that dot this coast. In bales are skins of suckling mothers dragged to the beaches, by boatloads are harvested the hides of the slaughtered breeders, and ever the cry of greed—"More, more, let tomorrow look to itself."

Surely day is here, for now Walker and his ragged men march by, to give place to a whaler five years out of New Bedford, every sail aloft as she proudly enters to keep her rendezvous in this club house of her guild and to trade news with sisters from every harbor and inlet in the world. After that the coaster seeking haven from the storm and the tramp hoping for a cargo of hides. Will I see the American battle-fleet sporting half a million tons or will a peon slip by in his hand-made dugout? It is all so old and yet so new. Chicago was holding her World's Fair while the first scientist was looking upon this land, but the explorers had appeared when Cellini was modelling his bronzes.

Now comes the first glimpse of reality, the outline of whitewashed walls just beyond the beach. Faster than the mind can interpret, more widespread than the eye can envisage, comes a crash of development in which time plays no part, and then the scene is complete. Magdalena the pueblo is drawn up in orderly parade facing us across a few hundred feet of water. Behind are hills, steep and ugly, peppered with dull bushes and spreading to either side, stony and hostile.

The pueblo doesn't belong in the landscape; the two have nothing in common, and nowhere do they blend into each other. The campo is as God made it, as untouched by human proximity as are the distant mountains and desert. To right and to left, as far as visibility extends, are water and beach, hill and cañon, but not a trace that is left by the hand of man. Utterly out of place and unrelated, huddled and cringing from the surrounding wilderness, are twenty houses. Only a telegraph pole on the knob and a midget graveyard in the ravine have strayed from the herd.

Magdalena has no outposts. It touches the desert but does not trespass. Its last wall is as solidly a part of the whole as are a ship's sides when holding back the ocean. There is to be seen nothing that is detached, no solitary house, no bit of cleared ground, no road, no break of any kind across the geometric line that separates. It is as though fear had crowded the village into a solitary dot on an inappropriate screen.

Considered item by item Magdalena is homely. Viewed from the bay, its waterfront is picturesque because the composition is artistic. A gravel beach, in a wide arc reaching either end of the hills, is the foreground. On the south edge of the town lies the three-masted schooner *Jewett,* an abandoned wreck fast succumbing to decay. She had been brought from the States a year or two ago on one of the fatuous attempts to remove sheep from Socorro Island and, after a series of mishaps which culminated in her encounter with a *chubasco,* was beached and abandoned. From the stranded hull to the last of the pontoons lies all there is of Magdalena—a dozen shacks crowding the gravel of the shoreline, another cluster about the wharf, half filled gaps on either side.

The only buildings to boast a second story are the home of the *comandante* and the stucco relics of Hale's experiment in commercializing desert weeds. Some of the town has been touched with lime, but for the most part it is virgin to the brush. It is a heterogeneous monotone, its only flare of green two sickly palms, and it aptly terminates in a cemetery of small boats, wrecked and decaying. Let it in justice be said, however, that Magdalena is an artificial settlement planted to supervise commerce.

The sunrise that had unfolded the town also disclosed the bay. There were four little boats anchored near us and, swimming through the fleet, were a dozen or so pelicans who had learned that sometimes tidbits are thrown overboard. Diurnal birds were coming from roosting grounds, flying low over water that stretched to the horizon line. We had been prepared to find a large bay, we knew that this was one of the few great harbors on the Pacific, but vaguely we had not expected to be so impressed. Excepting for the ocean barrier the smooth protected sheet everywhere disappeared into space, its accomplishments a parody on its potentialities.

There were other twilight risers aboard the *Least Petrel*. For the first time since leaving Ensenada we were not masterless in our wilderness and, in token of subservience, our signal flags were being flown. It was still early, by our clocks, when we were boarded by a rowboat full of officers. A half hour delay, a thirty minutes of friendly explanations and sincere willingness to help, and we had been granted the courtesy of the port. It was amusing to contrast our treatment with the storied experiences of many of our acquaintances. The position of port administrador in coastal Mexico requires a man of imagination, if half the tales are to be believed, and he who is most fertile in conceiving pretexts for fining visitors is he who prospers most. I have heard of penalties levied because of failure to send advance notice when no means were provided for delivering such a message, because of illegal entry when picked up on the high seas and towed in by a federal patrol, because of invoices so complete that there was no loophole for perquisites to local authorities. I have heard, too, many a tale of efforts, successful and otherwise, to outwit the Mexican authorities, of unvarnished attempts to swindle bragged of by American skippers. My opinion is that the man who plays fair and understands the customs of the country will seldom have cause for complaint.

After breakfast we went ashore to attend to errands and to do our sightseeing. We wandered down the main street, which is really the beach, and watched the inhabitants at their occupations. There is pathetically little to be done in such a place as this, no amusements, no resources, no outside interests, little reading or culture, and not sufficient work to keep either mind or body occupied. Naturally there is a drift toward animal-like inertia. Conversation is listless and possible topics are soon exhausted. It is a normal condition, in a town as isolated as Magdalena, to find most of the men and boys habitually out-of-doors, lounging, waiting for something to happen. It is said of them that in winter they follow the sun around their houses and that in summer they follow the shade. There is more than a touch of truth in the maxim.

Such was Magdalena when we stepped onto the beach. The apathy of the natives, however, proved to be more apparent than real. It was not the studied stoicism of the Indian. Curiosity was aroused both because we were not fishermen, the type of strangers to whom these people were accustomed, and because our wants, to them, were novel. They began to drift in from every direction and we were soon surrounded by a swarm of boys augmented by a sprinkling of men. Our unwanted escorts followed us from house to store, crowding close so as not to miss a word of what was being said. We asked for a laundress, only to learn that our washing could not be cared for in Magdalena; water comes in barrels from the boats. So we moved to a house at the other end of town and there, hemmed in by our army, arranged to have the clothes sent to Santa Margarita Island.

We next enquired for a pilot to take us to the lagoons.

There was much marching and counter-marching but in time we and the rabble found the man we wanted and a deal was made. Then we wheeled and in broken formation proceeded to the village store. Here we spent some time looking over the stock. We made a few purchases and our retainers melted away. Their curiosity had been satisfied; their easily aroused interests were not capable of being long sustained. They drifted back to the old routine and when later we reappeared upon the streets they paid us no attention.

In Magdalena the centre of life, if it can so be called, is the combined store and cantina housed in an almost bare rectangular room, a scant twelve feet by twenty. Lengthwise, near the centre, runs a rough counter behind which, with the floor for a bottom, are a series of bins. Deep shelves above are carried from one end of the room to the other. There, in full sight, is displayed the entire stock. The bins contain, separately and in bulk, corn, beans, flour and *pinocho*—the raw sugar of Mexico. The shelves are lined with clothing and rolls of cloth and with such household necessities as blankets, pots, or brooms. Peppers, stringed, swing from the ceiling; in one corner are fifteen or twenty cans of preserved food and, of course, there are cigarettes.

One peculiarity of the stock lies in the fact that no choice is offered the customer. There might be four brooms in the store; if so they would all be alike. If I wished to buy a coffee-pot I would take the one offered; any others that might be on hand would be duplicates. Salesmanship did not exist. If you didn't see what you wanted you would be told "no hay." An unvarnished statement that the desired article was not carried. In all these respects this little store was so typical of Northwestern Mexico that it almost made us homesick.

One corner of the room was devoted to the sale of liquor

and here a different method was in vogue. A few bottles stood on the shelf, the main stock being kept under the counter. Clearly a small business was regularly done with visitors. The storekeeper was familiar with American favorites and his supply, though small, was diversified and well selected. He labored under none of the restrictions that have been experimentally imposed in the nations to the north, being free to sell by the bottle or the glass and to whomsoever he chose. As elsewhere the saloon was a gathering place for the exchange of the news and gossip of the town.

We judged Magdalena by this store and, I believe, the criterion is just. That a hundred dollars would cover the inventory, excepting liquor, was our guess and the measure by which we gauged the purchasing power of the community. The absence of fresh vegetables or any substitute, of even the simplest articles of luxury or pleasure, of reading matter or anything cultural, told the story of the people. We left Magdalena with regret both because it interested us and because we had been so well treated, but even we could find little to say in its praise.

CHAPTER XIX

MAGDALENA BAY

THE two midday hours were spent sailing down one of the great harbors of the world. Eighty square miles with a depth of thirty feet or more lie adjacent to Entrada Point, and even they do not comprise the half of this inland sea. Almejas Bay of itself would be famous were it not an offshoot of Magdalena; and Santa Marina, where El Camino Real debouches, could, if isolated, become a great port. There are inlets and coves and bights. And the lagoons. It is a hundred nautical miles from Boca de las Ànimas to Laguna del Rancho Bueno, and a hundred miles spread over a long stretch of country.

Down from Tenaca comes a string of five islands, long reefs that in most places are low and narrow. They so nearly touch each other that they leave only one passage which shipping finds feasible. They are the barrier between the ocean and the sheltered waters and by their distance from the mainland they determine the width of Magdalena Bay. Windswept and sandy they are the hybrid creation of current and volcano.

Santa Margarita, the largest, in many respects is not typical. It is twenty miles long, averages perhaps five across, and attains a height of nearly two thousand feet. Highly mineralized, it is well known for its quartz and shale and especially for its extensive manganese deposits. Springs of fresh water are utilized by the cattle company, the owners of the island, and there is food for a fairly large herd. Hidden gardens of wild flowers crowd into the growths

129

of the desert. On her first morning ashore the Partner returned with a great armful of March blossoms, of night-shades, morning-glories, black-eyed susans, forget-me-nots and wild hyacinths.

We anchored in Almejas Bay opposite the comparatively level pass that cuts across to the sand dunes and the sea. It is a region forested with cardón and covered with sage and, intermittently, with heavy thorns. Mesquite is found wherever the roots of that ubiquitous tree touch water. Ocean fogs, too, have played a part. There is no definable change on this southern island, no breaking into a new botanical environment, but there is an appreciable increase in the amount of vegetation and, on its lower levels, Santa Margarita is more heavily covered than any desert point we as yet had visited. Nevertheless it offers a harsh landscape; favored spots and rolling country have not far to go to reach the interminable volcanic hills.

We scattered over the lowland in pursuit of our varied interests. Rogers was in the dunes looking for and finding old shell-middens. Peter and Gregory were collecting, and Tony and I, with the Partner, were investigating osprey nests. These Fish Hawks are the most conspicuous of the birds of Margarita; they have built freely in the arms of giant cacti and their great bales of faggots, occupied or deserted, become a familiar part of the scenery.

We had provided ourselves with binoculars and a light sixteen-foot ladder. With the glasses we tried to spot the parent bird before she flushed and usually we were successful, for the white head, peering over the edge of the nest, is conspicuous against the skyline. We used the ladder to save ourselves climbing the sahuaros. Tony, when necessary, will take his punishment and shin up those prickly limbs. I've seen him open holes forty or fifty feet above the ground, but even he prefers walking up wooden rungs and doing his work at leisure.

MOTHER ELEPHANT SEAL NURSING HER BABY

A CONTRIBUTION BY THE SAN BENITO MARSH SPARROW

WEST SAN BENITO ISLAND

We found few eggs; the birds are early breeders and most were on young, some just hatched, some nearly grown. The eggs were white, covered heavily, often almost completely, with rich red markings. They are unique, at least among North American eggs, in having a distinctive odor. It so strongly permeates them that for years after they have been stored in cabinet drawers they exhale unmistakable musk. Young osprey are alone among the birds of prey I have seen in being covered with a down that is not white. The striped, tan-colored babies harmonize with the nest lining of rotted kelp and, when disturbed, take full advantage of their protective coloration. They flatten themselves and pretend to be dead, maintaining their pose even when handled, but the little devils at no time will close their eyes. It is always surprising to look into a nest which apparently contains three dried bodies and then catch the glitter of those bright yellow fire-balls.

The conduct of the adults while we are near their nests varies with individual temperament. The degree of anxiety exhibited, on the average, increases progressively and very noticeably as incubation advances and as the young mature. Sometimes the parents fly to a neighboring cardón to sit quietly until we are gone. More often one bird, or both, will circle about us, uttering shrill and wholly inadequate cries. The radius of their flight may be quite long or it may not be over a few yards; that depends on individual timidity and anxiety.

A not uncommon practice is to dive from a considerable height directly at the intruder, keeping up the pretext of attacking until the last moment to swerve. Time and time again, as one or the other of us stood helpless on that ladder, we would hear the shrill peep and the rustle of the wings of a bird that was almost in our faces. None of them made any real effort to strike and we knew that they would not. Everyone has read or heard stories of large birds attacking people; such tales are quite an annual event in newspaperdom and usually involve a child and an eagle. I am making the statement, without qualification or exception, that they are not true. Certain species of owls, the Long-eared for instance, flutter in the act of striking, and will, though rarely, scratch a person who is too close to the owlets. They can do so safely because of their slow flight, but think of what would happen to the bird that swoops if he came in contact with an object that did not yield. At seventy-five or a hundred miles an hour he could not survive a sudden arrest. Every instinct of the bird protects the man.

One or the other of the parent osprey remains with the young until they are able to leave the nest. Caracara are plentiful on Santa Margarita and any juvenile, dead or living, is a welcome addition to the menu of this versatile bird. He is a strange creature, the caracara. He can run and he can fly, he is a carrion eater as well as a hunter, he is as aptly termed eagle as vulture, and neither in appearance nor in habits has he a feathered counterpart in North America.

Of smaller birds we found eggs of the Nelson Shrike, the Black-chinned Sparrow, and the Costa Humming Bird. The most interesting to work among are the little hummers. The male has nothing to do with the nesting and we pay no attention to him. But if a female flies about us and indicates, by her movements, that she is not feeding, we keep close watch. She usually betrays herself if she has been flushed from her nest. She will ordinarily return within fifteen minutes at most, going directly to her eggs without an effort to mislead or hide. If we can follow her we will find two babies or eggs that we would have been very unlikely to have seen if we had confined ourselves to direct search.

The nest of a humming bird is a tiny cup of plant down

held in place with spider webs. The signature of the species is plainly marked upon the structure. Some are more substantial than others, some are heavily and some lightly decorated with lichens, some rest on bases and some cling to vertical supports. The Costa usually places feathers in the lining, the Allen a superfluity of plant down, the Calliope builds sixty to a hundred feet above the ground, the Broad-billed three to five feet, the Blue-throated well inside the foliage of sycamores, the Black-chinned of tan down, severely plain, the Ruby-throated decorated to the point of oblivion, the Xantus over water and the Anna in willow bottoms. These and the other peculiarities of each race are adhered to so consistently—I am mentioning only those with which I happen to be familiar—that I can identify any of these nests if I meet with it in the field.

The reason for these racial minor differentiations has nothing to do directly with evolution, with survival, with the solving of life problems, with protective coloration, or with any influence not traceable through instinct. In our line of work we live with instinct, we study it and profit by it, we depend upon it to lead us to our nests and we have learned to gauge and understand it. Because so many writers of late have belittled it, have evolved substitutes to account for its manifestations, have denied its application whenever it stands in the way of their theories, have misinterpreted it to suit their needs, I feel impelled to define the word and to record the knowledge we derive directly from field experience.

Instinct is a racial mental condition developed under the influence of heredity and involves both the desire and the ability to do certain things. It is the result of the accumulated experiences of past generations. The brain that undergoes physical changes through memories of happenings or through skill acquired by practice reacts to the condition into which it has artificially developed in precisely the manner that does the brain which has grown into a corresponding condition during and as part of the maturing of the body. Predictable groupal reactions of individuals having identical or closely allied inheritances where coincidence is eliminated by mathematical laws of chance are manifestations of instinct.

Suppose I have flushed a Costa Humming Bird from her first set of eggs. Her mannerisms tell me she has a nest in the vicinity. Why does she carry out the details of conduct I have learned to expect? It is her desire. Why does she presently return to her nest? It is her desire. Why did she build that nest of particular materials and place it in certain surroundings? Such were her desires. How could I, if sufficiently expert, have predicted within close limitations what her conduct would be, what materials she would select, what surroundings she would adopt? Because I have learned to anticipate her desires. I have also learned, not from theory but in the field, that the group desires of the nine humming birds I have mentioned depend entirely on their heredities and not at all on their environments. I do not find the various species that inhabit a given district reacting alike but I do find all the individuals of a given species carrying their distinguishing traits into every environment in which they breed.

This is the first nest of the bird we have flushed, she has had no previous experience, has learned nothing from practice or experimentation, and yet to no nidologist, to no specialized expert, is there the slightest difference between the first nest and the fiftieth. The psychologist who, instead of discovering at first hand what instinct is, prefers to theorize on what will best harmonize with his preconceived ideas, will not agree with me. He will deny that the actions of the bird were impelled solely by the urge of an inherited desire, will argue that she was reacting to impulses acquired during her own lifetime, but can he explain the skill?

That nest is a wonderfully delicate piece of work—you couldn't build it, nor I—its construction is an exhibition of exquisite craftsmanship. Not with one lifetime of practice could the bird learn to use her bill, her feet, her body to construct that masterpiece of art. Even as the system has been worked out by nature she could not do it during her first months out of the nest. With maturity and through a process of normal, orderly growth her brain has reached a certain physical condition, a status at least equivalent to the one which it might otherwise have attained through long years of practice and a vast series of experiences.

The elaboration of these ideas and their application to man would require a separate volume. They are suggested here because they are an important part of our study. The proof of their truth is constantly before us and their application is an essential of our everyday work. Anyway I believed them, and used them, and proceeded to find three humming birds' nests. About that time the Partner espied signs of habitation and, being a good forager, must investigate the chance of securing edibles.

We entered a mesquite thicket through which we passed easily, along a trail. A browsing goat and her two kids disappeared into the brush and a dozen or more caracaras flushed from the shade. All were forerunners of an occupied house, the perhaps overly hopeful birds being quite given to keeping watch upon isolated huts with the hope of sometimes beating the dogs to a bit of scraps.

As we came into the open we saw a clearing with a house and two palm trees. There was a little truck garden —we noticed a few tomato vines and some peppers— enclosed in a tight fence made from the spines of palm leaves. The stems had been stripped, placed upright, woven securely into place with other stems, and held in position with mesquite branches. Four or five dogs rushed out to bark at us, scattering chickens and turkeys as they came.

The turkeys were unexpected. They caught the Partner's eye; then and there she made up her mind to have one roasted, and so we went to the house. Its walls were of leaves cut from the palm, its roof of the same material, and its timbers were limbs of mesquite. It had no windows, not even openings, and it had no doors, but there was a doorway facing us. The hut consisted of one room and a *ramada*—an extension carried on poles over the doorway, roofed with palm leaves but having no walls.

A middle-aged man lay on the ground in the shade of the *ramada*. He was on his feet by the time we arrived and, after the custom of the country, we all shook hands before the first words were exchanged. Then we went inside and each of us shook hands with every member of the family, the wife, the half-grown children, the younger ones and the baby. Mexican handshakes are too frequent to be energetic—there's no grip to them, no return from limp fingers. Seats were brought into the *ramada*—cylinders cut from a palm tree—and then conversation began.

While the Partner tried to lead up to turkeys I inventoried the furniture. There was a table of the same material as the fence, neatly lashed with *cuero*. There was a bed, a wooden frame with a bottom of criss-crossed rawhide. There were skins and two or three old blankets, a few on the bed, the others hung on cut boughs or strung along the fence. When I tried to divide the bedding among the old folks and the children and made reasonable allowance for younger ones who, like wild animals, went into hiding at our approach, I concluded that on cold nights all but a few slept in one huddle on the dirt floor.

The stove was out-of-doors under the *ramada*. Clay bricks had been worked into a solid base thirty inches high and about three feet by four on top. There were placed on this a few adobe bricks so arranged that firewood could be slipped underneath and cooking utensils placed above.

Of the latter I saw only a frying-pan, a coffee-pot, and an iron kettle. Cutlery and plates—I wonder what the system is, for surely there were not enough for everyone to eat at the same time.

The Partner had finally worked around to turkeys. The peon was willing to dispose of one but there were difficulties. He was in debt to the cattle company, of course, and, through arrangement, the storekeeper at Magdalena would not sell to him. As the company's policy was to compel him to buy from itself and remain in debt he didn't care for cash; he wanted to trade, especially for coffee. That couldn't be done, however, for we had paid no duty on any of our provisions, the understanding being that they were to be used only aboard.

The Partner wanted that turkey, she is persuasive and persistent, and in the end he agreed to sell. Then came more trouble. He would not let us take the bird; he promised to bring it aboard early in the morning. Poor devil. He wanted to see the boat and the crew, to find someone with whom he could talk, and he hadn't wholly given up hope of coffee. Maybe he was justified—I don't know. The Partner is not very hard-boiled and no one inventoried the cans when he left.

CHAPTER XX

MANGROVES

AFTER a night and a day in Almejas Bay we moved back to our anchorage off Magdalena. We lay there until dawn, waiting for the pilot whose services we had engaged on our first visit to the pueblo. He was to guide us through the maze of narrow waterways known as the lagoons. They are an endless series of uncharted canals interspersed with islands and camouflaged with deceptive branches that in the end are only blind leads. The channels are variant and obscure; they twist and double and swing so wantonly from one side to the other that even a man familiar with the watercourses navigates them with difficulty. They are no place for a stranger to take a boat, these lagoons.

Our pilot came aboard promptly at the hour agreed upon, which was gratifying, and brought a companion, which was characteristic. By sun-up their little boat was fast to our stern and we were under way. The pilot was a large man, fat and genial. His skin was dark beyond the shade usually associated with Mexicans and marked him with descent from aboriginal stock. In his build and in his physiognomy there were the traits of a mixed ancestry which included, unmistakably, the characteristic head shape and color of the Digger and probably of the Guaicuris.

This was our first contact with the Indian type. We know that the country through which we had been travelling had at one time held a considerable aboriginal population. Early colonial history is replete with allusions to

the number of Indians found in Lower California and mission reports bear evidence of the size of former congregations. Little of that native blood, even in adulteration, has
survived north of a line between Magdalena and La Paz.
In the vicinity of the Cape itself the primal stock has been
much more tenacious but even so virtually all of the citizens of the Peninsula are derived by colonization from the
west coast of the mainland. It is an illuminating reflection
on the fate of the natives that a survival of their blood
lines should be such a rarity as to have aroused our interest.

Whatever our pilot's ancestry, his seamanship was reassuring. We left to him the responsibility of the boat and
gave ourselves over to the enjoyment of a beautiful morning. Without a breath of air the bay was glass at this
hour of the wild fowl's awakening. Through early mists
and almost as soon as we turned from the village we saw
the black ribbon. It wavered over the surface in either
direction as far as it could be distinguished—a distance we
estimated to aggregate eight or ten miles. It was composed
of Brandt Cormorant. They were flying fifty abreast,
barely skimming the surface and maintaining a course that
took them through the harbor entrance out to their fishing
grounds.

We paralleled their line of flight for four hours. During
that time there was no diminution in the flow and no gap
in the girdle. Eventually we reached the bird island, to
find that ours was but one of three streams that were still
being vomited from the rookery, from the long flat bar that
barely protruded above the water. We landed, but saw at
once that it was useless to look here for signs of nesting
birds. As far as one would care to walk he would find only
footprints, only touching, overlapping impressions in the
padded sand.

It may be that it is possible to arrive at a numerical
estimate of what we had been watching, but a digit fol-

lowed by a string of ciphers is an anticlimax which I shall not attempt. Nothing can accentuate the line of flight we actually followed from sun-up to mid-morning. Nothing less than having been beside it can depict the stark tragedy revolving around the fact that each of these birds, individually, will kill several fish during the day and must do the same thing the next day and, it or its descendants, every day thereafter until the world changes. And for what purpose?

This is a dangerous line of thought. We ourselves had been fishing and had had no scruples about the two beautiful gold-speckled pescasierra that had conveniently snatched the jigs just in time to be fresh for lunch. That meal, however, evolved into a new source of complications when Juan gave another display of temperament. He is as strongly nationalistic as the Mexicans themselves and by that token every fibre of his pride revolted at cooking for and serving our two pilots.

Peace and good humor no longer reigned in the galley. As though from a miniature boiler factory came the slamming of pots and the crashing of pans and the doorway was passed only at the imminent risk of life. Was the flashing butcher knife that reached every corner and jumped from stove to gunwale merely a gesture or was there a lethal impulse? No one had the curiosity to ascertain, nor was there encouragement in the coldly serious face that had replaced the smile which always before carried wrinkles to eyes and forehead. In the end Juan had to yield—there was no alternative—but even the Partner did not care to press the matter when he withheld every suggestion of delicacies, even to butter and lemon sauce.

Soon after we had passed the roosting island of the birds we were among the mangroves. The tide was high, not a puff of wind had come, and so it was under the most ideal of conditions that we burst into fairyland. The sides of the lagoon drew together, they became densely bordered with clustering green bushes, and all the while the basin was filled to overflow with quicksilver. As we passed spearhead points or swung around bends new vistas opened invitingly with tributaries that came tentatively into our garden. Only because nothing artificial could have been so gorgeous was it possible to believe this scene was real.

Time passed; we watched no clocks. Miles slipped behind; they were not measured. Only the burnished plaque that pushed its way under eager foliage. Perspective gave movement and for no two instants did the picture remain unchanged. Haughty as a parading mannikin would a bayou peep at us, would open wide and then, before it closed again, tease us and tantalize us with a glimpse of yet other gems beyond. Compositions that were beautiful shifted until they became sublime. Deeper and deeper into the labyrinth slipped the *Least Petrel,* giving to us an hour that can never be lived again because never again can we be here for the first time.

There was no background. Green leaves on the nearest border were our horizon; above were only sky and sleeping clouds. Hazy, distant, and tiny, if looked for there could be seen the peaks behind Magdalena and even the dim summits of San Lázaro and Santa Margarita. They were far from us, far away in another world where they could not intrude on our privacy. They did no more than reassure us that there were no bounds to our aqueous garden and that its solitude, while we willed, was ours to hold against the world. A glory that had no end, a scene conceived for our delectation, a landscape that was our fee.

An island came to meet us, an island the size of a city block. One half was mangroves, one half was shells. The shells were a bit larger than those we had seen in Scammon's and were perhaps more brightly colored. Otherwise this spit was a replica of the larger island which had so intrigued us. There was no adulteration here, no fragments. In the bushes on the other end, half hidden in the foliage, was a flock of fifty Lower California Reddish Egrets roosting at ease, taking their siesta. Abruptly we underwent a change from nature admirers into collectors. Captain turned the *Least Petrel* shorewards and gently laid her bow on the sloping bed of shells. An armed band of pirates we jumped to land, dryshod, and shot the specimens we needed. They were beautiful birds in full nuptial plumage, but as the breeding season was yet to come there were no heartaches.

We found a feeding ground of White Ibis a few miles beyond and anchored, satisfied that this should be our destination. The channel had narrowed and shallowed and the lagoon had broken into a series of islands. There was no need to go further; in an entire season we could not have seen all nor even an appreciable part of this unknown, unsurveyed lagoon country. So we paid our pilot and sent him on his way. He didn't want to go, he had nothing to do in Magdalena, he had been enjoying our meals, and we were a break in the monotony of his life. There were some rather embarrassing moments before the little sailboat disappeared down the lagoon.

With our going ashore came disillusionment. The falling tide smeared our Eden with wide mud flats that were a blot on the landscape and a mire to cross afoot. The first breath of wind turned our silver sheet into a commonplace body of water and personal contact with the mangroves replaced beauty with unpleasantness. But we had had our morning; nothing could rob us of that memory. And lest we need reassurance that our impressions were not to be ephemeral there were many hours, in the days that followed, when returned conditions told us the picture had been no dream.

The *Least Petrel* had been making too much water on

ON THE TRAIL TO TURTLE BAY

A HALF-DECAYED STILLBORN MONSTROSITY

MISIÓN SAN LUÍS GONZAGA

the run down and Captain decided to do a bit of caulking. It was then that troubles began. He beached her at high tide and did his work very neatly while the hull was exposed, but in pivoting to get back to deep water he split the skeg. The timber should have carried the strain but didn't, nor did it profit us to satisfy ourselves that the fault lay with a shipyard in San Diego.

At next high water for the day we drove the *Least Petrel* as close inshore as possible and carried her hawsers to the mangroves. As the tide ebbed she began to settle on her side and by morning her deck slanted at an angle of forty-five degrees. In the cabin the effect was weird, for the eye was not conscious of the tilt. A pair of binoculars swinging from a strap, a hat on a nail, anything hanging, stood out at a sharp angle from the wall. Unless one concentrated on hand holds he would take nasty falls whenever he tried to walk.

Partly because our preparations had been somewhat hurried and partly because we had not anticipated to the full the discomforts of this Mexican drydock we had not made arrangements to camp ashore. Sleep on the boat was virtually impossible and was not seriously attempted. There were little things to be attended to from time to time and as to the rest we disposed ourselves to spend the night as best we could. Juan was the busiest—he baked bread on one side of the galley door and played poker on the other. The game came to a disastrous end early in the morning with a lurch of the boat. Beans were used to represent chips and when the jerk caused every player to grab for support with both hands the stakes accumulated in one heap on the floor. The baking was more successful. Juan took his dough ashore—Rogers swears he sleeps with it under his blankets to make it rise properly—and kept a watchful eye over it through all the digging.

That began just before low water and we were fortunate in being able to remove the skeg before the tide had risen too far. We had plenty of time after that to reinforce the cracked timber with lumber and bolts and anything that happened to be aboard. It was a close call, at the next low tide, to replace the skeg, and we just did manage to get it set. Our luck held when we warped off several hours later and brought one discomfort to an end.

It was low tide again when we landed on the mud flats and made our way afoot through the border of trees. At first we tried skirting the outer edges but gained nothing by so doing. Progress was slow and noisy—we sank to our knees and even to our hips and floundered helplessly most of the time. No quarry would await such an approach. The fringe proved to be the common mangrove, *Rhizphora mangle,* which in these waters reaches a height of about ten feet. It has become highly specialized in adapting itself to salt water and tidal flats and most of its peculiarities seem designed to make trouble for the man who tries to invade its thickets. The trunks are so close together that one cannot squeeze between them and they are too high to climb. The way is barred by cross-roots and branches that will not support a man's weight and yet are too strong to be pushed aside. Crawling on hands and knees or even on the belly means tussles with breather roots that are fitted, at low tide, to absorb air for the trees. Contiguous openings are few and hard to find.

How does one get through? By taking advantage of every gap, by disregarding bruises and torn clothing, by making an effort that cannot be sustained. To penetrate a short distance for the examination of a nest, for instance, or the retrieving of a specimen is possible almost anywhere but only if there be a fortunate series of spacings can serious headway be made.

A few steps into this jungle isolates one from the outside world. Overhead, just above the line of highest water, the canopy closes in a criss-cross of crooked branches topped with a closed roof of leaves. Naked stalks and hanging seed pods and loathsome suckers reaching downwards for the mire close the circle within a few yards. The footing is treacherous. It is a dull brown mud that may be firm or may, without warning, drop a man to his waist. In which case, if he seizes the nearest branch, it will usually break.

Avifaunal life is plentiful but one is apt to see only jays, birds which seem wholly out of place in this association. Whatever adaptations they may have undergone in order to survive in these environments their insatiable curiosity has not been affected. While the noise of crashing is driving away all other feathered denizens and is even sending red crabs scampering to their holes it is attracting these gossips of the mangroves, who must learn all about the intruder. Greyish-blue forms lurk in the outskirts, playing the game of trying to see without themselves being exposed.

Beyond the border of trees lies a low sand desert that only by accident comes in direct contact with the lagoons. Of its two phases one suggests dunes, with irregularly spaced growths of thorn and chaparral. The other is a shroud-covered graveyard. I walked through one of the armies of the dead where skeletons stood almost touching, where for an hour I saw no living bud nor a tint of green. Frameworks from which hung streamers of moss. Parasites stealing life sap wrested cell by cell from aridity. Grey vampires preying to the death upon their only source of existence.

Often for miles there spreads a jungle of head high stalks draped with the beard of the oppressor. It seems to me there must have been a day, and that not long ago as time is reckoned in this desert, when ocotillo and mesquite were masters. Then came increasing fogs or some other climatic change which gave advantage to the mosses. Surely the condition of today is not permanent. The hosts cannot survive indefinitely and carcasses must sometime decay. Can the marvels of propagation make replacements here? I cannot see how. Not unlike this plague spot are those human institutions whose history is of power overplayed to their own undoing.

Mammals find more sustenance than do songbirds. Seeds and buds are rare but browsing there must be, for deer abound. We found their spoor on every island, but our attempts to corner them met with no success. They have learned to cross the narrow waterways and they outguessed us whenever we tried to anticipate their line of flight. Coyotes, too, and the lesser carnivora pass readily from island to island.

There were unmistakable signs of primitive human life both on the islands and on the mainland. The artifacts here are recognizable without difficulty because flints are foreign to the country. The number we found and their wide distribution bespoke a one-time large savage population. As so often before come the unanswered questions—where did they get their water? On what did they subsist? What has become of them?

CHAPTER XXI

AROUND THE CORNER

WHEN we left our anchorage and definitely started for
Magdalena it was late in the afternoon, a little too late
as events transpired. An unexpected breeze coupled with
failing light obscured our channel. After we had lost the
course it was not long until we fouled a sand bar.

We had struck so hard that even with the aid of a rising
tide it took half an hour to work free. We churned full speed
astern, we kicked up floods of muddy water, we strained
and we floundered. With the engine racing we held a pole
against the side of the boat, one end on the bottom. By
watching its point of contact with the gunwale we were
able to measure our progress. As soon as we remained
motionless for more than a moment we shifted gears;
Captain did not care to let the propeller dig a deep hole
in the sand. He ran forward until the boat stopped again
then he reversed once more to full speed astern. Every
time he changed direction the *Least Petrel* responded with
a short rush. She slowed down almost immediately but
she always increased the length of the trough. Eventually
she opened it and we were again in deep water.

The sensible thing would have been to have anchored for
the night, but Captain was stubborn. He knew now that his
channel lay on the opposite side of the lagoon and for three
hours he tried to get across. It was a repetition of bumping
and backing and sounding, though of course, being now on
his guard, he did not strike hard. In the end he had to give
up, for we couldn't risk stranding by being caught at high
water.

Trivial as this experience was, it broke Gregory. He became more and more agitated each time the boat struck and while it was on the bars his conduct verged on the hysterical. He calmed during the short periods we were under way but when the anchor went down with the announcement that no further effort would be made until morning he simply went to pieces. He did and said a number of things which could hardly be called manly, after which he retired to his cabin. Whereupon he began to drink.

That is something he should not have done. Due to early dissipations he had a chronic weakness which alcohol intensified to the point of disability. Gregory fully appreciated that one of his greatest obligations to the others on the boat was to care for his health and so his collapse was even more serious than appeared on the surface.

We discussed the situation after he and Peter had gone. There seemed to be nothing we could do. The trouble lay in a combination of personality and environment, two factors over which we had no control. We tried to establish Gregory's point of view—not a difficult task, for he had expressed himself freely. It condensed into the feeling that he was lost at night in an uninhabited, unknown country, and that this hardship was the culmination of a series of horrors that began before we had reached Los Coronados.

Gregory wasn't educated up to the country. Where we had been impressed with the picture and had gloried in it he had seen but the frame and the wall on which it hung. His perspective was the mechanical reproduction of proportions and from that angle, we all were willing to admit, Lower California is ghastly. He had developed no appreciation of the beauty of a desert, he had no love for its solitudes, and he took no joy in struggling against its hardships. He was obtaining no return.

Favorable or adverse, whatever may be a man's reactions to other wastes, they will be many times intensified on the

Peninsula. In this thought we tried to find some palliation for Gregory, some measure of justification. But always the fact stood out, and it could not be controverted, that had he been a man of a better type he would have kept himself under control in spite of his emotions. We could forgive his mental attitude, or so we tried to persuade ourselves, but there could be no excuse for his response. Nor could we, would we, blame Lower California. She had not created the man; she had merely been merciless in laying bare his soul.

In the morning we found our channel without further ado, for by daylight we could readily trace the line of demarcation between deep and shallow water. In a short time we were out in the open bay and by mid-morning were back at Magdalena.

As we ran in there happened to be four fishing boats in port. Our interest in them was mild in comparison with their curiosity about us. As they looked the *Least Petrel* over through binoculars their gestures were so eloquent that we could almost hear the arguments as to what manner of craft she was. We satisfied them to a certain extent as, one after another, we hailed to ask if they could take care of our mail. But since they were all just down from the north and would be away from home a month or more, our little hope failed.

The Partner and I went ashore, she to retrieve her laundry and I for papers. By noon we were again aboard, cleared for the Cape. Magdalena's farewell to us was a continuance of wonderful weather, of water that would barely have rocked our canoe. It allowed us to crowd close inshore, almost to the reflection of the island hills. These were the most dreary of any we had seen on the bay. Mile after mile, without character or hope, theirs was a panorama of mediocrity. Steep and high, yet not impressive, brush bedecked with scant, dwarfed chaparral, their stony surfaces held no promise of ever becoming of value or interest.

THE FLIGHT OF THE *LEAST PETREL.*

A few miles beyond the village a great flock of shear-waters covered acre upon acre of the bay. We had seen these birds before, singly or in pairs, and had tried diligently to collect a few, but they had been shy and wary and would allow us no close approach. Now they were in a dense mass. Some, repleted, were merely resting; others darting about at random, feeding greedily, were too intent upon securing their own prey to give much heed to danger. They allowed us to sail right into their midst and to pick up the half dozen we needed. These proved to be Black-vented Shearwaters— a species that would soon be winging its way to burrows on Natividad.

As we neared Entrada Point we ran past a puzzling structure on the beach. At first we mistook it for the abandoned loading hoist of a gravel pit. It certainly was an old timer, of rusted iron and rotting wood. By its side lay a pile of coal, and that, too, was significant of age, for many years ago crude oil replaced other fuels on this coast. The answer came in a few moments from what at first appeared to be a curious geological formation. Our glasses revealed the skeletons of whales, great masses of bones piled on the shore. The machinery was an epitaph of bygone days of glory and a reminder that little is salvaged from these distant lands.

At the tip of Entrada Point we came abruptly upon the opening into the ocean. Can it be that we are looking at the Golden Gate? Not less than it rivals San Francisco's harbor does this bay vie with the northerner in sheer beauty of entrance. Two great ridges, each nearly twenty miles long rise abruptly from the dead level of the sea to reach heights of two thousand feet. They approach head-on, they pause, they leave unblocked a three-mile mouth. Dark against the prevailing tonelessness and isolated from other formations of their kind the function of these hills is to serve as perpetual threshold monuments to the wonderful harbor where unappreciated Nature has left a masterpiece.

Passing through this inspiring portal we came to the open ocean and once more turned our backs upon the swell. We entered the regular steamer lanes and followed them for eighteen hours, from Redondo Point to Cabo Falso. At no time during that run were we out of sight of vessels plowing their way northward. Freighters and liners came from the canal and fishermen, who had been scouting every corner of the coast, hurried from island or bank to the canneries at their homes. The tankers, exceeding in tonnage all other shipping combined, were returning from distributing California's oil to Mexico, Balboa, and even Chili.

The first twenty miles of our course led along the western side of Santa Margarita. From the water the island was more forbidding than it had been on the sheltered side. To seaward the volcanic origin is clearer and the slopes carry less vegetation. The sides are steep to precipitousness and the great bluffs are scarred by the battering of storms. The central portion of the island is marked with low sand dunes, unimpressive, but relentless in their march across the old mesquite forest. Over the whole is thrown a mantle of monotonously colored vegetation in which green fails even to modify the neutral brown. Giant cacti themselves are dwarfed into insignificance by their background in this seascape where details are kinder than perspective.

The day passed uneventfully. Our homesick pair, as usual, were calmed by the presence of passing ships and strains were eased in the absence of all allusions. Santa Margarita dropped astern and then, for the second time, we cut across an indentation in the Peninsula. The coast abruptly dropped from sight and hazy blue mountains far down on the horizon became dimmer and dimmer until they disappeared in the gathering twilight. Not again, on this cruise, would we watch the sun sink into the Pacific.

As dawn was breaking we picked up the twinkle from the lighthouse on Cabo Falso, the first aid to navigation south of Ensenada. With sunrise we could clearly see the solitary building perched on its two hundred and fifty foot bluff. Behind rose the Victoria Mountains, and once again we were entering into a new zone.

Gone were the plains of Scammon's and San Ignacio and Magdalena; the mountainous terrain now extended to the sea. Gone was the long slope upward from the Pacific, the uneven division of watersheds we had followed from Vizcaíno. During the night we passed La Aguja, where Lower California dwindles to a scant twenty-five miles. That sandy neck, low and brush covered, joins to the Peninsula the circle of the southern mountains. Many of the peaks became visible to us as the sun cleared away the morning mists, as our stage again was set for an unheralded scene.

The Victorias are a series of isolated peaks converging inland and northward to culminate at over six thousand feet in Santa Genoveva, Las Casitas and El Picacho. The terrain has the configuration of Southern Arizona—buttes of mountain size that are surrounded by flat and open country and contribute nothing to the ultimate sierra. The weird configurations of the typical desert, the table-tops and domes, have not survived the heavier rainfall of this southern extremity, but knife-like ridges with sides as steep as earth and rock will lie are still an essential component of every vista. The coast line is a series of high bluffs crowded by a range of hills of fifteen to eighteen hundred feet. Behind are other plateaus and still higher peaks and then more plateaus —of this erratic pyramid are built the Victoria Mountains.

We came close inshore at Cabo Falso and then our interest wavered between scrutiny of a new country and eagerness to catch our first glimpse of the famous Cape. The landmark won when, soon after the lighthouse was passed, there burst upon us a monument in every way worthy of the majesty of its site. For to us, at least, there is no land-mark in western North America that can vie with Cape San Lúcas.

From distant Attu Island, which is more easterly than New Zealand, extends a range of mountains that is one of the glories of the world. The Aleutian Chain of Alaska, the Coast Range of British Columbia, the Cascades of Washington and Oregon, and the incomparable Sierra Nevada, southward and ever southward, the Cuyamacas of San Diego, the Sierra San Pedro Mártir, the Sierra de la Giganta, and at last the Victoria Mountains, before they pass into uncharted depths, climax their orgy in a grand gesture of adieu.

The Ocean of Balboa and the Sea of Cortéz are forever held apart by the apex of a territory. No bluff or broken ridge is it, no quiet rounded point, but a half mile sandstone slab, set on edge, and carved by Father Neptune into the most inspiring of headlands. With half a continent for a base, with a mystic sierra for a pinnacle, with a worthy ridge for a support, gleaming white in the sunshine, the horizontal obelisk steps into two world-famous seas, a challenge to mankind.

The series of serrated pinnacles terminates in two sister rocks. Los Frailes are the Cape. One rises two hundred and twenty-five feet, the other exceeds three hundred. Tall as a fifteen or twenty story building these rounded wedges are thinner than any architect dare build. A flying bridge under which we might have run with ease, a solid rock, white with ages of guano, a monolith engraved by wind blast and storm, with clefts and crevices and overhangs, with carvings and turrets and bastions—Cape San Lúcas, the end of the rainbow.

CHAPTER XXII

SAN LÚCAS

Two miles of sand beach, curved to a gentle crescent, backed with dunes, flanked on one side by a stony mesa, on the other by the glory of the Cape. In one corner a tiny pier, nestling under towering rocks, mothering fishermen at anchor. Close by on the sand a frame of rough branches roofed with palm leaves, a *ramada* for those whose occasions call them into the glare. A dory drawn beyond the tiny breakers. A fifty-foot embankment of sand crowned with half naked mesquite. Tops of palms peeping above the rim. Beyond, far away, the hazy, intriguing pinnacles of the Victorias.

We lay hove to, rocking gently and sleepily, waiting, watching a stage on which there were no actors. An hour passed and then another, but we of the *Least Petrel,* having flown our flags, were barred from any further move. Over the crest at last came men. They launched their dory, slowly, they rowed over and boarded us, unhurriedly, but with the examining of our papers their indifference passed. They became our hosts, asking that we go with them to the *comandante*. So the Partner and Captain and I went ashore, to become acquainted and to explain our purposes.

As a beach on which to swim—or to land a boat—the cove at San Lúcas has no peer. The sand lies at so steep an angle that two or three steps give swimming depth. A clear bottom is this, with water fresh from an untainted ocean. Comfortably warm all winter long and refreshing in hot summer days, here should be the site of a great resort. The world does not have so much to offer that man can spare this little gem to emptiness and reverie.

SAN LUCAS

We crossed the beach and started up a trail leading over the barrier of sand. Fifty feet is no height and yet, so soft was the footing, the three of us were panting by the time we reached the top. The barrier, apparently thrown up by the trades, has every appearance of an artificial dike. The top is flat and narrow, while the bottom is two hundred feet in thickness. On the landward side, below us and almost at sea level, lies an open plain that, before this dam was built, might well have been an arm of the gulf. The scene-shifter who guided the destinies of our journey had chosen a remarkable site from which to display the pueblo of San Lúcas.

We studied the view in detail with mixed emotions of pleasure and disappointment. This was our first contact with an agricultural settlement. There was no doubt we were looking upon untainted Mexican life and that we would here find people working out their destinies free from American influences. There was not a flaw in the purity of San Lúcas, not a foreign note, and, most emphatically, nothing had been designed with the purpose of attracting tourists.

On the other hand we found no promise of picturesque features. Perhaps what we missed most were adobe buildings; not one stood in the pueblo—Captain explained that mud bricks would be promptly levelled by Cape winds, though I suspect the lack of proper clay. No two builders had chosen the same material for substitution and to describe the architecture one would have to list separately each of the fifty buildings.

There were houses of box-slats gathered on the beach and there were huts of palm leaves. Some builders had bought rough lumber and one or two used imported kiln-baked bricks. The new jail, which was being constructed, was of common brick set in mortar and plastered. It contained two cells, each about eight by ten feet and twelve feet high. A foot square window, barred, was set in the back of either room; the doors were simple grilles of iron. The building was in the open, isolated; its ventilation had been obtained at the expense of all privacy.

Excepting on the jail every roof we saw was thatched. The commoner practice is to cover the rafters with thick layers of date palm leaves, crudely clamped into place. Some house owners, having ambition, use rows of overlapping fan-palm leaves, fastening them to bamboo cross-rafters in or-derly lines after the fashion of shingle construction. If, as Captain insists, the *chubascos* flatten adobe walls what is supposed to happen to these roofs? Probably the natives figure on replacement every few years as part of life's routine.

Fences are anomalies. They are everywhere in the settle-ment. Some are well made of barbed-wire, others of per-pendicular stakes set in juxtaposition and held in place with interlaced horizontal tree-limbs. The crudest construction, which is surprisingly effective, is a simple wall of cut briar stacked about three feet high. Fences of adequate design are an outstanding necessity, for San Lúcas is a cattle-yard.

Cows and calves roam everywhere. The site of the pueblo is a former mesquite bottom many of whose trees have been saved. On these the cattle browse and there is left no leaf or shoot which they can reach. The resultant shade is a popular retreat for stock of every description. On the outskirts of the cleared fenced-in fields are clusters of protected mesquite under which houses stand. The impression we had from our sand dune was of a series of empty blocks interspersed with built-up streets.

There were no gardens and no attempt at making sur-roundings less tawdry. This, too, in spite of the fact that there is good soil and enough water to support fairly ex-tensive fields of vegetables, especially of tomatoes. Palms, scattered here and there at random, are inadequate in num-ber to add much to the picture. From a utilitarian standpoint one wonders why they are so few. A community such as this could almost subsist on the date and its by-products.

We walked down the slope of the dune and crossed half a mile of the village. Our business at the customs house finished, we explored. The home we had visited on Santa Margarita was here repeated time and time again and was the basis of the communal life of San Lúcas. It was apparent, however, that nothing was quite as primitive as had been the life of the island family. The people of the pueblo lived as did those on Santa Margarita, but they owned, on an average, perhaps twice as many things. Even that, of course, was pitifully little.

The tourist, the casual visitor accustomed to a comfortable home, looks pityingly into these peon huts. He sees an almost animal-like existence, one with no embellishments. He sees the physical necessities of food, clothing, and shelter cut to an irreducible minimum. The one-room, unfloored and almost unfurnished hovel is the measure of the ability of the owner to acquire. Ignorance, laziness, lack of character, economic surroundings, be the cause what it may, the millions who pass their days in this stark poverty and cultural vacuum are the losers in mankind's competitive struggle. That the standards displayed are voluntary is possible, of course, but if these people are reconciled and are making no effort to better themselves their acquiescence merely means that they are correspondingly low in the scale of human development. Through this stereotyped line of thought the peon is judged by his surroundings.

An observer who insists upon measuring the Mexican laboring class with an American yardstick is not approaching an understanding of their character. The peon is well aware of many of the countless things we regard as necessities. If he could be persuaded to formulate an opinion regarding them he would probably agree that quite a few are not beyond his power to acquire. They are not worth the effort, would be his reaction. There is no pressure of example to drive him toward accumulation. If he has a few pesos in his pocket he doesn't want to work—why should he? When it's gone he'll look around for more. If he has a little money to spend the last thing in the world he will purchase is anything tangible. He intends to buy pleasure, which is food or liquor, rarely a bauble. Life is to be enjoyed; its unpleasant aspects, when they cannot be evaded, at least are to be postponed.

My training is against believing or in commending such philosophy. Nevertheless it exists, nor do I feel that I am justified in damning any man simply because I do not approve. Otherwise what should I say of my own people, of whom eighty, or is it ninety, percent do not save a dollar? Even if I were to go so far as to preach to Mexico "I know you're wrong because you don't agree with me," dare I add the next step, "If your mentality were not so low you would not disagree"?

It is always a pleasure, be you Latin or Mongol, Nordic or Jew, to feel that the stock from which you spring is at least a little better than any other strain. Being Americans let us therefore assume that we have a racial superiority over the inhabitants of San Lúcas. That seems safe, especially as they are probably looking down on us. But if we are to make comparisons on a basis of blood lines we will find that we are dealing with fine distinctions. If the basic differences between peoples were great there would be more general accord on relative merits and opinions could be backed with definite proofs. In view of the practical level of human intelligence—some authorities estimate it at ninety-eight percent—we should be very chary indeed before we attribute our broader culture and our material advantages entirely to a more highly developed brain. We have paid a price, a price we think well worth while but one which, nevertheless, is very great.

If relative surroundings are not an index by which to compare peoples—and clearly they are not—it becomes interesting to judge the peon mind on its own merits. He is not a simple creature, like the negro. A wide acquaintance coupled with sympathy for his point of view, an intimacy with his daily life, and a check with the same type living in the United States, shows him to be far above the average in the scale of humanity. His fault is more a lack of desire than of ability. As an individual he seems to be temperamentally happy in his surroundings; nationally there is beginning to develop the ambition to progress.

We met the young woman who teaches school. She took a real pride in showing her classes and explaining her purposes. Every child in the village is compelled to attend and the hours are long. Study is not optional. The pupils face their taskmistress from the wooden benches and they read their lessons aloud. No chance to shirk, to let thoughts wander, as from early morning until late in the afternoon the steady hum of childish voices comes through the windows. Schooling is being taken very seriously by the authorities. They are endeavoring, and with surprising success, to reach into even the smaller settlements in their campaign against illiteracy.

In addition to homes and official buildings the town contained two cantinas. These, as was the case in Magdalena, combine the functions of saloon and general store. The two were so much alike and they so closely resembled the one we had examined further north that, had we not known they were characteristically Mexican, we might have suspected the three of being under single ownership. The proprietor of one of the cantinas, being an old-time friend of Captain, turned our call into a visit. Of course we fired a bombardment of questions and after a while his answers became a recital of troubles.

As a place in which to do business, apparently, Lower

California is not be recommended. It is a territory governed from the City of Mexico and undoubtedly is mercilessly exploited. In spite of the growing interest on the part of the last few governors and the commendable showing they have made on roads and schools, the revenues from the Peninsula have not been kept within its borders. Lower California cannot afford the contribution and has suffered accordingly. There is official interference in everything, duties are levied on imports from the mainland, and excise taxes are crushing. It is on the last point that our friend dwelt at greatest length. One of two cantinas in this tiny place, he paid a monthly tax of three hundred pesos. Summing up his grievances he expressed the hope that Lower California would follow the example of the States in adopting prohibition. "Then we Mexican saloon-keepers could make money too," he said.

The natives were of far less interest to us than the Partner was to them. Having the courage of her convictions she wore, in the town, either conventional riding breeches or else, if in a frock, went stockingless. Both styles were serious shocks to the staid community. No direct objection was made, nothing was said to the Partner, but Captain, being well acquainted in San Lúcas, did not get off so easily. The first time he came up town alone he was taken to task by half the women he knew.

"Who is that person? What do you mean by bringing her here?"

"I didn't bring her here—she's the owner's wife."

"The owner's wife? Where is he?"

"We saw you two in the village together?"

Captain tried to explain.

"Why doesn't she wear stockings? Has she no skirt?"

Poor Captain.

"An American custom," was the best he could do.

Coming back from a walk I cut across the dunes and

stumbled upon the most southerly home in Lower California. It was simple and small—six feet long. A gnarled mesquite root served for one side. This was patched where it twisted above the sand and had been made wind-proof with a few box shakes. The opposite side was a single board. The floor was composed of discarded rawhide saddle pads; there was no roof, unless the tree could be so termed. An empty kerosene box served for one end and two more saddle pads, held up by short stakes, for the other. The owner's wardrobe —his extra shirt—was rolled at one end and weighted with a stone, and there were two straw hats similarly held in place, one on the floor and the other on the dressing table— I should have said the box. There were two cans of which one showed signs of much use in fire, the other none. These were carefully suspended from the branches above and completed the taxable assets of the establishment.

The evening brought company. For dinner we had Sr. and Sra. Martinez and the Jefe Oficina, Antonio Ruiz C. Conversation was desultory for lack of facility with each other's languages, but oh you radio fans! With our little battery set we skipped about from Seattle to Havana, jumped all over the middle-west, passed through Texas to Cape Victoria, and settled down to a mutually interesting program from the City of Mexico. San Lúcas was proving herself a place to be liked.

CHAPTER XXIII

ONE evening we brought out our atlas. As Cape San
Lúcas was the turning point of the trip we thought it worth
our while to compare its geographical position with that
of some other well-known places. We were rather surprised
to find ourselves eight hundred miles east of San Francisco,
for, naturally thinking of the Pacific Coast as running north
and south, we did not realize how great was the drift away
from the meridian.

We traced our parallel of longitude northward to a point
between Salt Lake City and Denver, we ran it along the
eastern side of Yellowstone Park and followed it across
the continental divide in Central Canada. Carried south it
ran indefinitely over open ocean, passing not far from Easter
Island. In the cove we were lying just below the Tropic of
Cancer and so a girdle of our latitude traversed Havana,
Calcutta, Hongkong, and the Hawaiian Islands. Far south
of any point in Europe it crossed Africa over the Nubian
Desert and in Asia touched the Red Sea. We were eight
hundred knots from San Diego by the plotted steamer course
but we followed custom, allowed for the shoreline, and
considered the distance an even thousand miles.

We were in the tropics; at least so textbooks designate
the tip of the Peninsula. The transition was largely technical, there being no change in vegetation sufficient to indicate our leaving one zone and entering another. There were
still the desert growths with which we had become familiar,

162

cholla, pitahaya, cardón, mesquite and numerous species of thorns. The density of plant life still depended primarily upon associations. From the alluvial soil of the bottoms, or the salty flats of the plains, there was a progressively steady decrease to the stony surfaces of the mesas. Furthermore the Cape Region showed little specific variation from the more northerly deserts; there was an impressive increase in the size of individuals and in the abundance of plant life, but no accompanying introduction on a large scale of new forms. Shrubs which had been waist or even knee high, here assumed the proportions of small trees; the bushes of more arid surroundings became fifteen or twenty feet of congested thorns. Thickets, jungle-like and head-high, spread for miles with a notable absence of undergrowths. The smaller forms were either crowded out by crawling branches of briars or else, in open sandy stretches, were starved by roots of trees. Fortunately for our work the interlacing foliage which otherwise would have proven impenetrable was cut and crossed by trails, occasionally by roads, and often by main or lateral stream beds.

For the several days that the *Least Petrel* lay at anchor in the cove we busied ourselves exploring the surrounding country. We made a special search for Sanford Elf Owls, little bits of things no larger than a man's hand. They are insectivorous cardón dwellers who breed and spend their daytime hours in old woodpecker holes. In hunting them we used our wooden ladder, dragging it along trails or shoving it across the tops of bushes as we worked our way from one Giant Cactus to another. We rested by inspecting the cardónes. Holes dot the upper part of nearly every one of the stalks, especially of the older and larger plants, and our task was to determine from the ground which of the cavities showed signs of occupancy. When entrances were clean and polished, were free from dust and cobwebs, we knew that something had recently passed in or out. We climbed to all our best prospects and laid them open with an axe.

A typical woodpecker nest is a cylindrical cavity, one foot or more in depth by six or eight inches in diameter, excavated in the heart of the cactus branch. It has as an opening a round hole perhaps an inch in diameter. We examined more than a hundred before we left the Cape, an undertaking which tested our perseverance, for we did not find a single owl nor, for that matter, a feather of any kind. But the quest was not without compensation; a wide range of other animal life had usurped the abandoned nests. Mice were the most active. If we chanced to run into a family sometimes as many as half a dozen would bubble out of one nest, to spread over the landscape and, often, upon ourselves as well. Occasionally the prying hatchet brought to light a snake, a harmless constrictor but an unpleasant customer to meet from the top of a wobbly ladder.

Lizards were Charley's specialty; he rarely allowed one to escape. They came in all shapes and colors, some tiny, some so large that it did not seem possible for them to have squeezed into the holes. Wasps and other insects have followed the trail of the woodpecker and they surely did resent our intrusion. Bats, too, had found these hollows ideal places in which to spend the daylight hours. Later in the season a dozen species of birds will be dragging nesting materials into the prepared excavations or will be raising young upon the fine chips on the bottom. These Giant Cacti are laboratories in which to study adaptation. The interlopers are so far dependent upon woodpeckers to supply sites that in areas where carpinteros are absent there is little faunal life among cardónes. There would ensue a blighting and widespread biological dislocation if for any reason the woodpecker family should disappear from the desert.

On our last day in San Lúcas, worn out by mid-afternoon, I went back to the boat to rest. It was warm and I had worked hard, fighting the jungle for pyrrhuloxia and thrashers and cardinals. Everyone but Captain was still afield, even the Partner, though having deserted the cause of science, she was busy trying to fill her market basket with ranch eggs. As these are habitually eaten by the natives as soon as laid her system, I suspect, was to converse in the shady corner of some hut and wait for the hen to perform its duty.

Captain was lying on his bunk, reading. I knew a weakness of his and, in want of someone with whom to talk, brought up a favorite topic, the *chubascos*. They are the one thing in these waters of which he is really afraid and never have I known him to avoid an opportunity of impressing their dangers upon me. As they are seasonal storms, occurring only during the latter part of July and the ensuing three months, and as their zone is fairly well defined, Captain's purpose was to see that our itinerary was kept so arranged that we would at no time risk an encounter. All in the world needed to start a discussion was to the suggest that, in formulating our plans, he was overestimating the peril.

I cannot and hope I never shall be able to describe a *chubasco* from personal observation. Possibly I owe it to my education to cruise about the mouth of the Gulf some September until I work my way into a first-class tornado. But when I looked at the naked beach and remembered that it once had held a customs house, when I gauged two hundred and twenty feet of sheer rock and realized that water has been thrown above Los Frailes, I remained steadfast in my determination that whatever I learned about *chubascos* would be at second hand.

These summer terrors are so devastating that for three or four months in the year they close the Cape Region to small boat navigation. Naturally they have a wide ramification of influence. They affect such principal industries as fishing and truck gardening and, indirectly, they reach all the ordinary routines of life. *Chubascos* determine sailing dates and types of architecture, are to be disregarded in few major plans, and loom large among conditions that are to be accepted. They were very real to me, too, with the evidence of their prowess on one side and the arena of their action on the other.

"A *chubasco*," said Captain, "is a mighty strong wind, but just what kind seems to be a matter on which no two people agree. For one thing the word is local—in Lower California, for instance, it has a very different meaning than in Sinaloa and Nyarit and I guess that has a lot to do with the confusion. I was caught in one of the damn things once and so I thought I knew all about them. When I talked it over with other fishermen I found they had ideas that weren't like mine at all, if you know what I mean. I got interested and stubborn and went to the experts in the Weather Bureau and the Navy to get the dope straight and had to come to the conclusion that no one knows just what a *chubasco* is.

"To begin with there are two kinds of storms in northwestern Mexico—the straight hurricane and the revolving cyclone. In the second place the winds south of San Blas are very different from those about the mouth of the Gulf. Furthermore there are two distinct forms of cyclones, and, as there is no way of tracking any of them systematically, it's not to be wondered at that there's all this uncertainty.

"The nearer you get to the Gulf of Tehuantepec the worse the weather becomes and the longer the bad season lasts. In the summer, the rainy season, as far as I can make out there are violent rain storms that blow offshore every few days and usually attain hurricane proportions. These are called *chubascos* on the mainland. They have to do with heat-baked plains and cooler water and usually are not felt far out at sea.

"Mixed in with them are occasional cyclones that can be anything from a large whirlwind to a first-class tornado. They come up from the south and while their course is erratic they usually swing out to sea and back to land again before they pass Cape Corrientes. In the height of the season, three or four times a year one of them will swing over into Lower California or up the Gulf even as far as Guaymas, and then they too are known as *chubascos*.

"The one that caught me came in August—we were in a seaworthy eighty-foot fishing boat halfway between Mazatlan and San Lúcas, where we had no business to be at that season. There was an almost dead calm, but there was a humidity in the air, a storm feeling, that would have made us very uneasy if the barometer had not been holding. Clouds began to gather off to the southeast but even then we didn't suspect anything worse than a thunder storm until suddenly the bottom dropped out of the air. With a reading of 28.6 that gave us only half an hour warning, the wind and rain struck. It was dark—these things occur between eight o'clock and midnight—the seas became monstrous, with waves thirty feet high and the hurricane varying from eighty to a hundred miles an hour. Those figures are accurate—I'm a good judge and besides I checked them officially when I got home.

"You may well imagine we were in trouble. Our decks were swept by the first gust—everything went by the board except anchors and chains. Our dories didn't last five minutes as one great wave after another broke right onto us, threatening to smash our superstructure or roll us over. I don't know yet how we ever got through alive."

Captain was still frightened and it was clear that he was not going to tell much more.

"What did you do?" I hurried to ask before it was too late.

"It was oil that saved us. We ran before the wind, slowly, pumping from our fuel tanks. That kept the seas from breaking and in two hours the worst was over. Once is enough, sir; I'm not taking the *Least Petrel* into any *chubasco.*"

CHAPTER XXIV

SAN JOSE DEL CABO

FROM San Lúcas we travelled easterly, following the rock-bound coast. There were sand beaches and there were capes, but more often high mesas came to the water edge to end in rugged sea-walls. Always in the background were indistinct highlands, while the middle distance was a vista of untold miles of treeless hills.

We were making a short run. In a couple of hours we entered the indentation between Palmella and Gorda Points and, officially, had reached San José del Cabo Bay. As far as we could tell we were still in the Gulf with the so-called bay nothing but an open roadstead. Immediately upon our dropping anchor the *Least Petrel* began to pitch in the vicious chop and our discomfort made us more sceptical than ever about this being a harbor. Nature has been perverse to San José. She has blessed it with the rare endowments of fertile soil and abundant water and then, ironically, has withheld an anchorage, a gift with which, elsewhere in the Gulf, she is so prodigal.

We watched the breakers roll on the beach and no one, not even Captain, cared to challenge them in the dory. In time, through the waves, there came to us in a canoe two youths and an old man. While each of the boys handled a long oar the father sat in the stern, steering with a paddle. As they drew close we recognized them for Indians and their craft for a dugout.

Dugouts are an institution on the Gulf. They are what their name implies, single pieces of wood, sectors of the

169

trunks of large trees, shaped and hollowed. They come from the south, from the mainland, for in Lower California nothing grows to sufficient size. The workmanship is good, the lines well designed, and the surfaces, inside and out, are smooth and true. They are hand hewn and consequently are clumsy and very heavy, but so seaworthy that a trip across the Gulf is a commonplace. The canoe that had come for us was eighteen feet long, with a four-foot beam and a depth of thirty inches. Although neither in size nor in shape did it seem fitted for its task we decided to take a risk, for in no other way could we reach San José.

Four of us, the Partner, Rogers, Peter, and I, climbed in for the first trip. We sat on the bottom, making ourselves as comfortable as circumstances permitted, and in a moment were headed for the shore. The dugout was sluggish, it rode low in the water, and in spite of the reassuring skill of our boatmen, the closer we approached the shore the more menacing did the surf appear. Suddenly and before we fully realized that we were in shallowing water a great wave rushed upon us, curling and breaking on either side.

Came another and still another, until one caught us on its crest and fairly hurled us at the beach. Out of the confusion of sand and spray and running figures we found ourselves aground with a dozen men on either side holding our bow head on to the sand. While our helpers good naturedly took their ducking we waited for receding waves and stepped ashore, dryshod.

The beach was an impressive sight. Well above the water was strung a line of boats, dugouts for the most part, mixed with a few skiffs and cumbersome scows. A hundred men were scattered about the landing place, loafing or gathering around us in curiosity. Fully half were Indians, full-blooded for all we could tell, for theirs was the dark skin of the aborigine. Their legs were bare from the knees down, the blue overalls being either cut off or rolled. Their costumes were complete with wide-brimmed straw hats, nondescript shirts, and ever-present bandanas knotted about their necks. These handkerchiefs, tied across the face when the wind is driving its stinging load of sand or the air is choked with dust, serve a real purpose in protecting the throat. Their principal use on the beach at San José, however, is to cover the mouth after dark. In some way there has grown up a belief that night air is poisonous and almost without exception the boatmen of the Cape give credence to the superstition.

The waterfront activities held us the better part of an hour. A small steamer lying in the roadstead was the excuse for much scurrying and bustle in handling cargo and passengers. Not the running and confusion and barking of orders that would have marked a similar body of Northmen, but soft voices and chatter and much willingness to help. There was a fascination in watching canoes ride in on the breakers and in the always successful rush to keep the boats from capsizing when they touched the sand. A steer was driven down to the beach. We couldn't leave while they were hog-tying it and loading it into a canoe nor while it was being launched through the surf. In fact we waited patiently on the beach until a rope had been dropped about the animal's horns and it had been hauled safely to the deck of the ship.

We climbed over a dune not unlike the sand bank at San Lúcas; a mile or so away, across a level valley, San José lay on a hill. There was much in the scene to suggest that the scientists are right, that this is indeed the tropics. There were scattered huts with adobe walls and thatched roofs, there was a vista of palms and banana trees and sugar cane, there was a lagoon and a living stream of water and there was in the air, in the people, in the surroundings, the languor of the south.

We plodded afoot for half an hour across a corner of the most important agricultural centre in Lower California.

Through the ages the flow from the Victoria Mountains has been working on this garden plot, has been excavating a valley and covering the floor deep with silt, that most fertile of soils. Man has harnessed the water, has spread it across the plains in little unlined ditches dug in the soft earth. The oasis is large and the water supply generous— our path took us beside a stream which, though seven feet wide, represents only the surplus, the drainage from irrigated lands. Cattle are raised in this Eden, and peppers and onions and corn. A quarter of a million cases of tomatoes are annually exported and of sugar cane there seems to be no end. There is little that energy and determination could not accomplish in San José.

I am afraid, however, that this season may prove to be the last in which tomatoes can be grown in Northwestern Mexico. The sole market is in the United States; the natives, even if they wished, have not the purchasing power to handle any appreciable portion of the crop. American exports will be impossible under the new tariff; it will demand a tax virtually equivalent to the selling price. Yet only during the last few weeks of their season do tomatoes from the Gulf compete with those grown in any of the United States, the southern product ripening so much the earlier. According to the local point of view there is no reason for barring the Mexican vegetables and the feeling is general that they would not be excluded could the question receive individual attention and be judged on its merits. The duties will result in rank, stark tragedy to this community and, to the poor people, it is all so unnecessary and so pointless. Poor Lower California! Nature has not been generous and man consistently crushes what little chance she has.

San José del Cabo stands upon a knoll, a hundred feet above and surrounded on three sides by fertile flats. Our introduction was a domestic scene, a dozen or more women washing clothes from the banks of an irrigation ditch. We climbed the hill, leaving below the cane fields and the gardens and the palms, we entered a narrow street of one story adobes, we traversed a few blocks of rural Mexico, and made our way to the plaza. That small park centres about the inevitable bandstand and is dotted with benches and shrubbery and trees. Over a vista of oleander and magnolia and in the shadow of mission ruins, came the first impressions of San José.

As values are reckoned through Lower California there is wealth in this district. The brothers Canseco have an emporium that carries an elaborate mixture of American and German goods, of furniture, crockery, household utensils and dress materials. Ready-made clothing only is a native product, for this store, unlike those we saw on the West Coast, handles no food. Indeed, there was hardly an article to be found in Canseco Hermanos that we had seen since leaving Ensenada.

Evidences of the goods stocked were to be found in the homes of some of the people, of the fortunate few, for there were families who at least aspired to standards and so, perforce, became the local aristocracy. There were houses built about gardened patios, exotic entrances through open hallways lined with potted plants. There were cement floors and walks, shade and the privacy of individual rooms, hinged doors that opened inward. There were glass windows, curtained, and walls of stucco, white, usually, but sometimes ambitiously green. There were such comforts as furniture, bedding, chinaware, and almost always an old-fashioned hatrack. Everything primitive, simple, not to be gauged by our ideas of necessities, and yet, unpretentious as they were, a long step in advance of San Lúcas and a sufficient factor in the community to result in a store such as Canseco's.

This is only a part of the picture and, I'm afraid, by far the smaller. In most respects San José shows no progress. The workers, Indian and Mexican, do make money, it is true, but being virtually all of the type found in San Lúcas, they take their surplus to the cantinas. There, in the only way they have learned, perhaps in the only way open to them, they break the monotony of their lives. Their homes are the huts of the West Coast. The Indians on the northern side of town congregate in even simpler hovels, in make-shifts of cane that are little more than *ramadas*. Necessities are bought in stores not unlike those of the other villages, though an exception might be noted in the case of the Chinese shop-keepers. The orientals are a trifle more progressive; as a rule they handle no liquor but do have a somewhat better stock of merchandise.

One of the Partner's errands was to buy fresh beef. We found the butcher after we had searched the town—since everyone was supposed to know the location of his shop he had not seen the necessity of displaying any sort of sign—and it was characteristic of the country that he had nothing left. He had killed early in the morning, had put his stock on sale soon after sunrise, and by seven o'clock all the desirable cuts were gone. We did not arrive until the middle of the morning. His meat, while on sale, was in no way protected from flies, when purchased it was not wrapped, being carried away in market baskets, in the hand, or with miniature baling hooks that often allowed it to drag in the dust. I wonder to what extent the suffering of these people would be alleviated if they would but take the most elemental of sanitary precautions. The answer is suggested by the tragedies that are concomitant with the almost universal absence of birth control and with families that average few adult children.

We had passed two sugar mills on our walk to town. Both had been abandoned, but on the further side of the plaza we were fortunate enough to find a third, and this one was in operation. We could see the process almost from the planting of the cane, for there were no board fences, no

"Keep Out" signs about this mill. Came twenty burros buried under loads of stalks that flapped rhythmically with every step. Ears peeping above, legs to the knees showing below, the train slovenly moved through the glare of dusty streets, through roadways that have no sidewalks and are bordered simply by house walls. Sometimes the children in the streets, or the dogs, or the goats moved aside, sometimes the donkeys turned, but always the train dragged along on the way to the mill. Arrival marked the first step towards sugar making.

The cane is fed by hand into a crusher, big metal wheels with interlocking teeth. Power is supplied by a steam engine whose boiler is fed with cane refuse. If ever anything mechanical earned veneration as a museum piece it surely is this antique. The crushed stems were pressed by being placed under a threaded screw which was turned by a patient burro. He walked in a circle at the end of a revolving pole, his fading ambition being revived by a boy seated beside the path who methodically struck him every time he passed.

The sap was boiled in open vats, in great kettles bricked up so that the burning refuse transmitted its heat both to the sides and to the bottom. There were spread upon a bench a series of home-made blocks of mesquite, perhaps a foot square and four inches thick. These had been studded with cone-shaped holes an inch across and two inches deep, forming molds into which the syrup was poured. One man emptied a ladle into the centre of each die and two helpers, using flat sticks, scraped until every mold was full. When cold the *pinocho* is a dirty brown color. It was dumped into bins and crated by hand into bird cage effects of criss-crossed sticks.

Not only does refining stop at this point but, crude as the process is, every step had been shiftless and sloppy. Burros, dogs, babies, and loafers stray everywhere and the sheds are open to swarms of flies that drive one almost crazy. The molds are washed, or at least moistened, before use by being dipped into water that has not been changed this season. Ladles, cane, blocks, anything and everything not in active service accumulates on the floor to be kicked or dragged through dust and trash. The story of the meat is repeated —fastidiousness, even decent cleanliness, is not practiced in connection with food.

The Partner and Rogers and I lunched in the patio of a house not greatly changed since it had been a private home. The table was set out-of-doors under the roof of a veranda. There was an olla hanging in the shade, caged birds under the eaves, a well cared-for garden at our feet. As course after course was served, soup, spaghetti, beef in chili sauce, squash cooked with peppers and tomatoes, fried beans, tortillas, coffee, we compared notes on the things we had seen and discussed our impressions of the town.

San José del Cabo, we agreed, had no counterpart on the Peninsula. Its were the rustic attributes of a tiny pueblo, yet it was tinged with the urban characteristics of a larger town. Its limited progress was more than offset by the extreme simplicity of its Indian population. The not inconsiderable money that was made showed little indication either of being saved or of being wisely spent. More industry here, more real work, yet a most abject surrender to the demoralization of the tropics. Sleepy, content, sunny, a fascinating hodgepodge, kin at once to the thirst of a desert and the spell of a South Sea Island.

CHAPTER XXV

INTO THE GULF

THE so-called bay at San José del Cabo was no place for us to linger. We had arrived aboard the *Least Petrel* and were under way again before dark, but there had been a narrow escape from unpleasant consequences. We had cut the time of departure too fine, for no one wanted to leave the town, and when we did arrive at the beach we found that the breakers had become so much heavier since morning that the boatmen no longer wanted to embark. Only after considerable persuasion, coupled with three times the regular ferriage, would our Indians agree to undertake the risk. We slipped through the surf in safety, but the margin had been too close for comfort.

Our introduction to the waters of the Gulf was not being made under auspicious circumstances. The waves were no higher than some we had encountered in the ocean, it is true, but the *Least Petrel* was shipping far more water than on any other run. The long swells of the Pacific she had ridden, but here the distance from crest to crest was so short that if she rose to meet one wave she poked her bow squarely under the next. We closed all our doors and portholes, we battened down the hatch and made fast everything that could not be removed from the deck, and we took a drenching from the green water that continually raked us from stem to stern.

I certainly envy Captain and Juan on occasions such as these; their seamanship was something very different from

177

ours. They seemed literally unaware of the rolling and pitching and certainly did not allow it to interfere with their duties. Captain as always held to within two degrees on his steering and Juan merely smiled and spread a cloth if his dishes slid all over the table. We, on the other hand, could not yield to the motion. We tried to maintain balance at the expense of wearying muscles and, in the end, were physically exhausted.

With Peter the night was worse than one of bodily discomfort. As long as the lighthouse at San José remained in sight he had been content, but when it no longer flashed to us he reacted as he had done off Cedros Island. Captain had remained close enough inshore to keep in touch with the coast line and Peter knew that no other bearings were available. We all recognized Captain's ability to follow headlands at distances from which our less experienced eyes could discern nothing, but Peter could not accept safety on faith. Again he was threatened with invisible reefs and breakers close to hand, and once more came hours of uncertainty, of peering into black voids, of stark fear of a sea empty and unknown.

We all had hoped that his break at Cape San Eugenio had been a flash from which he had recovered, and so his lapse tonight was a great disappointment. Coming as it did under circumstances less provocative than before it showed that time was undermining rather than strengthening his courage. It was now apparent that during the interval fear had constantly been with him, that when he was not in a state of active fright there was a dormant but continuing dread of the future. This was the key to his course of puzzling conduct.

He had undertaken, one after another, to bully everyone on the boat. He met with no success, of course, but that did not disguise the fact that he was trying to save his own face by bluffing a rôle of super-importance. Another pose—

he worked the two together—was to belittle us and our purposes as well, to sneer at our accomplishments and at our plans. He enjoyed nothing so much as making someone ridiculous and he allowed his desire repeatedly to carry him to the point of untruthfulness. This conduct was simply one of the aspects of his attempts to regain self-respect, but I doubt if the results were any more satisfactory to him than pleasant to us.

These things were not serious matters, were accepted as among the incidents of the trip, and were generally ignored. They were annoying, of course, and did result in a growing tension, but of themselves were hardly a cause of worry. Where real danger lay was in the fact that Peter's morale was breaking and that there was no predictable limit where he would stop. We had barely touched the frontier of the real emptiness of the Gulf, of the conditions which he seemed unable to withstand. In a struggle between himself and the country Peter was on the verge of a defeat that I feared might evolve into a rout.

Meanwhile we were working our way into the Gulf. About four o'clock in the morning, worn out by the incessant pitching, we voted ourselves a few hours' rest, and ran into Muertos Bay. We slept peacefully till breakfast time, waking to find ourselves in an anchorage typical of these waters. There was protection from winds over something more than half a circle, there was good anchorage and there was a sand beach that was perfect. Muertos Bay is surrounded by the foothills of the Victoria Mountains. Rising at first sharply from the coast for a thousand feet or so they ascend more gradually as farther in the interior they build up the cone-shaped sierra. Their vegetation is similar specifically to that of San Lúcas but it is far less luxuriant. The decrease is palpably indicative of an abrupt lessening of rainfall as the Gulf is approached.

On the beach are an abandoned warehouse and pier—

relics of the days when silver was brought to the coast from the mines at Triunfo. The unsalvaged shed and the little wharf, intact and virtually unchanged since last utilized, are among the mementoes of failure which strew the southern Gulf coast. Lower California would be fortunate if mistakes committed within her boundaries did not leave such conspicuous aftermaths. Corrugated iron and timbers and piling, deserted and not worth the cost of salvage or of stealing, serve too well to warn the cautious investor.

Anchored near us in Muertos Bay was a fishing boat, one of the larger types that carry a crew of ten. A Japanese outfit from San Pedro, it apparently was not having much luck, for it still rode high in the water. It was evident that the fishermen were making strenuous efforts to fill their hold, for they hardly awaited daylight before they appeared on the beach. They had a long narrow net of fine mesh with which they were trying to catch the needed bait by surrounding schools of minnows. With excited and voluble chatter one group held an end on the shore while others, in a dory, swung around the half circle. At eight o'clock, as we were leaving, they brought in their seine empty for the third time. We collectors are not the only ones who have off days.

An hour out of Muertos found us in Ventana Bay slipping between the mainland and Isla Ceralbo. This, the first of our Gulf islands, was something of a shock to those of us who never before had been in the Vermilion Sea. Ceralbo is a ridge so narrow and so steep that, though only four miles wide, it attains a height of twenty-five hundred feet. A volcanic uplift, abrupt and tawny and hot, the ugly mass lies a few miles offshore, uninhabited, unwatered, and unused. Even its mineral wealth has resisted exploitation, and only a limited amount of vegetation, hardly enough to soften the glowing cinder, has straggled from the mainland and in some manner contrived to subsist. We were well

OUR DRYDOCK

MAGDALENA VIEJA

FRIGATE BIRDS

content that the representation elsewhere of its flora and fauna relieved us of obligation to struggle with this wedge of ash and lava.

We passed through Ceralbo Channel out into the open Gulf and then ran northwest until we entered the treacherous passage between Arranco Cabello and Lupona Point. San Lorenzo Channel, studded with rocks and reefs and foul water, is a trap for the unwary, safe only if the navigator makes no errors. Captain found some buoys, in which he placed little confidence, and a familiar bluff, on which he relied implicitly, and in the course of time we found ourselves past Dispensa Point and in a body of water that has no analogue in all the wide world.

We looked across twenty miles of what should be a famous bay to where were spread the graduated terminals of Sierra de la Giganta. Indistinct in the distance and the haze they nevertheless revealed themselves as desert mountains crowding the shoreline of the Gulf. To the south they faded away but northward they developed ever increasing proportions until they blended into the outlines of San José Island. Behind was the ten-league line of a virtual peninsula through whose centre we had passed and whose northern end was Espíritu Santo Island. The inland sea, from our position, was landlocked. We could not see the twenty-mile opening between the two islands; our horizon was a closed panorama of mountains pushing into the water, of mountains rising triumphantly out of the waves. Not a cloud, there seldom is, not a shadow, nothing but a glaring circle of water held within a pottery basin.

This is La Paz Bay, paradise of anglers seeking big game fish. Those for whom tarpon and tuna are too docile come here for the greatest of swimming fighters, the swordfish or for that most immense monstrosity, the sunfish. The dorsal fin of the latter, high out of the water, is a sight too frequent to cause comment, but one, nevertheless, always exciting because it betrays the sleeping giant below. The leaping of the swordfish as ten times, twenty times in rapid succession, thrusting with his sword and striking viciously with his tail, he hurls himself high in the air, is a revelation of power and vindictiveness. I wonder if in sport there can be a greater thrill than hooking one of these killers with rod and reel. Some day, with arrangements made to take the necessary time, I'm coming back to pit my skill against the most fiery inhabitant of this lava-beaded sea.

Coming out of San Lorenzo Channel we turned almost north, to follow the shore of Espíritu Santo Island. This is smaller than Ceralbo, being twelve miles long, averaging three or four across, and having a maximum elevation of two thousand feet. We ran close beside it for an hour and found it to be another volcanic cinder, steep, inhospitable, and pitted with deep cañons. In places the soil was bare, though, for the most part, it was touched lightly with brush. The mouths of some of the arroyos were small mangrove-bordered lagoons backed with heavy brush and running into valleys of sahuaro and lesser cacti.

We came to anchor under the wing of Isla Partida, as the northern end of Espíritu Santo is named. In days gone by there was an active volcano there, one that bubbled and spouted and built itself a crater of goodly proportions. Then came subsidence, with half the volcanic cone below the level of the sea. Tides and currents ate an opening through one side, the Gulf poured in, the sluice was widened, and there has resulted one of the most remarkable little harbors the mind can imagine.

We spent three days under the misshapen lava walls of the old volcano. Comfortably protected from random winds and from vagaries of cross-currents we should have been content. Instead we were depressed by the sheer ugliness of our surroundings and by the open hostility of the rock-covered slopes. We were busy every minute and were well rewarded for our work, yet we were under constant pressure, anxious to finish and to leave.

Rogers was surfeited with material. He found in unbroken sequence artifacts that carried him from the fishermen and pearl divers of today back to most primitive of aborigines. His difficulty lay in separating the ancient culture from the modern, especially on those sites which had been used in common. The peasant type that now camps on Espíritu Santo builds crude windbreaks of stone and is little less primal than were the first who left their hallmarks here.

Each of us, in proportion to his youth and strength, climbed the talus or worked along the shoreline in search of specimens. We collected a small series of birds, but only as opportunity offered, for ornithology was made incidental to mammalogy at this station. We caught several ring-tailed cats, shot four or five black jack-rabbits, and set long trap-lines for mice and rats.

On every one of the larger islands in the Gulf small mammals are to be found. Obviously each of the various groups is in a state of geographical isolation and there is abundant evidence to show that separation has existed over a long period, even as biological time is reckoned. The separated communities, relatively small in component numbers and existing without intermixture with each other, almost without exception have developed into recognizably distinguishable races. Contrasted with the condition in the Gulf are, for instance, the islands of the Great Lakes. Although on them there is also isolated mammal life it is homogeneous at least to the extent that separate subspecies have not been named. In the northern example separation either is not complete or else is comparatively recent.

The Gulf islands are ideal mediums in which to study certain aspects of variations in heredity and processes of evolution. Let us assume that we have under examination a series of skins of bush rats. We have examples from the

Peninsula, from the mainland coast of Mexico, and from a dozen islands. We find that no two groups are alike. Those which come from the larger areas show the least tendency to vary—a logical condition in view of the fact that the more widespread the re-introduced inheritances the more likely are they to be absorbed and to disappear.

That the racial distinctions are accidental rather than either systematic or utilitarian is as nearly proven as a matter of this kind can be. There is no progressive development, say from the northerly to the southerly stations, but instead errant appearances which no man would venture to predict. The most painstaking checking, made on location, fails to reveal any connection between the separable traits and factors which have even the slightest bearing on relative chances of survival.

The Gulf islands show, with a clarity that is nowhere surpassed, the results that flow from individuality. In minute details the component members of any given race are not identical nor do they breed true to type. If the ancestors of the various groups had been precisely alike, if father, son, and grandson were exact replicas, we would have had no new races and there would be no such thing as evolution.

In theory the islands were once a part of the mainland. When they became separated the rat population remained. Thus were established a number of isolated groups in each of which, it may safely be assumed, there were individuals possessed of peculiarities. We may add the further hypothesis that novel characteristics would appear from time to time, owing to the fact that inheritances are not facsimiles. Most of the abnormalities would die away, would be absorbed back into generic standards. If as often as once in a century, however, some trivial quality, instead of being bred out, became established in the racial inheritance, then evolution's first step would have been taken. A point to be borne in mind is that this change need not be construed as necessarily meaning progress. The new quality itself, if not a definite drawback, would almost invariably prove to be neutral. An advantage that can exert any really beneficial influence on the occasion of its first appearance, before it has been augmented by development and stability, is possible, of course, but so extremely unlikely as hardly to deserve consideration.

On the contrary an abnormality, if important enough to have a bearing either way, in the vast majority of cases will be a disadvantage. There are many minutiæ without which an individual cannot survive and a conflict with any one of them must necessarily disappear. Furthermore competition to live is so intense that, in a state of nature, an animal even slightly handicapped would have little chance of stamping his peculiarity on offspring and eventually on his group.

There remain changes which are harmless and those which may be a step towards eventual betterment. These, naturally, will be transmitted and a fixed percentage will be permanent. Espíritu Santo gave us an appreciably increased understanding of this situation, and a definitely clarified perspective as well. In this isolation we could realize, as never before, that evolution is essentially a negative process. If we assume that one variation in x accidentally, blindly points towards progress, then one in x^2 will represent a second step, one in x^4 a third step. The time will arrive when the development has become actively instead of potentially valuable and then, but not until then, will survival of the fittest become a factor. The process, as we saw it displayed, up to the final stages is one of elimination rather than of survival.

CHAPTER XXVI

LA PAZ

WE were running south down a tortuous channel. Hills ahead and to port were miniature mountain ranges, a series of steep ridges and branching spurs only a few hundred feet high and yet unbroken in harshness of contour. Slopes were geometric ascents forking from drainage gutters and crests were weaving ribbons running at random along the skyline. The landscape was monotonously painted a dusty brown; only where it met the haze of distant clouds or ended on the edge of the Gulf was there contrast to relieve the eye.

When first we saw La Paz it was a tiny bar of white against this field of tan. It twinkled and glistened, a microscopic line of contact between land and water, as much an entity unto itself as a single star in the heavens. A drear and empty wilderness, this, with no sign of habitation, with no visible man-made mark, with no preamble or introduction, and then a blur slowly evolving into a clear-cut rectangle. Eventually there developed details, walls and trees and boats, but still the city disclosed no closer relation to the desert at its back than to the waters at its feet.

A belated and unwanted pilot came aboard. As he was merely guiding us to a near-by anchorage already selected we bundled him into the pilot house and promptly forgot his existence. We were watching the growing waterfront and esplanade with its background of low houses. Palms and ornamental trees began to reach high above roofs and to peep at us from behind white walls. There was promise of shade and gardens and rest in this old metropolis; there was a foretaste of hospitality in the close clustering of the houses. Aligned with the edge of the esplanade, shoulder to shoulder, they fronted us as a solid street of friendly buildings. La Paz comes down to the sea to welcome her visitors.

Avenida Alvaro Obregon extends the length of the water-front. It is faced with a masonry sea-wall which rises so little above the level of the Gulf that on high quiet tides the embankment is the border of a courtyard fountain. Near the centre runs a toy pier and along the edge are formally spaced concrete benches and trimmed palms and a double row of pruned ornamental trees. Over the greater part of its length it is bare, unshaded, glaring in the heat of noon-day, an empty stage waiting until dusk calls the actors.

The esplanade of La Paz is flanked on the east with a palm grove and on the west by a desert and a lagoon. At anchor is a small flotilla of boats—pearlers for the most part, and little catboats from up-gulf ranches that have no roads, a visiting yacht, perhaps, and a few makeshifts in government service. There are passenger vessels scarcely larger than our own that run all over the Gulf—Mazatlan and Santa Rosalía and Guaymas. During our first day in the harbor came the freighter *Washington,* whose route connects the inland seaports with Alta California and whose cargo is a clearing house of Lower California's trade.

Little things—rowboats and dories and dugouts—were drawn up on the beach beyond the town or rode at the end of short hawsers or were paddled and rowed aimlessly through the fleet. They swarmed at a respectful distance as long as the port officials were aboard us. The moment the men of the *adjuana* left four native boats came alongside and a dozen men and boys climbed onto our decks. Curious idlers and, I suppose, not beyond petty theft, their ideas of private rights did not coincide with mine and we drove them off none too kindly in spite of their uncomprehending protests.

The *Least Petrel* in La Paz was no longer self-conscious. In other waters she might be an object of ridicule, here she slipped gracefully into the scheme of things. Near her were a couple of small power launches—old whaleboats fitted with engines of discarded automobiles. Half a dozen hulls twenty to thirty feet long rotted for lack of paint, an old-time excursion boat had been pressed into pilotage service, ugly scows, two channel buoys awaiting *mañana* to be repainted and reset, an eighty-footer with racing lines and burlaped cargo—the outcasts of the world were assembled, reshaped from their original purposes regardless of harmony or final appearance. Only the dugouts were appropriate; they alone were Mexican.

We went ashore, crossed the esplanade, and sauntered up the nearest side street. The first step took us into the heart of a purely native city. Stores there were, sandwiched between dwellings, but we saw none of the ornate symbols which Americans associate with commercial activity. Not a lettered delivery truck, not a glass-fronted display window, not a blazoned advertisement. At most a modestly painted board was set above an open doorway; from without there was usually no indication of the business carried on within the sombre room. A peep into a typical store showed, as before, a crude wooden counter and shelves or bins for merchandise. The *almacéns* of this town were not basically different from those we had seen in the country.

Chinese stores, we had observed, became progressively more numerous as communities increased in size. In La Paz, as in most other west Mexican cities, the Asiatics do not control the larger places of business but, on the other hand, their small establishments ordinarily are an improvement over those offered by the natives in competition. Not to the extent, however, of strangling the Mexican merchants. For

ESPLANADE AT LA PAZ

MUNICIPAL WATERWORKS

PEARLER'S QUARTERS IN LA PAZ

one thing the Chinese seldom carry more than a few simple commodities. Medicines, as an example, are handled only by Mexicans or Germans in *boticas* that are more purely drugstores than their American prototypes. The stock in trade consists largely of endless assortments of patent medicines imported from the United States; the principal side lines are Mexican and French perfumes.

The closest parallel to our commonly called specialty shops was a shoe store in which we found an assortment ranging from sandals to boots. Home-tanned leather from the ranches was worked with the aid of only the simplest of machinery and the clerk was the shoemaker himself. He was almost unique in having an idea of salesmanship. Instead of the customary discouraging and final "No hay," a bare statement that he did not carry the desired article, this man tried to ascertain what the customer wanted and there was nothing he did not offer to make to our order.

In the retailing of merchandise La Paz is primitive. Small stocks and small turn-overs, customers who buy rather than merchants who sell, purchases in centavos far outnumbering those in pesos, storekeepers waiting with infinite patience instead of rustling business, delivery into the market baskets of the shoppers, and no suggestion of service. A *mozo* is hired by the upper classes to carry the smallest bundles. Even Juan could not be trapped into going shopping with the Partner because his pride would not allow him to walk through the streets with packages in his hands. Lemonade carts with insipid drinks offered unattractively, pastry vendors peddling from baskets carried on their heads, drinking water dispensed from rawhide sacks on burros, and swarms of boys with boxes and brushes to polish shoes.

The American finds the streets interesting, fascinating even, because the scenes are so distinctly different from anything in the States. Nevertheless the dingy walls of adobe are ugly, standing, as these do, flush on the property line and paralleling each other or branching interminably with a sameness that is disappointing. No character develops, no segregation of residence and business, of richer and poorer sections, except in the extreme outskirts. Walking along the narrow sidewalks one passes the barred windows of homes, the open doorways of stores, and the potted entrances of patios. One sees much that is naïve, one catches intimate glimpses of Mexican life and of hidden gardens, but of beauty only an undisplayed intimation.

There was life on the streets; men, women, children, dogs, donkeys, horses, and automobiles of the smaller models driven with constant sounding of horns. The keynote, simplicity, missed appeal because it too obviously was the earmark of poverty. The picturesque features were the frequent and sometimes surprising evidences of survival of ancient customs. A carpenter passed us. He carried his tools neither in a chest nor in his hands; a leather garment fitted with adequate pockets held saws and hammers, planes and nails and chisels, and about his neck hung a brace and bit. Two women, a mother and her grown daughter, walked by, each with a five-gallon can of water easily balanced on her head. When Cortéz came the ancestors of this couple were similarly carrying *ollas*—often it seems to me that all the progress made in the last four hundred years has been the change from pottery to tin.

A funeral procession moved down the street. Out of respect for the custom of the people we stepped to one side and waited, bareheaded, until it had passed. The coffin was carried by four men who staggered under the weight. Others, ready to relieve, walked alongside; being pallbearer was not an unearned honor. On foot came the mourners, seventy-five or a hundred, the men in advance of the women and children. There followed one man riding alone in a model T— it would not have been Mexico had not two or three urchins been clinging to the spare tire on the back.

The crowd straggled along without order or formation, picturesque only because sincere. The most interesting features were the accessories, the four huge candelabra carried singly, the unpainted cross of wood, and the garlands in the hands of mantilla draped women.

A few feet from the sidewalks, though on the other side of the walls, are the hearts of homes, be they mansions or hovels. There are in La Paz a few families, at most half a dozen, who possess means with which to indulge themselves and yet none of whom number seclusion among desired luxuries. Old families with German furniture and Spanish chests and French linen, with ancestral furnishings, with traditions traceable to Europe far more than to the United States, are snuggled against such neighbors as have been provided by shifting chance. Even to those who dwell in the most pretentious homes custom has not given an urge for offsets and front lawns and exterior displays.

As was natural our first day ashore proved to be the most interesting. The Partner in a linen dress and five of us in white ducks proceeded to investigate the town, our special objective being a regular café dinner. As we tramped along the Partner yielded to the lure of candy, so we all filed into a *dulcería*. Choice was limited to cocoanuts, either whole or else cut and sweetened, and to *pinocho* and its derivatives. Of chocolates or imported delicacies there were none.

We supplemented with strawberries—small fruits peddled on the streets in little homemade baskets—and, munching, passed on to see new sights. We happened into a little house in the front part of which belts were sold—of leather, plain or exquisitely hand carved. Buckles ranged from the cheapest kinds to those ornately designed in silver derived from coins. The maker's stock was small and our wants and waist lines variable, so we had our orders filled to measure.

We did not find the mission ruins, for our guides always insisted on taking us to a modern church. We wandered through Rufio's large store, to be impressed with its size and its stock. It was interesting to compare sources; furniture was American, shelf hardware, glassware, crockery, and toys were German, linen, dress-goods, perfumes, and dolls were French, shoes, hats, and the coarser cloths were of Mexican manufacture.

Still no hotel nor even restaurant worthy of the name. We were eventually formally introduced to a señora who offered to prepare and serve a meal in her semi-private patio. She did her best, kindly soul, and the garden was lovely, but her ways were not our ways and, one and all, we ate our remaining meals aboard the *Least Petrel*.

CHAPTER XXVII

PEARLERS AND SAN JOSÉ

OUR second morning at La Paz found us a half cable's length from a pair of thirty-foot sailboats. They had been made fast to each other in order that the combined crews could assemble on one vessel to partake of communal meals. The stove was a gasolene can, the fuel was cut lengths of mesquite, and the fire hazard approached arson. In their happy-go-lucky disregard of consequences these men were but following the established custom of the Gulf. How it is possible to make a practice of cooking on such a flimsy hearth without having ships constantly being burned is one of the puzzles of the country. It is done almost with impunity, however, for I have not heard of a single instance of fire on a vessel being attributable to the open air oven.

Amidship in each boat could be seen the tops of metal wheels, parts of the obsolete hand-driven air pumps that earmark the pearler. Diving for gems apparently is not a lucrative pursuit; it would be difficult to imagine life more completely reduced to elemental necessities than was that of the eight men we watched. They were gathered about a coffee-pot, and they owned in addition a frying-pan and a pail for stewing—these three kitchen utensils and no others. Dried beef was hanging to the boom, red underwear for use while diving was fastened to cross-ropes, and in the stern were water-casks and a quarter sack of corn. The men had the tackle needed for their occupation, but it was to a jumble of wretched hand-made, patched, and obsolete junk that they daily trusted their lives. Not a luxury was aboard, not an unneeded article of comfort, not an item designed to bring fleeting pleasure or recreation into stark empty existences.

Were they who drew in things material no more than bare sustenance recompensed for their dangerous labor by the sustaining fervor of the gamester? I do not believe so, for neither in the men beside us nor in any other pearlers we had seen was there evidence of the singleness of purpose or the hopeful waiting that marks the devotee. Rather was there uniformly an air of apathetic discouragement, a display only of hard labor and small returns for all concerned. The system under which the crews work does not inspire them with the optimism of gamblers. They have no capital; acquiring a surplus is not a part either of their creed or of their training. So a *padrón* interposes, the holder of a government concession and the owner or charterer of a boat. The diver has no direct means of knowing the value of the shells he finds; to open them is not permissible either to himself or his companions. There is a shed in La Paz to which I have seen the fruit of their collecting brought just as it comes from the sea. A dozen peons with sharp knives and nimble fingers were seated about a long table upon which great hampers of the potential pearl bearers were dumped. The bivalves were slit and opened with dexterous speed, the empty shells being piled in loose heaps for commercial use. The men who do the preliminary work are not those to whom comes the excitement of success. That passes on to responsible employers, yet even of them none can experience such unbridled exaltation as came to the early Spaniards.

No burlesque compares in fantasy with the opening history of La Paz. To conquistadores drunk with the sack of the City of Mexico came the wild imaginings of Sebastián. That negro had been one of a small party which actually crossed the continent from the Atlantic and his report of the gold and the jewels he had seen was limited only by the bounds of a vivid imagination and the ability of credulous hearers to grasp descriptions. He was followed by the monk de Noza, who allowed himself in no way to be outdone, and by other explorers who, meeting with misfortunes, lied freely about where they had been, substantiated what had been told before, and added everything that fertile fancies dictated.

In this orgy of ridiculous exaggerations and pure fabrication there was only one reality—the pearls of La Paz. Ximenez, in the interval between murdering his chief and his own assassination, had been the first of European blood to land in Lower California. That was in 1533, only twelve years after the Conquest. Neither he nor his followers had been able to profit by his discovery of pearls, but two years later Cortéz himself travelled to what, at the time, was known as Santa Cruz. Then began the accumulation, the forced labor of the natives, and the usual cycle of spoliation.

The search for the Seven Cities of Cíbola proceeded merrily, filibusters and raiders and pirates laid in wait from the Cove of San Lúcas to the Bay of La Paz, crime was rampant, treachery, bigotry, and incompetence were supreme. Lower California, for a hundred and fifty years, fulfilled no other rôle than that of post of call or destination of expeditions of discovery. When the century and a half had passed there survived out of all the bloodshed and misery only pearls in the coffers of Europe and hatred in the hearts of the Indians. Trivial matters, perhaps, yet nothing else endured and but for them the history of Lower California, from its inception to the founding of the missions, might well remain unwritten. No one came who had a thought of work; not a house of permanence was built, not a field was tilled, not a spot was colonized.

As we crossed La Paz Bay from north to south we

passed half a dozen little pearlers running before the wind
or lying at anchor under the bluffs of Espíritu Santo.
Some were white specks in the distance, some were close
enough to give a friendly greeting and at San José Island
we succeeded in establishing a limited and formal friendship with a crew actually at work. I spent a couple of hours
one afternoon seated on their rail watching the diver walk
about on the bottom. Two fathoms was his limit and at
that depth the white sand threw back enough light to
enable us to follow every movement.

We could see the distorted figure bend over shells, either
to pass them by or to place them in his wire basket. Three
hours was his shift and during that time a few dozen
oysters would be about all he could collect. The captain
watched constantly, feeding the life line and the air hose,
skillfully preventing tangling. The diver kept pace with the
boat as it drifted under the guidance of a sailor, two men
at the pump-wheels pulled and pushed without pause or
rest, and at regular intervals great bubbles of air burst
from the undersea helmet. Operations were slow, leisurely,
and quite in keeping with my spirits. There was no method
of resting more appropriate to the surroundings—the swell,
the sun, the wind, the scenery—everything combined to
lull nervousness and proclaim the folly of hurry.

I found myself contrasting the shells this man was taking with those to be found on the eastern side of the Gulf,
on submerged lagoon rocks and mangrove roots. The mainland oysters, thick and small and gnarled, are appetizing
beyond words. Those of the Peninsula are smooth and flat
and thin; they are as large as a saucer and give the impression of delicate construction. The separation of the genera
of these mollusks on the two shores is a striking example
of the most intriguing biological riddle I have ever encountered. In my notes are the names of bird after bird, and
mammals and reptiles, insects and plants, which, without

apparent rhyme or reason, occur on one littoral and not on the other. Of course there exists a logical cause for this condition, but so far we have been unable to offer any plausible explanation of why a hundred miles of inland sea should develop separations comparable with two thousand miles of open Atlantic.

San José Island is a volcanic uplift twenty miles long, averaging three or four across, with a central ridge of some two thousand feet. The higher levels are the steep brush-covered wastes which, all over Lower California, we had encountered to repletion. The lower coastal slopes, however, for their greater part are comparatively gentle and fertile. They support a heavy desert jungle, a medley of cacti and briars conspicuously punctuated with cardónes and in many ways resembling the valley floors of Cape San Lúcas. The thicker areas are difficult to penetrate and careful planning is often necessary in order to avoid becoming pocketed. It is not a light matter to be caught where progress is impossible and retracking a matter of painstaking difficulty.

In spite of its not inconsiderable sterile area and the forbidding greyish blankets of thorns and stickers San José is one of the two most fertile islands in the Gulf. Carnivoræ are abundant, coyotes, for instance, and a particularly interesting endemic Ring-tailed Cat. Everywhere we picked up the trail of deer, though, because we could afford little time for their hunting, we did not secure any of the much wanted venison. Cattle are run on a large scale, which means wells and water and an hacienda. Rodents are common and birds abundant. But in spite of all the promise it offered we were able to give the body of the island only a most superficial exploration. We concentrated on the spit where we had pitched our camp.

A canal a hundred yards wide cuts from the main body of San José a triangular stretch of cobbles and hills and lagoons. The isolated wedge covers two or three square miles and, in addition, on the easterly side of the channel are a thousand acres more of mangrove swamps. The study of the biology of this peculiar region had brought us to San José Island and demanded every hour of the few days we could remain. We landed near the outer end of the point at a spot where favorable conditions and an abruptly sloping beach enabled us to anchor close inshore. Here we proceeded to remove half the cargo of the boat, ferrying load after load in the dory. We piled on the cobble strand a great stack of supplies—bedding, food and water, equipment for preparing and serving meals, clothing and canvas and boxes of paraphernalia for our work.

The *Least Petrel,* manned only by Charley and Captain, left as soon as she was unloaded. The skeg we had patched in Magdalena was still in place and apparently as strong as ever, but ours had been a makeshift job and we felt that safety demanded better materials. There is, on the Gulf, no cradle upon which little boats can be drawn out of the water, but at La Paz there were facilities for holding the *Least Petrel* on level keel after the tide went down and there were men who would excavate a trough under her propeller. So it had been arranged that we would remain upon San José while the repairs were being made in La Paz.

Like an army of ants we marched backward and forward from the gulf edge to the camp site, moving our accumulation of supplies. The water keg was the most difficult item to handle; it had a talent for making trouble. In La Paz it had required hours of time, half our party and four *mozos* to scout out the small barrel, clean it of tequila, drag it half over town to where there was good water, and put it aboard the *Least Petrel*. We had almost lost it getting it ashore and then we had to work it across two hundred yards of rolling boulders. Our headquarters were on the narrow strip of salicornia grass between the cobbles and the mangrove fringe of the lagoon. It was dark and we were weary long before our work was done. The night threatened to become stormy and though we missed the help of Captain and Charley we did not blame them for wanting to reach the lee of Espíritu Santo as soon as possible. Out at sea the waves were already assuming menacing proportions.

We made our final camping preparations with the aid of electric torches, selecting the sites on which to spread our sleeping bags and smoothing shell-beds and roots as evenly as was possible in the shadowed light. Scarcely were we settled when there rose the minor noises of the night, soon to be drowned in the insistent yapping of coyotes. The sharp staccato notes, varied with prolonged wails, proved too much for our cook. The beasts were endowed with ventriloquism; Juan didn't know whether they were miles away or at the edge of the camp. My last recollections before dropping off to sleep were of the Basque slipping under his blankets with a loaded rifle still in his hands. At midnight I woke to find that the wind had quieted and that the replacing calm marked the beginning of the most distressing three days of our entire spring.

From the lagoons, from the mangroves, from the grass at our feet came gnats and mosquitoes. In hordes they rose, ravenously hungry, and no defense we could make gave any measure of protection. Out-of-doors our Flit guns were inadequate and citronella at best brought only local and temporary relief. We snuggled down into our bedding, but the gnats always found some opening by which they could penetrate. Exposure to swarms of mosquitoes, I presume, is an unpleasant experience familiar to every traveller, but the smaller pests are another matter. The almost microscopic flies poisoned the blood to the point of mild sickness and raised welts until our bodies became a mass of tiny painful sores.

Then, wonder of wonders, it began to rain, a soft, misty drizzle that, except for one afternoon, continued without let-up for three days. This was only the second time in years of travel that I had seen precipitation south of the influence of Sierra San Pedro Mártir and naturally we were caught unprepared. The humidity of the air was not far from the saturation point; there was a very close connection between the dampness and the clouds of gnats. We were cold and life was dismal, we could not dry our garments nor endure for any length of time the smudge of our fire smoke. We tried every expedient we could devise before admitting that there just was no solution.

Our first task in the morning had been to stretch a canvas by roping it to mangroves and to poles cut from near-by trees. We banked two sides with brush, but the limit of our resources left us with a *ramada* rather than a tent. We made a table of boxes and set up our gasolene stove under the shelter and we built and maintained a cheerful bonfire just outside. After the first night we slept packed like sardines where at least the falling rain drops could not strike us. When the annoyance became unbearable we tried to find relief by taking frequent swims or long walks beside the water edge. Drowsing and scratching and seeking diversion where we could we somehow managed to pass the long dark hours. Daytime brought betterment through incessant activity.

In the centre of the spit is a large tidal lagoon. It is fringed with mangroves and contains several insular patches of the salt water trees. It drains through a narrow half mile channel into the main canal and to the open gulf beyond. We had dragged our canoe to the lake and spent no small part of our days exploring the shoreless waterways. After months of arid hills and desert vistas we were exhilarated by the movement, the life, and the rich green foliage itself.

Conceding that relative scenic grandeur is largely a matter of personal reaction I nevertheless insist that the lagoon of San José is the most beautiful spot in Lower California. It calls for a canoe such as ours—nothing less is fitting—in which to wind and twist along tortuous lanes and to glide through openings that may end in an impasse or may lead to a fairy sylvan pool. The soft ripple and the quiet paddling caught avian dwellers unawares and allowed us to read, as from a blind, the secrets of the slowly unfolding panorama. Above the gardened borders of our roadway we watched the flight of all-unsuspecting herons and ibises and egrets, and perhaps of a darting flock of sandpipers or dowitchers. Always, as we moved, so did the hill peaks, their changing perspective moment by moment giving new composition to the picture.

Here we worked and studied and, in so far as permitted by mosquitoes and rain and gnats, enjoyed ourselves. We explored the large canal in motor and dory and we crossed several miles of open water to visit outlying rocks. We climbed hills that overlooked the series of intricate waterways and we studied the ruins of old barricades. Time was when the lagoons of San José had been of military significance and the sites of old sentry boxes were still plainly marked. We worked our way along the edge of the bluffs, hoping to surprise a Duck Hawk, or out at sea we trolled, with jig and line, catching fish for the table. We shot some White Ibis, after much stalking, and for one entire morning we chased an American Egret that at no time allowed us within gun range.

On the flats beyond the mangroves we found Marsh Sparrows, but no signs of breeding. Of the eight or ten members of the heron family only the Great Blue had begun to lay, so we had to content ourselves by identifying, as well as we were able, the large number of last year's nests of other species. We studied Belding Plover where the gulf waves threw food upon the long terraced rows of cobble and we tracked elusive Frazar Oyster-catchers across the little jutting sand dunes. We trapped rats and mice and Ring-tailed Cats, we hunted deer and gathered shells. Some boxes we filled with gorgeous intricacies and others with microscopic specimens scooped by the handful from tidal drifts. The days, crowded to overflowing with work and exploration, were bearable because of movement. The nights were wearying and dismal, the clotted sores already were inducing low fevers, and there would not come normal winds to clear away mists and pests or sunshine to dry our clammy clothing.

On the outer edge of the swamps were the homes of Mangrove Warblers and Belding Rail. The little singers were tame and saucy, as they watched from retreats half hidden among leaves into which they dared us to follow. Often, indifferent to such harmless invaders as ourselves, the male, yellow of body and wearing a striking hood of chestnut brown, displayed his charms to the coy little greenish female. In a month or two they will be stripping bark from dry seaweed stems and weaving nests five feet above ground in mangrove crotches. One egg or two or perhaps three will be laid, white, heavily speckled with brown, and then the mother will sit so close that she will sometimes have to be lifted if one wishes to examine her clutch.

We found old nests of Belding Rail and from them learned, I believe, all that is known of the Gulf breeding habits of these rare birds. Their demand is for salicornia —an iceplant-like growth associated with food requirements. In salicornia patches are usually stunted mangrove bushes, dwarfs that have been able to obtain sufficient nourishment to live but not enough to flourish. They are to be found sometimes in clusters, sometimes isolated, and are characterized by branches forking often just above high water line.

The preference of the rail is for one of the outlying bushes and for a nest-site which is barely above the highest tides. If he cannot find a fork ideally placed he may go into heavy growths to build and often is driven to use crotches three or four feet above the mud flats. In previously published accounts of his life history it has been said that he nests in the heart of mangrove thickets, but that surmise is incorrect. The nest itself is of twigs and salicornia stems roughly worked into a flat dish.

We saw many things on San José which we would not willingly have missed, and yet our experience there was more than an annoyance—it was real punishment. It tested the mettle of everyone in the party, and the response was courage and fortitude. Perhaps to Juan goes the greatest credit, for his smile was unfailing though all was new to him; this was the first time he had ever slept out-of-doors. Perhaps to Rogers, who suffered most from the poison, and yet talked only of the mounds he had explored, of the old camp sites he had found, and complained of nothing but the difficulty of separating ancient culture from modern. Perhaps to the Partner, who maintained her rôle of hostess and whose only expressed thoughts were for the comfort of others. The naturalists had submitted to added suffering while at the skinning table, but they proved themselves experienced campers and, on the whole, came through in fine shape.

There is a redeeming aftermath of experiences where pain and pleasure mingle. A recital of unadorned details may be simply an indictment of the whole adventure, an account of drawbacks which cannot be overbalanced. But time will erase the memories of suffering or at least reduce them to shadowy backgrounds. A few days, or months, will erase the pencil marks of the sketch and bring into relief the clear cut lines of ink. So it will be with San José; the hardships will become incidentals and the three days will eventually be looked back upon only with enthusiasm.

CHAPTER XXVIII

THE SEA OF CORTÉZ

MATHEMATICALLY there was a possibility that the *Least Petrel* would be back by the evening of the third day. So many hours to La Paz, one tide on which to remove the old timber, another to set in place the new skeg, the wait for high water again and then the run to San José—we could make estimates and total the time and we all hoped, rather than expected, to sleep aboard that night. As may well be imagined it was not a matter to which we were at all indifferent. On the contrary, so anxious were we, that although it rained miserably and visibility continued poor, yet from twelve o'clock on of our last afternoon there was always someone scrambling to the high point of the cobbles to take another look into the south.

Not long after mid-day we descried a small power boat and our hopes ran high. She was too far away to be recognizable, however, nor did she turn toward us, but passed up the channel, bound for Loreto. Later on we twice picked up ships that, after long waiting, proved to be pearlers. Even with supper finished we followed hopefully a pair of red and green lights that came abreast, but they also ignored us and continued relentlessly up the channel.

Oh well, this is Mexico, where things are not done in the minimum of time. When the *Least Petrel* did arrive she caught us unprepared; our first intimation of her approach was the noise of the engine as she made for the anchorage. Did we welcome her? Late as it was we gathered together what we needed, bedding mostly, and went aboard. Dry clothes, hot toddy, and surcease from our troubles put a very different aspect on life. I'm sure I caught the Partner making faces at the gnats, but what can one say when a lady denies?

Some years previously there had been another occasion upon which a small party of us had camped upon an island in the Gulf. We, too, had watched our little tender disappear into the night and the storm as she ran for the shelter of a bay on the mainland. Our water supply was limited and, being almost without food, we were subsisting largely upon bird eggs as we waited for a break in the weather which would permit the boat to return—if she had not foundered. The situation had been too much for one of the men. He had gone to pieces with fear; he had spent the daylight hours perched on the highest peak, gazing as in a trance towards the distant shoreline.

His was a really pitiable condition, for he had often shown himself to be a man of unusual bravery, but in the predicament we faced neither pride nor reason served to bring him under control. The incident had made a lasting impression upon me and I naturally was apprehensive, while we were on San José, that there might be a similar break by some member of our present party. It was, of course, the Easterners who caused me the most concern.

Gregory, I feel sure, was not affected. He seemed to be satisfied with the fact that a definite program had been established and his imagination apparently did not carry him so far as to picture the results of a dislocation of the schedule. We had brought only wine, no hard liquor, from La Paz, and, perhaps because of that fact, the hardships of San José seemed actually to have had a favorable result upon him. Peter, too, had passed the test as well as could be hoped. How far the manifestation of certain disagreeable traits of character were due to the strain of isolation

I have no means of knowing, nor yet of how great was the moral influence of the reassuring presence of the hacienda. Whether or not he was on the verge of another explosion I will never know; in any event none came and the return of the *Least Petrel* apparently closed the incident.

I wanted a day on San Francisco, a thousand-acre pile of lava and ash that lay a few miles south of our camp site. So, the first thing in the morning we back-tracked for the better part of an hour. We found an anchorage between two bold reefs that run out from the southwest corner of the island. Here we had for company our friends the pearlers, who had come ashore for water.

They were taking advantage of the fact that some of the rain had accumulated in a string of small basins along the bottom of one of the ravines. The Mexicans had brought ashore six or eight empty gasolene cans which, with considerable labor, they had filled and had carried back to the beach. The pearlers had foraged the island, too, for they had found several trios of baby ospreys which they had brought down to their boat to be cooked and eaten. Once again I had cause to marvel at the omnivorous character of the appetite of the natives. I will admit, academically, that before we criticize them, we should recognize their right to regard our prejudices as narrowmindedness, but sometimes, as in this case, it is hard to do so with sincerity.

We were disappointed in San Francisco. We had come to hunt for murrelet eggs and found ourselves in advance of the laying time. For some reason entirely beyond our ability to explain the seasons in 1930 were about three weeks later than those of average years and so the divers, instead of being in their little caves attending to home duties, were swimming about in the open Gulf, mated pairs and empty nests.

We put in a hard day and were rewarded by only four sets of eggs divided among five collectors. Nevertheless I believe everyone enjoyed the experience, for a peculiar fascination attaches itself to an island small enough to be walked around. San Francisco's size is ideal and yet it decidedly proved itself to be no toy. It has a height of nearly seven hundred feet, reached by severe slopes on the west and precipitous bluffs on the east. A high rocky head along the southern end is connected with the main body of the island by a sandy neck. The Partner and I were especially interested in this knob, in its windswept, barren sides and its great wall marked with red and yellow bands. It seemed as though we never would tire of looking down upon the wild seascapes of the Gulf, with rocks and spray and seals and flying birds under our feet.

We started up San José Channel late in the afternoon. We passed Seal Rocks and Coyote Rocks and Cayo Islet, an outcropping that looks like a railroad embankment set in water, and we were midway up the channel when a flock of a dozen Brewster Egrets crossed our bows. The wonderful birds were passing from the lagoon on San José to a little bay behind San Evaristo Point on the mainland. We immediately changed our course to follow.

In nuptial plumage, we were all agreed, there is nothing as beautiful on the Peninsula as this rare bird. Bill and legs are black, feet and toes yellow, plumage an immaculate white that has no artificial rival. From the shoulder hangs the aigrette of commerce, the laced filigree that, gorgeous in any setting, is of transcendent charm when worn by its true owner. Aigrettes were that day displayed to us in an idealistic environment. They were decorating the manikins posed on the wave-washed rocks of San Evaristo.

We succeeded in slipping into our anchorage without disturbing the quarry, but that was as far as our good luck held. No trick of woodcraft enabled us to get within range of the wary birds, though we tried determinedly until dark and resumed our quest with the coming of day. Once alarmed they would not alight near cover from which they could be stalked and our only attempt to approach in the open sent them scurrying back to San José. Yet I, at least, did not regret the time they had cost. Backed by the cliffs of Sierra de la Giganta which rush up to and fall abruptly into the Gulf, scintillating on their rocky perches among other birds of less resplendent white, multiplied in silvery reflections from the waters below, they epitomized at once the beauty and harshness of their untamed surroundings. It is memories such as they left that recompense one for the hardships of Gulf travel.

Midmorning found us once again in San José Channel with tide and wind working at cross purposes to kick up a nasty sea. We soon gave in to our punishment and once more crawled under the protection of the great Sierra, running for shelter into the bight below Nopolo Point. Here, where we spent the rest of the day and also the night, tragedy, in the form of a toothache, overtook Captain. We shot his jaw with novocaine and put our pliers to the offending tooth, but we lacked the skill properly to apply strength and were physically unable to extract the molar. Poor Captain was a wreck and we in none too good shape when eventually we were forced to admit failure.

A toothache is not a thing to be taken lightly even with a dentist an hour away. In a situation such as ours there was nothing to be done but grin and bear it. The nearest relief, and that problematical, was in Santa Rosalía; the only comforts were those to be found in our medicine chest. Captain gave a splendid exhibition of courage—I dread to think of the consequences had I been submitted to his ordeal—he suffered when he must, he rested when he could, he carried on and would permit not even a discussion of giving up our work to hasten his relief.

Most of us spent the afternoon ashore at Nopolo, spreading over the valley in pursuance of our individual interests. We were at the mouth of a dry stream bed, an expanse of coarse gravel and small boulders hidden under a heavy stand of mesquite. The drainage basin was not large, for the crest of the sierra was literally on top of us, but there were pans of fresh or brackish water. These springs were at least semi-permanent, for we saw countless Xantus Humming Birds among the trees. There were a few quail here, a bird very like the plumed knights of California, and there were jays and thrashers and wrens and cardinals. The valley was narrow and deep, the walking difficult, but reward came from the grandeur of the desert scenery.

Lower California, over the greater part of its length, has but one side. From the Pacific the land, be it plateaus or jumbled hills, mesas or eroded cañons, slopes steadily upward until the crest is reached. A hundred miles of unbroken ascent, of drainage lines feeding to the west, of cooling trade winds blowing off the ocean, and then the country ends, sky-high in space. Down from heights of two thousand feet or four thousand or five the long, long climb is balanced by a sheer drop to the level of the sea. There is left a face cut by the awful strength of Nature, a longitudinal cross-section in which lie exhibit-like displays of strata and sedimentary deposits. Cut, yet broken too, the declivity, only in part a polished face, is comparable to the shattered trunk of a half-sawn tree that has fallen from the tremendous weight of its top.

In such a spirit did Sierra de la Giganta come to meet us. Its oldest talus has been rounded into foothills, has even been mellowed until it supports sahuaro and thorns. Its fragments have been cut with cloudburst tracks and eroded into systematic watersheds, into valleys half horizontal and half vertical. Always is its eastern side unfinished, an unhealed wound of partition, an age-old fragment abandoned by man and God alike. Towering into distant height sterile soil and pigmented vein are massed into a fragmented wall, a hideously fascinating back stage prop of the great terrain that faces the ocean.

The little storm blew itself out during the night and so, as soon as there was light enough to see, we again pulled into San José Channel. As we came opposite the northern end of the island we were attracted by signs of habitations in Dolores Bay, on the mainland. Once again a pin-point of trees and houses appeared upon an immense vista of brown barrenness. Captain, in better shape this morning, was appealed to for information and rather reluctantly admitted an intimate knowledge of Dolores Bay and its hacienda.

The only vessel that he had ever lost lay rotting on the beach. She had sprung a leak at night, water had come in faster than pumps could control it, and there followed a barely won race to the shore. An old comradeship came to an end when she struck; more was gone than her value in dollars. Though years had passed to Captain she was still a personal friend, a living charge that had come into his keeping, a personality that he mourned. He forgot for the nonce that he was a hard-boiled old salt and, when he told of the *San Diego,* betrayed a high degree of human sentimentality. A battered old fishing boat, she had given her best and to her memory was due love and respect.

Captain wanted to see her again, wanted another look at the old ribs and keel. He would not directly admit the desire; he accomplished his purpose by persuading the Partner that she should visit the hacienda. That was not a difficult task; there was little the Partner was willing to miss. We all had been intrigued by the frequent signs of hidden life in the face of the Sierra and we welcomed the opportunity of acquaintance with the mysterious inhabitants. What kind of people were they, we wondered, and how did they wrest a livelihood from mountains of lava? So we turned into the bay and anchored.

THE FLIGHT OF THE *LEAST PETREL*

The hacienda ran down to the Gulf. Our first glimpse told us that we had come to what was primarily a banana plantation. Plentiful, though less conspicuous than the herbaceous plants, were mangoes and figs. Here were not the orderly orchards of California planted in geometrical rows, carefully cleared of underbrush and neatly pruned. Instead clumps of trees and irregular vineyards grew beside earthen irrigation ditches whose meanderings were determined by the natural or diverted flow of their water. The plantation followed the stream bed, a ribbon of irregular width that filled the cañon. Controlled but untrimmed and uncultivated a bit of wild jungle pointed into the mountains and, being only in part domesticated, it worked out its destinies largely under the influence of Nature.

Our first steps ashore brought us to a series of sheds, storage centres for exports and our introduction to the final economic contribution that centres in Dolores Bay. Here freight is assembled to await the irregular arrival of some coaster who will distribute it to Guaymas or Mazatlan, to Santa Rosalía or La Paz. Every article that goes out, every item that comes in, is trundled across the beach. No roads connect Dolores Bay with towns on the Peninsula; no other point of contact is there with the outside world. No trucks or even wagons bring to it the products of the far-flung rancherias and the isolated peon huts. Trails and nothing more converge at the beach.

Back from the water where the fertile soil began we passed through a gate into a half wild garden. Grapes in profusion, venerable vines knotted with age, were trellised over beams of palm. Dates and bananas and figs, stretches of vineyards and clusters of palms, a wild orgy of flowers and then the rambling walls of a large house. Here was promise of—well, who hasn't dreamed of the one-time glory of California with every Don autocrat of his own principality. The more clear the vista through the vines and trees and shrubs the higher rose our hopes, for new walls and wings were unfolding a rambling one-story palace.

The Partner and I by now were alone, Captain having remained with his beloved boat and the others being scattered over the desert that crowded against the oasis. We had barely stepped onto the clustered path when we were met by a fine-looking middle-aged gentleman who welcomed us with a hospitality as formal and as cordial as anything we had pictured. He conducted us across the wide veranda into his parlor, and then disillusionment came like a blow.

Art once again had foundered on the rock of finance. Labor costs were negligibly small, clay and space were gratis, and so size had been attained with as little effort as meaning. Room after room had been built, patios had been enclosed, walls had run into ells that were lost in the tangle of flowers, and yet we were in an almost empty warehouse. Building had been virtually free, it is true, but in this corner of the world furnishings were prohibitively expensive. In the seldom used parlor itself a serious effort had been made to create an atmosphere, and this largely by means of the cheapest and ugliest of American furniture. Of course to us it was disappointing and tawdry, but I have no doubt that it made an impression on the occasional visitors, and certainly our host's effort to raise himself above the common level was an ambition to be commended. But bowl after bowl of paper roses while the garden blossomed luxuriantly could hardly be forgiven.

Our tour of inspection was more satisfying, for in the back rooms we found home-made furniture that was both attractive and appropriate. Mesquite, palms, and untanned hides were the materials used. A chair with a palm stalk for a back and criss-crossed rawhide or even a solid pelt still retaining its hair, or a hammock of pure palm fibre were not the articles which we would have relegated to obscurity. They were incomparably more picturesque than the plain chairs of oak which were so much more highly prized.

We wandered on and on through the irregular pile, finding within its walls rooms adapted to many purposes besides being parts of a home. There was, for instance, a tiny store in which trade was had with the little ranchers of the interior. There were sheds devoted to the business of farming, where hides were baled and cheese was made and fruit was packed. There was space for the storage of implements and crates and products. *Ramadas* that furnished a bit of shade were integral parts as were sections that served for granaries. There was even a special room for saddles. The profusion of potted plants in the patio entrances and under the roofs of verandas were in constant contrast to the almost bare quarters of the workers.

Through the medley the busy Partner made her way, buying beef and chickens, string-beans and cheese. For the choicest cuts of meat she paid forty centavos a kilo, which approximates eight and a half cents a pound. Other prices were in proportion. The hens were cornered and caught and the vegetables picked while she waited, for no surplus was carried, even for immediate household needs. The native cheese is white, rather dry, not at all rich, and being an article of export was ready crated. Shopping was slow but accumulative, a semi-social event participated in by nearly everyone on the hacienda before a boatload was dispatched to the *Least Petrel*.

The most interesting incident of our short stay was the arrival of a burro train from the highlands of the interior. There were brought on the backs of the pack animals hides and cheese, tanbark and firewood, all destined for the little ship that was expected within the next few days. The drovers were of the peon class, in shirt and overalls, barefooted and wearing wide-brimmed hats of straw. A small keg of water, a coffee-pot, tin cups and one blanket apiece constituted their full equipment. They traded rather than sold, coffee and sugar being the chief needs, flour, beans, and bolts of cloth coming under the head of luxuries. It is only when one appreciates with how little they are content that he understands how they can survive along the borders of this furnace.

The proprietor himself, distinctly of the upper middle class, was a type whose rarity in Lower California is one of the reasons for her backwardness. He was a producer on no small scale and his was the clearing house for an integral unit of the Peninsula. His economic status was decidedly beneficial; men of his stamp, if encouraged and protected, could do much to help the country progress. In a simple way he had assumed many of the functions of our small-town bankers.

We saw in Dolores Bay another class of men who, for want of a better name, might be termed vacqueros. Small groups, usually mounted on mules, freely rode in and out of the hacienda. The bodies of their wiry little animals were almost covered by great stock saddles that represented the financial ability of the owner to make a display. There was an excess of heavy, deeply carved leather, on the stirrups were long *tapaderos,* and from the horns hung decorative saddle-bags. The other ornaments, indicative of the rider's taste and purse, included everything a Mexican saddle could have. There were used both ropes of horsehair and lariats of rawhide, neatly coiled and tied. Often a thirty-thirty rifle was attached, revolvers being rare and shotguns unused. Bridles were conspicuous with massive Spanish bits, with martingales and heavily hand-carved silver trimmings.

The clothing worn was representative of Lower California and unlike anything to be found along the United States border. The leather jackets, always short, varied in color and material according to the taste of the owner.

They might be of deer hide or of cow leather tanned to a burnt orange. The chaparajos were drawn in at the waist but flared at the feet until they covered the sides of the animals. Fringes of the brightest colors, of orange or red or blue, were nationalistic, if indeed, not purely local. Sombreros were heavy and elaborate and massive spurs with absurdly large rowels were worn upon shoes, never on boots.

These riders are the most picturesque characters we had seen. Their mounts were so tiny that by the time the long leather dust coat had been thrown over the rider's shoulders little remained visible of the animal. When the mount selected was a donkey the effect was laughable. A finishing and appropriate touch came with the decorative knife, conspicuous and ostentatious because of its large bone handle and its heavy silver inlay. The men themselves were no less interesting than their costumes. Their primitive courtesies and their interest in us—the Partner was the first American woman most of them had ever seen—won us from the start. We left the kindly people with more than a tinge of regret. The hacienda had shown us the best and by far the most appealing side of the Mountains of the Giantess.

Not the least of the fascination came from the appearance of isolation. We knew that, scattered and hidden in the hills, were many a ranch and peon hut tributary to the hacienda. We knew, also, that a few miles up the cañon were the invisible remains of La Vírgen de los Dolores, one of the earliest of the missions. Nevertheless we actually saw only a prosperous combination of ranch and farm standing alone in an infinite desert. As we returned to the beach and were being rowed back to the *Least Petrel* there persisted the illusion that the people of the hacienda had no neighbors and that their lives were bounded by a circle tangent to the line of travel of undependable trading ships.

CHAPTER XXIX

AMONG THE ISLANDS OF THE GULF

FROM our anchorage in Dolores Bay was visible a great white rock. It lay a mile or two offshore, dull white from its guano covering, a thousand yards long and a hundred feet high. Safe from marauding coyotes it had every qualification of a master rookery. Hopes ran high even after we had approached near enough to make out details through our glasses.

There could be no doubt that once the little island had been covered with breeding birds, great flocks of boobies and, probably, of pelicans. In this almost rainless land we had no means of determining how long ago its abandonment had taken place; we were sure only that there had not elapsed enough years to have washed away the guano. We circled as closely inshore as Captain dared to go and we observed, all told, less than a dozen birds. We studied the sloping top and we ran binoculars up and down the coves and the clefts that opened in the tall sea-wall. Disappointed, of course, yet as always we reacted to the spell of waves breaking over half submerged rocks and shattering themselves against perpendicular facets. When in other respects explorings and pryings fail, they always reveal, as compensation, unsuspected spots of barbaric appeal.

We did not land on Habana Island; we could see that to do so would be a waste of time. To be sure we were interested to know what had driven the birds from their one-time homes, but the answer would not be found upon the rock itself. The question revolved rather around the disappearance of the fish, the little so-called sardines upon which the steganopodes depend for food. Tuna and their kindred had likewise become rare in these waters, and as a consequence fishing boats were returning empty more often than fully loaded. The little episode we had witnessed at Muertos Bay, when the Japs had been unable to secure bait, was less an accident than a change that has taken place along the whole southern half of Lower California. The biological effects of the absence of minnows and bait were far reaching, but the reasons were too complicated for our determination.

Morena Rocks were less than an hour's run from Habana. They, too, had once been a rookery and were now abandoned, so from them we laid our course for San Diego Island. Here it had been planned that Peter and Gregory should camp for a week while we crossed the Gulf to Sinaloa, but when the time came to make final preparations both men positively refused to leave the boat. Theirs was a disappointing decision which reduced materially the sum total of what could be accomplished on the trip, but neither former promises nor obligations to their employers were of sufficient weight to induce them to carry out their part of the program.

Fear was the impelling motive of Peter—he said so frankly. San José had been a more severe strain upon his courage than had been apparent at the time. He was not afraid of the hardships of camping; it was the thought of being on the little island, helpless, unable to leave, and the *Least Petrel* definitely beyond the range of his sight, that drove him to the verge of hysteria. He did not possess the moral courage to endure the thought that she might become wrecked, might break down, might in some inconceivable way leave him stranded, to die of thirst or starvation. He was not amenable to reason or to demonstrable proof that, if anything happened to the *Least Petrel,* he was safer ashore than aboard. Argument merely drove him to added bluster and so the matter was dropped. At that I don't believe he took into consideration his only real danger, the fact that we might all be so wearied with him that we just wouldn't return.

Gregory followed Peter's lead, but did so without protest and I suspect that his decision was largely determined by a preference for Juan's cooking. In any event he flatly refused to camp alone, so that question was settled. Personally I did not care to spend any time on San Diego Island; there were too many other places that seemed more important. I told Captain to run as near to the shore as was safe and then to proceed north.

San Diego Island is not large—a mile long and little more than seven hundred feet high. It is a repetition of the endless volcanic uplifts; it differs from the others largely because it gives the impression of being merely the tip of a submerged ridge. From a little distance it was easy to believe that the sea was a bed of clouds surrounding a mountain peak supported by foothills and resting on a pedestal of normal slopes. There were the earmarks of a summit, the wedge-like shape, the corrugated sides, the barrenness, and the unshadowed monotone.

Less than an hour's run farther north we came to Santa Cruz Island. It is four times as long and twice as high as San Diego and, excepting in size, the two resemble each other very closely. The narrow gravel beach near the southwest end of Santa Cruz is the only point on which a landing can be made. The western side slopes at a forty-five degree angle from the shore; the eastern face is one of the stupendous spectacles of Lower California. Bluffs rise almost perpendicularly from the water itself, reaching upwards along a wavering crest from a minimum of three hundred feet to the awe-inspiring height of a thousand. Unfortunately our route and schedule did not give us the opportunity of seeing this wonder at its best, but we left determined to return sometime, to study and enjoy and to photograph in a proper mid-morning light.

Until dawn we lay at anchor in the lee of Santa Cruz and then laid our course for Santa Catalina. How familiar are the names, how well known along the southern half of California's coast! During breakfast we discussed our plans for the immediate future; the decision of Peter and Gregory not to camp made some changes imperative. We agreed that we would not land at all on islands to which we did not care to devote at least three or four days. Cármen, as far as we could determine, was the best prospect and so we turned twenty degrees to port and headed for Danzante Channel. There was still quite a sea, enough to make going ashore of questionable expediency; rough water was not the least of our reasons for seeking shelter.

Santa Catalina Island lay about eight miles to starboard at our point of closest approach. It is the least well-known of the larger Gulf islands and more for that reason than for any other I was disappointed in not being able to give it a thorough study. The waves were by this time so high that we did not even consider making the attempt; I contented myself with another of my resolutions. We could see that Santa Catalina, while several times as long as Santa Cruz, was of practically the same shape and height. There was the inevitable ridge—here with two pronounced peaks—and the steep sides gave the impression of a raw fragment of brick inappropriately lying in water. On the lower edges there was doubtless land more nearly level but from our position the base lay below the line of the horizon.

Captain insisted that the weather maker of the Gulf had a special grudge against us and had arranged the series of storms in such a way as most completely to interfere with our plans. If we lay in a snug harbor for a few days there would not be a breath of wind, if we planned a long run there was sure to be trouble from the hour of departure, and if we could land at some desired point only in a calm there certainly would arise a sea which would balk us. Today it appeared as though Captain were right because even before we came to the protection of Monseratte the waves had dropped until they were no longer an annoyance and the Gulf seemed determined to show us how nice she could be.

Monseratte Island, like the others we had been passing, is of volcanic origin. It is four miles long by two wide and, as its highest peak rises less than seven hundred feet, it is comparatively level. We passed it on the western side where, its dangers being well known to Captain, he took us close to the shore. We could see that it was almost barren and that its yellow ridges, virtually unprotected by roots, had been deeply eroded even though rain fell only on occasional years. More than anything we had recently passed Monseratte reminded us of the ash piles of San Bartolomé Bay. For some reason the less steep the lava slopes the more repellent is their sterility.

We wasted no regrets over leaving Monseratte, our only landing in its waters being on an offshore rock to which we were attracted by the presence of Western Gulls. On the little island a hundred of these large white scavengers were assembled, scattered at fairly regular distances, almost all in mated pairs. We found the beginnings of many nests where the birds had started to pile bits of seaweed in open blow-holes, but we were still well ahead of the laying season. The breeding habits of these Yellow-legged Western Gulls are a peculiarly interesting example of adaptation. All their close relatives lay on sand or soft earth or in shallow saucers and are content with a light lining, even with a flimsy ring of twigs. In the Gulf the large gulls usually place their eggs among the cobbles of the beach, upon the landward extension of ledges or behind boulders under sea-walls. Such surroundings require nests of large proportions and accordingly enough weed to fill a bushel basket is frequently used. First there is laid down a pad that affords protection and then a basin of sufficient size for three big eggs is so constructed that shells and stones cannot come in contact. Here, clearly, is a necessity which has been adequately met; pity is we cannot trace all of the long series of steps that are involved in the process of differentiation.

We made short work of Danzante, merely passing through the three-mile channel which separates it from Cármen. Danzante is a fairly level island in appearance not unlike Monseratte. Excepting where the sand beach occupies the southern end it is surrounded by an unusually high sea-wall with cliffs fifty and even seventy-five feet tall. There is a shallow channel that separates the northern tip of the island—a little strait too full of submerged rocks to be safe for any vessel. The coast from Dolores Bay to the northern end of Danzante is studded with outlying rocks, some pinnacle, some tidal, and not a few established islets that have been named. Where narrow channels, as that between Cármen and Danzante Islands, lie between two much larger bodies of water, the flow of tides is concentrated and exaggerated until currents become unbelievably strong. All things considered the section through which we had just passed includes the most dangerous and treacherous of Gulf waters.

Cármen Island is of irregular V shape. Near the apex, on the inside, lies the well-sheltered Salina Bay. At its head is a small village and beyond are a lagoon and extensive beds of salt. There is a railroad connecting the mineral deposits with a landing place from which exports are made on a comprehensive scale. Feeling that the presence of people in numbers would interfere with our work we made no investigation of this part of the island, choosing instead to run up the western side. We were reminded of San José Island as, for a couple of hours, we coasted past alternating bays and points. Often we saw *ramadas* or even huts near the beaches and we knew that large herds of cattle were being maintained.

Of course Cármen is volcanic and a desert, and, but for the fact that we had learned to appreciate and value almost any vegetation, would have seemed barren, if not sterile. But in the valleys there was mesquite, showing the presence of subterranean water, and on the ravine sides were sage and cactus and brush. The hills in the background climbed as high as fifteen hundred feet—the usual naked wedges. The monotony of the country had become so oppressive that there was but slight relief in the fine distinctions we were able to draw, here and there. We were all glad to end the day by dropping anchor in Puerto Balandra.

This little bay is a half-mile circle. It is formed by two modest headlands connected by a sweeping arc of sand. Behind lies the mouth of a valley covered in part with two small mangrove bordered lagoons and in part with a five or ten acre level stretch of head-high brush. Above rise lava hills that surround the amphitheatre with the inevitable reddish brown waste. We watched the occasional herons flying over the swamps or standing motionless and with marvellous patience, waiting for an unwary fish to come within striking distance. Only pelicans gave an atmosphere of life to the scene.

There were always present a few dozen, young of the year being in the majority. The diving of the juveniles was not wholly a matter of instinct, for their movements were more awkward and their technique less finished than that of the older birds. In the clear water of the bay it was not difficult for us to follow the movements of the fishers sufficiently to realize that diving was a complicated procedure involving a multitude of factors. There was wind to be considered, for one thing—sometimes the birds struck directly downwards, sometimes turned a half spiral so as to finish facing in a direction opposite to the one from which they had started. A sufficient depth was essential, for pelicans do not scoop their food. They half fold their wings and strike almost along the line of the perpendicular, often so hard as to submerge themselves. Under such circumstances contact with an unyielding bottom would have disastrous results.

Size of the prey must be properly judged, for only danger would follow an attack upon too large a quarry. Position and species and guessing the route of escape, knowledge of where to hunt and how, visibility—altogether the process is as much a science as an art. Their system has proven itself to be an effective one, for there are a million of these birds in the Gulf. Still, in appearance, they are so awkward that one wonders how they hold their own against better formists, boobies, for instance, who are vastly superior in flight, or the graceful tern, who seldom miss their prey.

We spent a day, a wonderful day, in the cañon that runs back from the bay. We passed through a narrow gorge where two great walls of red lava, blown with potholes, almost close the gap, and here we found the home of a family that had charge of cattle. At first the Mexicans were suspicious of our invasion, for every one of us carried a gun; they probably believed that it was our intention to add their veal to our ship's larder. Once satisfied, there was nothing they would not do for us; our coming was an event that broke their monotony and would furnish them with topics of discussion for the rest of the year.

AMONG THE ISLANDS OF THE GULF

The rancher held the responsible positions of supervisor and guardian of the northwestern corner of the island and yet his home was only in slight degree more pretentious than the primitive houses which are standard in Lower California. He had fenced the narrow gorge and had built a corral; by using the enclosure in connection with controlled water he had complete domination over all stock. He had shade from tall mesquites that had profited by the overflow from the drinking trough and he had shelter from the wind, both the high bluffs and the heavy underbrush serving as breaks. Apparently his family was comfortable and satisfied but, however much more fortunate than people of purely peon type, the advantages involved only the most trivial details. The house was little more than the lair of an animal, not only physically but also in its atmosphere of mental stagnation.

As the Partner has often pointed out to me, the absence of reading matter, of toys, of any tangible assets not wholly utilitarian, of anything designed to amuse or to give mental relaxation does not necessarily mean that brains have become atrophied. Arouse the interests of these people, children or adults, and they will prove themselves alert and quick to understand. So it was with the islanders. The Partner enjoyed swimming ashore from the *Least Petrel* and visiting them. There was in the house a cradle made of reeds bound together with rawhide and fitted with an untanned piece of skin. Judging by the step-ladder family it had probably been in constant use for many years, a child being removed only to make room for its successor. The occupant at the time of our visit was about three months old. The Partner tried to show the inconsistency of allowing the older children to run about dressed in a single garment or less while the baby, even on hot days, was swathed under layers of rags that covered the body, the head, and often the face as well. Her advice was listened to with smiles of acknowledgment, but was never followed. She brightened the children's days with cookies and candy and in return was rewarded with the gift of several live snakes.

We went up the cañon and found that it opened into quite an extensive valley. There was a wide band of gravel that wound down from the hills, the inevitable dry river-bed. Here the pebbles were coarse and rounded and the unusually heavy riparian growth suggested a rainfall abnormal for this country. The level bench above was more nearly barren and open, being dotted sparsely with chaparral and cactus. Here we hunted White-winged Doves for the table and assembled a worth-while series of rarities for our collections. The resident land-birds were virtually the same as those of the adjoining mainland, the intervening miles of salt water not being a deterrent to the urge to extend racial ranges that comes to all species that have reached their saturation point. We found that the little brush lovers, sparrows and wrens who dislike ever to expose themselves, had at some time boldly launched their tiny bodies in a grim gamble of life against death in a flight to the hazy island.

I truly believe that sufficient time and patience would reveal on Cármen all the avifauna and virtually all the flora of the adjacent parts of the Peninsula and I know that representatives of most of the species of migrants that travel up and down Lower California make use of it as a station. The mammals, of course, are isolated, and their presence is a matter of very ancient history. So, too, with the snakes and lizards, though in their case, strangely enough, they have seldom developed differentiations sufficient to warrant the naming of new species.

Captain's tooth had responded to the Partner's care and to her hot water bottles and so we stayed on in Balandra Bay without much regard for time. These were among the happiest days of the trip and it seemed as though every hour disclosed some new surprise. We were well protected from the vagaries of the weather, we had won the friendship, even the coöperation of the natives, there was nothing to cause friction aboard—we had plenty of hard work but no troubles.

For recreation we swam and we fished. Our canoe was of the well-known Oldtown type, sixteen feet long and quite light. I played hookey from work on several occasions to paddle it around the bay, to the headlands, or even out into the Gulf when weather permitted. I trolled with a spinner at the end of a six thread line, using an eight ounce rod. I have always been an ardent deep sea fisherman, I have tested the systems in vogue in Avalon and along the beaches and I have subscribed to all stereotyped forms of the sport. I feel qualified to maintain that those who have not tested a canoe in the Gulf have no conception of where the real thrills lie.

One man to paddle and one to fish, we keep well out from the rocks, for we are after livelier game than garoupas. There is a satisfaction in canoeing itself, a subtle feeling of artistic interpretation in moving over rather than through the water, and a touch of kinship comes from the lapping of waves through paper-thin sides. Leisurely, for speed is needless and would be inconsistent, with the shining silver minnow glistening and swimming behind, trolling itself would be abundant reward if never a fish were seen.

But one cannot long drag the bait without having a strike. Perhaps it is only a two foot bass—but once my lure was taken by a twenty-three pound tuna. A hundred feet of line, a hundred and fifty and the run was checked. At least so it seemed, for I held the fish with my thumb on the leather brake of the reel, but his rush had only relatively been stopped—we were following in the canoe. I was too busy from that moment to have much conception of time or distance. Tony, keeping the canoe off the rocks and at the same time bow on to the fish, was no less occupied. During the ensuing series of mad rushes I did not have to give my quarry any more line. I played him with the rod and with the canoe itself; I eased the shocks and for the rest took a tow. I do not remember ever having felt as completely satisfied with life as when Tony finally gaffed the worn-out fighter. Even then it had to be killed before we dared bring it aboard. The power boats and automatic reels of Catalina are factory products compared with the delicate hand-work of canoe fishing in the Gulf.

CHAPTER XXX

LORETO

IT was sunrise in Puerto Balandra. Preparations were under way for our run to the mainland and Juan was busy starting a breakfast to be served while we were in the channel. The Partner and I, having given our instructions, were resting. Seated on our favorite spot, the hatch of the glory-hole, we idly watched the color changes as the sun began to crawl above the silhouette of Cármen Island. We were at peace with the world, relaxed, unexpectant of the spectacle that was about to be displayed.

We have seen many a sunrise together, the Partner and I, but never one that either in beauty or in romance of setting equalled the glory of this morning. For half an hour we were enthralled spectators, motionless, silent, forgetful alike of surroundings and of the outside world. Only one remark broke the reverie. "I dare not describe this," I told her. "I can't hope to make anyone who has not seen it believe that a painting so exquisite could exist."

Art and simplicity. The canvas was lava rocks and water, nothing more. The tone was pink; there was no other color. Only a God striving for a masterpiece could conceive such shades, such blendings and such contrasts. No lesser artist could so express meaning on an empty sea or a sterile hill. When the far-away slopes of Sierra de la Giganta became softly glowing embers of both incandescent and reflected light, when the headlands of Cármen were glorified frames for a picture no gallery approximates, when all outdoors was attuned to the point where every detail was a realized ideal, even then not half the story had been told.

229

For we were watching something living, something that changed and shifted with the seconds, something that revealed combinations immeasurable in number, yet all equal because none could be surpassed. We watched with awe a series no dreamer could hope to own and yet one for which the least acquisitive would grasp with miserlike desire. Ever the single motive, mountains across the harbor mouth; ever the single color, soft, celestial pink. Ever the subtle changes that flowed without pause or break with the perfection of music.

Then came to us the realization that the landscape and the seascape were old, old beyond the power of the human mind to conceive or understand. In all the scene there was not a detail that had been touched by the hand of man, not a change that had taken place in the four hundred years since first the Spaniards sailed this Gulf, nor, except where some rock had moved, any variation during incomputable centuries, eons that run back toward the creation of the world.

Romance added all that man can add to such a setting, for as we passed the harbor headlands our bow pointed at history. The beginning of colonization in Lower California, the commencement of its conversion, the inception of its economic and social status, all are expressed with the one word, Loreto. Let those who have built into almost sacred annals the Coming of the Pilgrims make dramatic comparison with the birth of the opposite corner of our nation.

Errors in the calculated circumference of the globe resulted in early navigators being sure that Mexico was an insular outpost of Asia. The first ships to be launched in the Pacific and to explore the Gulf made frantic, desperate efforts to find the passage that must exist. Ants on a tree that had collapsed and fallen into the stream they rushed to every extremity, spread to every forlorn hope, and clung with almost ludicrous tenacity to their beliefs.

Then came the era of searching for the passage through the new continent, the strait that had often been reported and of whose existence there was no doubt. Popular belief at first connected it with the Gulf of California and for that reason the shores of the inland sea were, from the outset, recipients of otherwise disproportionate attention. The lure of the Seven Cities and of an easy passage to islands of spice and pearls and wealth, but never a protest against downright robbery or the stealing of the property of others. Was gold of less value because held under lawful ownership?

Next is the era of Manila galleons, of pirates lurking in the Gulf, of scurvy-stricken crews to be saved only in some secure harbor. There came at last, after proof that California was not an island, attempts to populate and colonize. Military necessity had not sufficed to establish a settlement, and pearl-trading, it was found, prospered best in private hands. The fact of the matter was that Lower California was not worth the expense of acquiring and holding. So there followed for generations heated discussions and abortive attempts, concessions and charters and impracticable proposals, and at the end the Peninsula remained almost unknown and occupied only by Indians.

The country was old, as we in America reckon age, and from the days of Cortéz to those of Father Kino lies a very appreciable part of Western history. Yet it was not until the inspired Padre and his even greater disciple surmounted obstacles and inertia, treachery and dishonesty, jealousies and enmities, and stamped themselves as being of the truly great men of the world, that religious zeal succeeded where national policies and economic desires had failed. Measured by obstacles overcome or by indomitable and sustained determination we would have to seek far in our own colonial history for characters as wholly admirable as were these two men.

It was not difficult for us to imagine that this was the year

1698—we knew we were on the identical water sailed by
Salvatierra and that we were watching landscapes he had
studied. From where we were he had looked forward to
the establishment of the first colony in Lower California,
to the conversion to the Catholic faith of thousands of
natives, and to the fulfillment of what had been, many,
many times, but a chimeric hope. He had already founded
the Pious Fund, but could he, possibly, foresee its increase
and the resultant series of missions that would spread from
San José del Cabo to beyond San Francisco Bay? He did
picture and then erect the first of the missions, but, no more
than John Winthrop visioned the great republic, did the
Padre dream that the culture he inaugurated would spread
up the coast and become the California of today.

We slipped out of Puerto Balandra and continued west
until we crossed the trail of Salvatierra. We approached
the mainland along the line he had followed and watched the
development of the landscape that had been his inspiration.
We saw the same headlands and islands and deserts, unchanged in detail, until there began to take shape the hazy
outlines of a village. We neared the beach and finally dropped
anchor well offshore in an open roadstead. We ran up our
signal flags and presently an official boat came out to us, to
make us realize that this no longer was Father Kino's day.

The illusion would not wholly dissolve. We rowed ashore
as we might have done two hundred years before, we dragged
our skiff high upon a beach which, over most its length,
was as bare as Salvatierra had found it, and the few roofs
we could see inland were types of no era. Palms, thinly scattered, tossed their tops just behind the sand and again there
was much to suggest a South Sea Island. We walked along
the beach until we came opposite a wide street recognizable
because it was a straight ribbon free from trees and undergrowth. A quarter mile away lay Loreto.

The site was a large sandy valley with low hills on either

side and the great Sierra not far behind. The floor was not
the typical dry river-bed and yet it clearly had been formed
by the age-long swinging back and forward of some sort
of intermittent stream. It was covered with mesquite of
fairly uniform size, half bush and half tree. It was less a
jungle than a spaced dwarfed forest. There was almost no
undergrowth in the sandy plains where cactus was noticeably absent. Unlike the other villages we had visited Loreto
spreads with indefinite boundaries out into the brush. Here
and there, sometimes at considerable distances from the
pueblo itself, often isolated and usually hidden under mesquite shade, the wanderer is forever stepping out of the
thickets, unexpectedly and suddenly coming to a clearing and
an adobe hut.

Loreto lies an appreciable distance inland, the space between the beach and the town being open and dotted with
half a dozen houses, most of which are governmental cottages. To reach the plaza we passed through a lane fenced
on both sides with mesquite stakes. The frequency of front
porches and gardens contrasts strangely with La Paz and
other towns where adobe walls consistently rise on the
property line. We entered a number of the enclosures by
opening small gates hung on rawhide hinges and found ourselves always in a medley of coarser growths, unkempt and
half abandoned. Delicate flowers there were, but suspended
in pots hanging beside bird cages from veranda beams. We
entered many such homes in our search for pyrrhuloxia and
cardinals; the Partner always brings from her trips a few
cages of birds for her aviary in San Diego.

Life centred about the plaza; there the spirit of Loreto
stood revealed. The bandstand was very old, as were its
accompaniments, and over all its surroundings was thrown a
pronounced atmosphere of decay and dejection. The long
ago enthusiasts who had been fired with the courage to build
have left descendants lacking both the ambition and the

energy to maintain the inheritance. One cannot be long in Loreto and not feel the spirit of stagnation and depression.

Here was built in 1698 the first of the California missions of which traces remain. It was ambitiously conceived and its designs were carried out with infinite pains and labor in masonry and imported carved woods. It is today in a state of collapse, its crumpled ceilings and the talus of its walls being fenced off to prevent injury to those who might otherwise stray within the ruins. We looked through railings at tunnels which brought to mind abandoned mineshafts, though here and there rooms which still remain safe are unofficially used for worship. There spread, from the old chapel, walls which, being roofless, promise to endure. No historian is needed to detail the train of events—the failure to be self-supporting, the cessation of over-seas assistance, and the abandonment by all save the faithful few who can do nothing to preserve.

Loreto has saved some things out of her past. The mission relics, for instance, include woodwork whose heavy relief is covered with gold leaf—the broken picture of bygone beauty. Old homes, several of which, in part at least, are still occupied by the families of the builders, a long street under a community veranda, and, strangest of all, a social prestige that permeates and dominates the east coast and spreads even to the mainland. In surroundings little less squalid than the simplest we have seen in other pueblos live people whose pride of ancestry is as strong as is such feeling in any other part of America. Moreover the claims are admitted and the influence of the impoverished aristocracy can hardly be exaggerated. Loreto is the Back Bay of Western Mexico.

We met as charming an old gentleman as one would care to know, the mentor and ruler of the community. From what era he had taken the fashion of his hair I do not know; it was trained so as to cover the top of his head to a thickness of several inches and to spread widely on the sides and in the back. He usually had it pinned in a handkerchief, so careful was he of its shape. His clothes were old and cheap, his office dingy, and his cottage hardly worthy of the name. But he was a man. He showed us a box filled with calling cards from American naval officers and from world-famous travellers who had stopped here, and he served us a wine mellow with age whose formula surely was a secret of the mission padres. I could easily believe him to be a survival of the old-time war-impoverished Southerner.

We left Loreto with a feeling akin to that which comes from visiting a sick friend. We had found what we had expected but we had not been fully prepared for the extent of the ravages of time. We saw quite a bit of agriculture, it is true, but there was not enough. Only from the deck of the *Least Petrel,* with a foreground of unprotected beach and a fringe of palms, only from a hidden spot, here and there in the centre of town, where realism and decay chanced to be invisible, did we encounter anything picturesque. Of all the towns we visited in Lower California this is the one that taught us the most; it is the place that connects yesterday with today, the spot that must have inspired the great Diaz to his famous phrase: "Pobre Baja California."

We had planned to make a direct run from Loreto to Ildefonso, but the Gulf willed otherwise. She chose the afternoon for a display of temperament and proceeded to pile up one of the choppy seas that are so uncomfortable. Tide, wind, and currents combined in effective team work to throw across our stern quartering waves that rolled us without mercy. We closed all the doors and portholes on the starboard side, we moved from one room to another as seldom as possible, and a trip to the pilot house was accomplished only by holding firmly to the rail and taking a thorough drenching.

The anchorage at Ildefonso offered no protection against

this blow from the south and so we turned toward the shelter of El Púlpito on the mainland. We spent the afternoon ashore among associations typical of the eastern side of Sierra de la Giganta. We worked in thick groves of cardónes, but found only lizards and mice in the woodpecker holes. We explored the watershed and collected a few sets of eggs of jays, thrashers, and Cactus Wrens. We enjoyed most of all our close acquaintanceship with El Púlpito, for it is one of the famous landmarks of the coast.

As we came up from the south this five-hundred-foot knob appeared to be an island; it is joined to the mainland by a comparatively low isthmus. The great rock is rounded and shapely and the source of its name is quite evident. It is visible from a long distance in either direction and unofficially marks the boundary between the influences of Loreto and Mulegé.

To Rogers it was another milestone of prehistoric mankind, for even here he found mesquite-covered mounds that held free water at no great depth. To us it was the portal to Ildefonso, one of the greatest bird islands in the Gulf. Ildefonso is an almost barren rock little more than a mile in length, less than half as much in width, and nowhere reaching four hundred feet in height. The top is sprinkled with low brush and, in places, with cholla and there are a few substantial bushes along the eastern ravines. Its fame has spread wherever ornithology is studied and sunrise found us headed directly for what we hoped would be one of the high lights of the trip.

CHAPTER XXXI

ILDEFONSO ISLAND

HIS Majesty the Duck Hawk! To describe Ildefonso is to tell of the king of the cliffs who, throned on a towering pinnacle, overlooks his suzerainty and levies tribute upon his terror-stricken subjects. In season he garners toll from gentle Craveri Murrelets whose plucked frames and whitened skeletons litter the talus beneath his butchering rock. He seizes without mercy the Eared Grebe who does not dive quickly enough when it has been outmanœuvred. If a petrel carelessly rises too high above the water, if an Elegant Tern allows himself, at the wrong time, to become isolated from his flock, if a shore-bird momentarily neglects the safeguards with which he has been endowed, another living creature will be carried to the aërie, another pulsating, breathing body will be torn to shreds.

The Czar is too proud to content himself always with prey smaller than himself. He habitually drives to earth and kills the predatory Heerman Gull and no duck is large enough or fast enough to be immune. There is not an enemy who dares attack the tyrant or in any way disturb his rule. There are only two classes of birds on Ildefonso, those to whom he is indifferent and those from whom he takes his daily kill. Sometimes, when considering human oppression that is approaching a breaking point, it may be well to revert to this island, if for no other purpose than to realize the extent of the hardships under which life can at least endure. It might repay to compare this living tragedy with classic or legend or folklore that has for motif the supreme

gift and sacrifice of maidens and youths to imagined monsters. Nothing in storied tale dare approximate the red dragon
of the bluffs nor his annual levy of a thousand helpless lives.

The rulers are not wanderers over the face of the earth,
free to come and go as they will. Their kingdom is a rigidly
limited area, a vatican in which, like former popes, they are
moral prisoners. They own the eastern slope of Ildefonso,
a narrow strip a mile long, a terrain of cliffs breaking to an
irregular bench, marked with gullies and boulders and outcropping teeth to the very edge of the sea-wall. Of the world
beyond they know little, but within their self-established
boundaries there is not an intruder, not a movement, but is
of vital and immediate concern. From one year's end to another the rental they pay is unrelaxed vigilance against
usurpation.

Once upon a time, in human development, there was
but a negligible distinction between rulership and ownership. So it is on Ildefonso today. The surface of the land and
all rights to the air within their circumscribed portion of
the earth is the private property of the peregrines. They are
capitalistic landowners with an estate from which they derive a regular income. Their title, immeasurably old, has
come in unbroken succession from a past that might well be
reckoned in centuries. The fee has been maintained against
all the world and its perpetuity is assured by a system proof
against death or disaster. No more certain are the capital
and interest of a conservative trust than are the dividends of
this particular realty.

The title came from possession; the pair of birds
ruled and guarded from pinnacles that overlooked the estate. They were well aware that the property which kept
them in comfort, often in luxury, would not, if divided,
save them from starvation and poverty. It was incumbent
upon them to preserve their dividends entirely for themselves and to fight to the death any other Duck Hawks who

might trespass. Seldom would the struggle be severe; the owners would combine against the interloper, would attack him with coöperative team play against which he could not long pit his individual strength. As landless birds do not mate only the rarest of circumstances could bring two at once against the established proprietors. Even in case of a comparable equality in the struggle the determinant would be the morale of the residents. Theirs is the courage that comes from being in the right, from the terrible consequences of defeat, from being accustomed to victory, and from being established in familiar surroundings.

Usurpation from within is estopped with equal finality. The falcons normally lay either three or four eggs and it is to be presumed that most of these develop into young that leave the nest. From the hour that incubation commences until the juveniles are experienced hunters they are guarded and fed and taught with all the zeal that could be expected from such magnificent parents. Comes a time, however, when food is decreasing fast, when the collectable rental no longer will suffice, when thoughts turn to the babies that are to be reared the following season. When the day of atonement arrives the youngsters are driven from their homeland. Battered and bruised in proportion to the resistance offered they are definitely and permanently deprived of the revenue of their heritage. Once again is the kingdom under the unchallenged sway of its rulers.

What of the young? It were pleasant to picture the dispossessed wanderers, in the full power of adolescence, spreading to the wide-flung corners of the earth and founding new dynasties to enhance the glories of their kind. Unfortunately, however, since immemorial time every pasturage that can support a pair has been preëmpted and every border-line field has been tested and has been occupied just as long as its productivity lasted. The debutantes find themselves confronted by a monopoly stringent beyond the dreams of anything human, by a system age-old and unbreakable, against which they batter themselves helplessly and pitiably until they meet miserable deaths by starvation. Nature needs a few, a very few, of each year's crops; for the others she makes no provision and literally leaves them no place to go. Chased and fought the pariahs struggle against the pangs of hunger until their sufferings come to a merciful end, around the corner, perhaps, or possibly in unfamiliar surroundings a thousand miles from home.

We who have studied Duck Hawks in areas where every falcon is charted have observed that occasionally a pair becomes established in a region that had been unoccupied the previous year. Ordinarily the introduction is due to changing economic conditions which more or less temporarily fit a new area to support a family of these birds. It is possible, of course, that a suitable claim has simply been overlooked, but that condition is rare indeed under the intense strain of competition. Whatever the cause no one can appreciate better than a collector how pitifully few of the enormous annual crop are saved to posterity by luck in finding a vacancy.

One other chance has the newcomer—he may meet with a bird of the opposite sex who, while still maintaining title, has lost its mate. In such a case, if mutual fascinations appeal, he will drop into the lap of luxury and his troubles will have come to an end. He will have profited by the system of perpetuation that has proven the undoing of his fellows and has drawn an impermeable circle about their hopes of existence. In proportion to the good fortune of those who win in this lottery are the almost infinitesimal chances of drawing a prize. The life of an established Duck Hawk is long, his exposure to accidents slim, and never does he offer a challenger the opportunity for even combat.

It happened that the birds on Ildefonso had aided us materially in tracing these life histories. For three years to our knowledge and for an indefinite preceding time they

THE SITE OF LORETO: FROM PUERTO BALANDRA

MISIÓN SAN FRANCISCO XAVIER DE VIGGE

THE LAIR OF THE GIANTESS

had maintained their suzerainty and had bred upon these marginal cliffs. There were several means by which we had been able to recognize the identity of the birds. The eggs themselves were the most positive; they were determinable as having been laid by the same individual and would have enabled us immediately to have become aware of a substitution of the female. We had grown to know the birds themselves by their coloring, by their voices, and by their conduct when we approached the nest. Just as the poultry fancier learns to distinguish the individuals of his flock so had we become personally acquainted with many of the more highly developed birds among which we worked.

Our purpose in coming to Ildefonso had been to study murrelets, but our first move after we landed was an attempt to secure a clutch from our old friends. Overhearing the discussion the Partner declared herself in on the collecting and insisted that it would be she who would do the climbing. Tony and I joined in putting her in her place, in explaining that Duck Hawk eggs involved the sportiest of oölogical takes, and that no woman had any business doing anything so dangerous. The result was that the end of the next hour found her on our rope ladder with an especially equipped creel at her waist and a hundred feet of sheer drop beneath her feet.

In spite of her bravado I doubt if she was interested in the scenery, in the breakers rushing into the cove, a dizzy distance below, to spatter the black sea-wall. I know she did not give a thought to the gullies that looked like pencil marks as they crawled under low bushes and reached for the foot of the precipice, or to the scattered array of boulders that, propped up with ridiculous dignity, spread over the slopes. Yet there was grandeur in the bold carvings and in the long fissures of the innumerable lava cinders and pinnacles. Far below ghostlike birds patrolled the beach while, from the sea, protesting barks of sea lions maintained unremittent chorus. Far away, across a sheet of water which, when smiling, cannot be rivalled for beauty, rose the dim hills of Sonora. Why toil and strive in such a setting? What more can man ask than indefinitely to hang his feet over the lip of the cliff and search for new combinations of beauty?

Tony was busy, having assumed the responsibility of advising the Partner. The Duck Hawks were nearby, flying to and fro in fifty-foot circles that kept them above us and out from the face of the cliff. They were scolding with a shrill penetrating cackle that is music to the collector; it tells of a treasure that is near. The female, of course, was much the larger and, in this case, the more fearless, for she threatened many an angry swoop while her more brilliantly marked mate contented himself with hoverings and, perhaps, encouragement.

The aërie was on a yard wide shelf ten feet down from the top of the precipice. The Partner arrived safely on the ledge and, holding the life-line, began her hazardous search. She knew the eggs might be on any one of several selected sites, for the habits of the birds are against using the same nesting spots on consecutive years. On the other hand they will not go outside their private claims to breed and that limits their choice, for there are not apt to be many places that will fulfill all their demands.

They prefer a pothole or ledge set in the face of a cliff, the higher the better, their object being security from marauding enemies. They subscribe to the instinct whether there is real danger or whether they are on islands free from snakes and all mammal life. The chosen nesting ground is preferably sand or soft earth; it must be able to hold the eggs securely, for the parents build no nest. It is not conceivable that an untrained dog would pile up empty boxes so that he could jump over a fence, nor could a Duck Hawk be suspected of bringing a twig to keep her eggs from rolling out of place. Such an improving of a nesting site are among the things which one can be definitely certain this bird will not do.

The Partner finally found the set, four beautiful red eggs nearly spherical and decidedly larger than those of hens. She packed them one by one in the prepared sections of her basket and climbed safely back to the top of the bluff with a prize which will always have a place of honor in our cabinet. Her reaction, now that the struggle was over, was of pity for the bereaved hawks. They would have their moment of grief, it is true, but time would quickly heal the pain and in three weeks they would be laying a second setting.

We turned our attention to the other birds of Ildefonso. Several pairs of Osprey, breeding on the pinnacles near the shore, did not compete with the peregrines, for the fish-hawks were far too slow of flight to capture alates. Western Gulls and Ravens occurred in small numbers; we found three or four breeding pairs of each. Both, at heart, are scavengers to whom nothing edible comes amiss, but they, too, are beneath notice unless they carelessly intrude into the presence. Sparrow-hawks and Burrowing Owls are allowed to glean lizards and mice and insects; they infringe no royal prerogatives. Neither do the bobbing Rock Wrens nor the other small land birds which struggle, without much success, to wrest a living from this barren island. Great Blue Herons, the goal of European falconry, nest on Ildefonso without appreciable interference.

On a flat near the southern end of the island a great colony of Heerman Gulls were preparing to lay. They had no amiable rule of first come first served, nor did they await the approach of the great event before staking out their claims. By the thousand one of each pair stood patiently upon the spot which he and his mate had selected, allowing no closer approach than the reach of his bill. For weeks, in relays, every pair had maintained its alert vigil in order that, when the necessity arrived, there would be obtainable a plot in which a shallow saucer could be scraped. The nest itself would be little more than an encircling halo of twigs. Quarrelsome birds are these gulls, with no friendly feeling towards the world or for each other. They breed in dense colonies and fly from their nests to the water in a compact flock because of fear of the Duck Hawk. They know he will not enter their ranks even to secure his prey.

The steganapodes are the most conspicuous of Ildefonso's birds. Seriously, solemnly, stupidly they go through the routine of their fishing, unmolested because too powerful and heavy to appeal to the falcon. The pelicans breed near the southeastern corner of the island, building huge discs of twigs on bushes or outcroppings or even upon unprotecting soil. Some nests held the full complement of three eggs, others contained incomplete sets or even were empty, while in many were black, naked babies. This colony is one of a dozen scattered among various islands of the Gulf, and, like the others, is prospering. The birds, rather to our surprise, are numerically holding their own in spite of the decreasing supply of fish.

Two genera of gannets, the Brewster Booby and the Blue-footed Booby, swarm about the caves and ledges near the southwestern corner. They are much alike except in coloring, these stepping stones between the pelican and the shag. They abound from one side of the Gulf to the other, sometimes in separate colonies and sometimes, as on Ildefonso, mixed indiscriminately. Their life histories and their requirements are identical, as far as I have been able to ascertain. However, there must be some point that we have as yet failed to catch, for the Brewster is by far the more common in the northern part of the Gulf while the Blue-footed preponderates in the southern and eastern sections.

With their problems indistinguishable, with breeding sites and seasons overlapping, there is significance to be attached to the differences in their nesting habits. The Brewster Booby assembles coarse twigs and large wing quills and arranges rather than builds them into a coarse structure. Long before the young are grown the flimsy saucer will have disappeared, have been dissipated by the storm winds of the Gulf, leaving the fledglings to fare as best they can on naked rocks and ledges. Only during incubation does the body of the parent keep the fringe in place.

The Blue-footed Booby, on the other hand, deposits her eggs on bare earth. She is as incapable of collecting or using building material as is the Duck Hawk. I have noticed that she shuns the more open sites chosen by her cousins, seeking rather the floor of caves, overhanging rocks, or sandstone ledges on the higher sea-walls. This may be attributable to the fact that there is more likely to be soil in such locations, for I have not infrequently found colonies of Blue-foots in draws on insular mesas. Their one consistent demand is soft earth or sand which can be smoothed into a shallow plate by the rotation of the body.

What reason can be given for these radical distinctions? Were the theory of survival determinant, then the less advantageous of the two systems would in time give way and the other would be adopted by both species of the birds. Divergent instincts and inheritances are, of course, the explanation. Pages could be filled with examples to show that in nesting and in egg markings associations are negligible when compared with ancestral influences. This is observably consistent and it demonstrates that proper correlation of data on the point would be of great aid in reconstructing the highly desired biological tree. Somewhere lost in the history of the races is the true solution of a question seemingly trivial and yet whose answer would revolutionize the science of ornithology. Why do these closely allied forms build nests that are not alike?

On Ildefonso is the most concentrated of the known

colonies of Craveri Murrelets. These divers breed only in the Gulf of California and until recently little was known of their habits. We have by now ascertained that, in greater or lesser numbers, they probably resort to every available island and large rock in the Gulf. They are strictly pelagic except during the breeding season, they spread far over the ocean and, in autumn, are commonly to be found as far north as Central California. They return to home waters during the last weeks of winter, and, before incubating, are commonly seen swimming on the surface as mated pairs.

In March they go ashore to lay. They build no nest, contenting themselves at most with scraping the sand a bit. They crawl under boulders where the wind has worked an opening, they squeeze into fissures and crevices in the lava, they work their way among recesses of caves and deep into volcanic blow-holes. Their one demand is a protected site where, in complete darkness, they may lay and incubate.

The eggs are normally two in number, long ovates, burnished, and widely divergent in color. These are very large in comparison with the size of the parents. This is an indication—not a proof, for there are many exceptions— that it is Nature's plan to carry far the development of the chicks before they emerge from the shell. Father and mother alternate in incubation, but there is no fixed arrangement, females at night, for instance, and males in the daytime, as is the case with pigeons. Sitting birds exchange places with each other an hour or two after dark and again shortly before the daybreak, choosing these times in order to be safe from the Duck Hawk. The parent leaving the nest flies straight for the water, keeping herself as near the ground as possible, for in this way she is least exposed to attack. Once at sea she can safely browse upon the tiny marine life on which she lives. She can dive from danger in the sky and fly from underwater attackers.

The day after the chicks hatch both father and mother swim close to the shore and call to the tiny black puff balls. The babies respond at once, be the nest on the edge of the waves or a quarter mile inland. The little things crawl to the opening and fall, they roll to the edge of the cliff and fall, they scramble to the top of rocks and fall, they reach slides and fall, down, ever downwards, over the sea-wall, through the boulders, into the breakers and at last to parental care and guidance. We read their after history as we meet them in family groups everywhere on the Gulf; none will again return to land until driven by the instinct to breed.

I cannot explain how the Duck Hawk bests a system that appears impregnable. I simply know that he does. He goes about it so easily, so surely, that the measure of his need is the number of his kill. The years have established a balance and, from season to season, there is no material variation in the number of murrelets. I see Ildefonso as a slave-driven factory in which a swarm of breeders toil and struggle, gasping with the effort of raising young fast enough to prevent extermination. Thousands of murrelets, toiling and suffering, devote not only their own existences but also all the fruits of parental love to the one purpose of feeding their majesties, the Duck Hawks.

CHAPTER XXXII

It was just sun-up as we left Ildefonso. We had plotted a circuitous course for the day and the run would require broad daylight by which to recognize the various headlands and make the needed turns. For the first few hours we skirted the edge of a long peninsula that wedged in between us and the now distant Sierra de la Giganta. Moisture seldom and rain almost never is in the winds that blow over the baked hills on our port, and as a result we watched the unfolding of a landscape but slightly less harsh than the one we had seen on Cape San Eugenio in the Pacific.

We were now directly opposite and little more than a hundred miles east of San Ignacio Lagoon; since leaving Cape San Lúcas, we had run northerly half the length of the Peninsula. The chart showed us to be near San Bartolomé Bay but the country itself told of a very different part of the world. The basic distinction between the two coasts lies in the fact that the western, as we had observed, is broad and susceptible of division into a number of zones, while the eastern is extremely narrow and virtually homogeneous its full length. There are variations in width and shape, it is true, and as we progressed into higher latitudes the rainfall decreased and water in the oases became correspondingly less plentiful. Neither these changes nor the drainage channels that now and again were large enough to break monotony served to divide the foothills of La Giganta into separable parts. From the Victoria Mountains to Sierra San Pedro Mártir the Gulf fringe is an entity of its own.

We drove our furrow through a sheet of glass; there

248

was not a wave to disturb the level nor a breath of air to ruffle the surface. Shearwater of several species were to be seen resting on the water, petrel were skimming with their swallow-like alternations of zig-zags and sweeping curves, gulls and boobies were overhead, murrelets and grebes at our feet. Even more interesting than the birds were the great fins of which one or more was usually visible. Sharks and swordfish, sunfish and mantas—the Captain claimed to be able to recognize them all but the latter was the only one I learned to distinguish with certainty.

This Blanket-fish, *Manta hamiltoni,* is well named. A captured specimen I saw was roughly circular. It was dark above and almost white below and weighed, on the scales, twenty-five hundred pounds. These great rays love to sun themselves by swimming just beneath the surface, a lateral fin on either side being held a foot or two out of the water. Native belief is that they capture their prey by swimming under it and folding up like a cloth.

An incident of the morning tends to confirm the Mexican idea. Dead ahead basked one of these monsters—whales excepted, they and Elephant Seals are the largest living creatures in Lower California—with the bow of our boat pointed directly between the exposed fins. Not a movement from the fish until our keel struck its backbone, whereupon it closed on us with a viciousness, a strength, and a speed that were sickening. We could hear the slap and feel the simultaneous grasp on both sides of the boat and water enough was thrown up to douse the pilot house windows. Small wonder that the pearl-divers dread these rays more than all other perils combined.

Soon after leaving Ildefonso we made our way past San Bruno, the Plymouth Rock of the Californias. If Salvatierra earned his claim to immortality by the wonderful qualities he displayed in founding Loreto what shall we say of the last twenty years of his life? Hardly a day during that time

249

but his little series of missions was on the brink of disaster, hardly a month elapsed that the institutions were not so seriously threatened as to be saved only by his greatness. His personal accomplishments were but the half—his ability to inspire his disciples and to teach them to perform was as much a factor in his success as was his own manhood. For the length of a generation he and his followers did the impossible, carried through their miracles and maintained the churches whose continued existence no less than their foundation was dependent on his sustaining genius.

Salvatierra and his padres built on rock; their work was so well done that it lasted a hundred years and more on that most hopeless of coasts. In another century the pioneering achieved fruition in Southern California. Can anyone, I wonder, cruise along that dreary desert and fail to appreciate something of the man, of the tender-hearted, sympathetic tower of strength? Most of us aboard the *Least Petrel* were Californians, at least by adoption, and we very willingly paid our share of the tribute the whole southland owes to that wonderful company of persevering Jesuits.

We were not long in reaching Concepción Point, a rather indefinite curve in the coast line. It is marked with perpendicular bluffs and here, going close inshore, we slowed down to catch fish. We needed two or three for the table and, having had no luck with the more desirable deep sea swimmers put pride aside and went after garoupas. This local name is apparently a synonym for the English word groupers and is applied to the genus *Mycteroperca* and, vaguely, to all the dark bass of the Gulf. It includes everything from jewfishes to the two or three pounders that are the most numerous of the larger edible fish.

In unimaginable numbers, from one end of the Gulf to the other, garoupas haunt the rocky ledges off coasts and islands. If a jigger is trolled at a speed of about four miles an hour over the proper bottom there is no question of catching something—the only gamble is species and size. The slogan "a ton an hour" can often be bettered. The second fish caught that day—Tony was our most inveterate Waltonite—proved to be quite small. While we were over-applauding and joshing with suggestions of "leaving it on for bait" a great shadow came from the bottom. A jewfish grabbed the smaller bass and the hook as well, and then trouble did start.

The hand-line was strong, but Tony made no effort to pull in his catch; he had learned a lesson on a previous trip to these waters. Everyone aboard at that time had been hurt through having his hands cut by fish he could not hold, so Tony at once wrapped the line around the rail. Then as many of us as could get a grip began to pull and to take up slack whenever the big bass gave an inch. Finally the brute was brought alongside and killed. How much it weighed we never will know for it was far too large to bring aboard. Juan and Charley butchered it from the skiff.

Rounding the point we entered Concepción Bay. It is a curiously shaped body of water, being twenty-two miles long by three or four wide with straight, parallel sides. The eastern border is a monotonous stretch of sand and pebble beaches backed by land that slopes gradually to the mountains of the small peninsula. The southern end, a section known as La Pasajera, is a flattened semicircular continuation of the beaches. The shoaling of the bay is here so gradual that we made no attempt to approach closely, contenting ourselves with what we could see through glasses. We picked up a lagoon but passed on as it did not appear to hold any details of special interest.

The western side was in decided contrast. It is rugged in outline—a series of promontories and inlets marked with high bluffs. Toward the northern end of the bay the rough country disappears. Near Gallito Point, which marks the western entrance, the coast is low and shoal water extends well out to sea.

Concepción is shallow and, though long and narrow, is straight. As a result a northerly gale from just the right direction will sweep unchecked down the bay and harry the surface into tremendous waves. There is very little tidal movement and currents are unappreciable and so the waters have stagnated under the desert sun until they have taken on a color and composition all their own. The bottom is nearly everywhere of sand, white and very fine, and it reflects enough light to be visible at a depth of several fathoms.

Sea-growths are variable—heavy in some places, absent in others. We saw scattered shells and dove for many, making a number of welcome additions to our collection. Sharks and porpoises were plentiful but small fish were either rare or else well hidden. Birds were not at all common—a few flocks of boobies, but no breeding colonies. We stirred up a large octopus—at least we never before had seen one that measured three feet across—and the squirming ogre emitted enough black fluid to surround himself with several feet of opaque ink. But after all it was the absence of life that was of biological interest. Concepción may be listed among the places where all higher forms of life are rare.

We spent several days in Coyote Bay, exploring its islands and the adjacent mainland. There are half a dozen islets scattered over this five square mile indentation in the western shoreline of Concepción Bay. Our experience with Habana Rock was repeated here. There was the complete isolation and the guano covering, but there were no rookeries. We found nesting only Great Blue Herons, Ospreys, Western Gulls, Duck Hawks and Oyster-catchers, and none of these were plentiful. On one of the islands we encountered a condition unique in my experience. A flock of quail night and morning made a flight of half a mile across open water. Their purpose, or at least their accomplishment, was to secure a roosting place inaccessible to prowling coyotes, wild cats, and other nocturnal vermin.

Traces of mankind of many eras were found on almost every island. There was evidence that clams had once been abundant, for there were any number of great piles of some large species of these bivalves. Shells of pearl-bearing oysters were more common ashore than in the water. So many factors had contributed to make collecting easy that this bay had been among the first to be exploited and scoured. The most interesting of the relics were to be found in the caves that still bear traces of primitive men. I remember particularly one of the larger dens whose shell dump was as big as a house. Even an inexperienced observer could satisfy himself that he was looking upon handiwork that ran back through misty ages.

Neither details nor geometrical terms describe Concepción Bay. It is more than an arm of the Gulf with elongated dimensions and peculiarly shaped shorelines. It is a marvellous anomaly of desert and water. It is more than an inland lake with borders of sloping soilless and treeless clods of lava. It is a cinema no two of whose pictures are alike, no one of which remains unchanging. It gives in alternation all that the Gulf has to offer in beauty or viciousness, all that the desert holds in enchantment or brutality. It opens an encircling panorama pushed back to effective perspective and yet kept within the range of observable detail. In Coyote Bay the combination reaches its acme.

You may anchor in that island-sprinkled harbor and see the meeting place of waste and ocean at their worst and at their best. You may declare it to be the world's most gruesome hell-hole, and I'll not disagree. So much depends on the point of view, on the personal equation. If you believe it is one of the most appealing of all enchanted spots then I will take you to task and argue that you have not half stated the case. For if you are a lover of the desert and the sea, if your idea of natural beauty is a wide sweep where no two items are the same, if you prefer a landscape that ends in a blur of haze to one that stretches endlessly over tree tops or terminates abruptly against a near-by wall, then, to you, scenic Coyote Bay possesses a charm that cannot be surpassed.

It has been known since the earliest times, this bay that has been a hiding place for those whose intentions were evil. It has been a haven of refuge from storms and from enemies for mission founders as well as for pirates. It has seen successively paddles and sail and steam and internal combustion. They who have sailed upon it have watched the glories of its dawns, some enthralled, surely few without appreciation. They have seen soft matutinal colors fade into uncompromising greys that endured throughout the shadowless glare of noondays. And they have awaited the coming of the sunset and the softening of all nature as the failing light blotted out the mountains, the rainbow sea, and one by one the encircling islands. The lure of Concepción comes not to those who rush in, make a quick survey, and leave. The prize is for the patient waiter who is receptive, who is content with the momentary jewel, and is satisfied if its pricelessness compensates for its rarity.

Two miles north of Gallito Point is Equipalito Rock and the mouth of Río Santa Rosalía. The stream is neither a normally unremittent flow nor is it one of the common underground rivers. It is rather a series of pools fed by water which sometimes flows, sometimes seeps, from one pond to another. It rises in the mountains which here happen to be so shaped that a large watershed drains into one cañon, but the presence of the so-called river is accidental, not indicative of a change in the country. Much of the flow is diverted for agriculture but enough remains near the mouth to form a series of lagoons. On one of these and two miles back from the Gulf lies the mosquito ridden, malaria infested village of Mulegé.

Before the pueblo had become overshadowed by Santa

Rosalía it had been the economic and governmental centre of a widespread area of Lower California. Its official status has gone with its commerce, its mission life has slipped into history, as did its pearling, and it is now a farming region which supplies the greedy markets of the mining town. Looked upon from a little distance, from the bordering highland mesas, the valley appears to be a solid jungle of palms. Canoeing through its lagoons carries one back to the tropics, with pygmies and miniature huts and mud flats backed by a solid towering wall of rough stalks and monster leaves.

The little settlement itself might well be a part of the simpler quarters of La Paz. The main street edges along a few blocks solidly built with adobe walls, one house running into another. There is the usual mixture of stores and homes —the type and size of the doorways as usual determining the character of the room within. There are the low, thatched roofs, the sandy, dusty streets, the children and the dogs and the glare. A newly built brick church, entirely out of keeping with its day and place, looks across the river from the southern bank and accentuates how severely time has dealt with Mulegé.

We had brought a picnic lunch ashore, as we so often did, and we found a lovely little spot where spreading mesquites threw a welcome shade over the clear sand of a lateral stream bed. We had hardly made the first move to unpack when out of the bushes came a little old man dressed in the conventional three piece outfit—straw sombrero, brown shirt, and blue overalls. Our Spanish was not sufficient for his understanding nor did we quickly grasp the meaning of his gestures. It finally came out that we were flirting with danger in our little dell, that it was a notoriously bad spot for malarial mosquitoes, and that we must immediately move to higher ground. We certainly appreciated his kindness and consideration. His conduct was more a characteristic of the far away people who seldom come in contact with strangers than an isolated act of unselfishness. Just another national gesture of welcome and hospitality.

Of course we lost our enthusiasm for Mulegé and so returned to the *Least Petrel*. We pushed north again into Santa Inéz Bay and visited the three outlying islands. They were small, low, and very flat—quite a contrast to the long series of volcanic uplifts that lay between us and Ceralbo. The Santa Inéz Islands apparently have been thrown up by currents; they are too recent to hold special interest for us. We found many relics left from the days when pearling was in its prime, perhaps traces of still earlier civilization—we were not sure. The islands were too small for mammals and for some reason held no appeal for birds. We could read traces of many visitors but nearly all had proven themselves to be transients.

We had one break of luck at Mulegé. We learned that a dentist was on San Márcos Island and so we headed directly for the gypsum mines. Dr. Denney is one of the institutions of the northern half of Lower California. He travels from pueblo to rancheria, stopping long enough at each place to care for whatever teeth are ailing and to spread the news of whatever is going on in the world. Around and around the circle, like a planet he makes his annual pilgrimage; there is no estimating the relief he brings to sufferers who simply could not go to the States for treatment.

Dr. Denney is a pleasant little man, always well groomed and friendly and welcome personally as well as professionally. He had set up his office in the corner of a shed, spread his instruments, and installed his lathe. The latter was a machine driven by foot-power, for Denney ordinarily had to do without electricity. In spite of the limitations under which he had to work he extracted Captain's tooth in fine style, and that incident was closed.

San Márcos is large, being well over five miles long and averaging nearly two in width. Its color and vegetation are

TEMPERAMENT

YELLOWTAIL AND GAROUPA: TWO MEALS

COYOTE BAY

those of the neighboring mainland and consequently it is more barren than most of the islands we had examined. It is hilly rather than mountainous and it nowhere attains nine hundred feet. We found a few birds upon it; Great Blue Herons were common and Osprey abundant, but the more usual sea-birds seem to find it unattractive.

It is the only island in the Gulf on which there is industry of any considerable proportions. The southern end of San Márcos is a solid bed of gypsum which is quarried and ground and loaded in bulk into steamers. The output, which exceeded a thousand tons a month when we had been there in 1928, did not seem to have lessened in 1930. The principle on which the quarrying is done is the blasting of great chunks which are run, by gravity as far as possible, into the crushers, and then conveyed on a fifteen hundred foot belt to ships or barges. The motive power comes from a low grade oil which, together with fresh water and supplies, is brought down by the Seattle boats. The island is wholly without resources of its own.

The political and economic effects of this big plant are at once demoralizing and laughable. For instance both the Federal Government and the Territory of Baja California claim title to the island and, as neither will concede the rights of the other, there is nothing for the company to do but to pay taxes to both. There is a general antipathy on the part of Mexicans to being exploited; they are not at all favorable to the removal of their natural resources for the benefit of foreign investors. On the other hand they appreciate the value to the Mexican laborer of being able to obtain employment and wages. On San Márcos the strain of these contradictory policies has been abetted on one hand by stubborn resistance to the customs of the country and on the other by an unjustifiable amount of petty interference. There has been a great deal of lost motion and too much unpleasant feeling. I can see both points of view and feel that neither side is wholly blameless.

As between the American business man who believes that a contract, however obtained, is religiously to be kept and the Latin to whom an agreement never ceases to be a matter for finesse and diplomacy there are bound to be disagreements. Roy Clark, manager in 1928, used to complain that he had to spend twice as much time straightening difficulties as he could devote to his real work of getting out rock. Charges of graft I listened to here as everywhere in Mexico, but I am yet to be convinced that the southern republic approaches our own in official corruption. We at home have grown accustomed to certain forms and take them as matters of course without realizing how inconsistent we are in damning the Mexicans simply because they develop unexpected angles.

Gypsum is mined, and has been for many years, on some workable basis. Political heckling of business urged on by demogogues and radicals has worked more injury to the people themselves than it has to those against whom it is aimed. But that is true everywhere in the world. I might note a recent law that requires an employer to give three months notice before he discharges any laborer. In practice the result is virtually a bonus in wages, for there is no possible way to make the man work while waiting for the three months to elapse. Usage goes even further; anyone who quits voluntarily can go into court and win his claim to the bonus by swearing he was so abused that he was forced to leave. The effect on discipline and, in the end, on wages paid, can easily be perceived.

We left San Márcos with the feeling that the situation was a muddle and that, while a great deal was being accomplished, more was being lost by lack of coördination. Such a law, for instance, as that petty theft should not be punishable if the offender could prove real need for the articles taken reflects a commendable sympathy with the man who is down and out but not good judgment in political science. We had hardly scratched social conditions in San Márcos, of course, though it was one of our old-time stamping grounds. As to real study of Mexico's problems, that was beyond our field and our resources, but at the same time we could not fail to see many mistakes and unnecessary crudities. Our combined impression, as we headed for Santa Rosalía and the big break in our trip, was that too much substance was being sacrificed for empty form.

CHAPTER XXXIII

SANTA ROSALÍA

SMOKE off the port bow, great clouds of grey spreading across the valley and half effacing the volcanic parapets, swooping down to the town and streaming up the coast, an oasis of industry in a desert of lassitude. Then the sea-wall, a massive bulwark of masonry that encloses a few acres of rectangular artificial harbor. Against the outer side lies the stripped skeleton of a multi-masted sailing ship. It is a German merchantman that was interned at the outbreak of the war and is now a scaffold for roosting shags and gulls and vultures.

The *Least Petrel* slipped through the doorway between piers of rock and came to anchor in the middle of a pond, the front yard of a town and the shipping point of a mine. The great tanker *Argyll* was pumping out her cargo of crude oil, food and drink for power-house and smelter, the steamer *La Providencia,* warped to the jetty, had just brought the touch of home from distant France, and a scow in tow of a tug was outward bound, to dump her refuse in the Gulf. Railroad tracks and sheds and cranes massed into a background of orderly confusion.

To the west lay Santa Rosalía. A lumber yard, the customs house, the end of a wide street running back into the town, and an interminably long machine-shop filled the water-front. A spindle wharf paralleled the shore at a distance of a few yards, and between lay interminable rowboats and the little passenger-ship from Guaymas. This was our introduction to one of the great copper mines of the world.

At Santa Rosalía there is no other industry. The Compagnie du Boleo has a jealously guarded concession and the energies of its people are limited to the one purpose of extracting metal from the hillsides.

We underwent the usual customs-house formalities while watching the scenes in the busy harbor. *La Peninsula,* not much larger than the *Least Petrel,* was anchored near us, discharging passengers and cargo from the mainland. The stone walls used by ocean-going ships were too high for her and the water by the landing wharf too shallow and so she was being unloaded with the aid of dories and scows. Baggage and freight were handled by a small army of *mozos.* Pitiable they were, wading into the water dressed only in overalls and shirt—tattered garments that freely betrayed the absence of underwear. Overworked when there was anything at all to do, they gave the impression of being starved in mind and of chronically not having enough to eat.

Walking toward the village we came to an open stretch several hundred yards across, flat, dusty, bare. Then to an incomplete foundation for a statue and afterwards to a small seldom-used school playground with slides and swings and parallel bars. Santa Rosalía, we now could see, lay on the level floor of a ravine. The buildings of the town spread a quarter of a mile, from one steep wall to the other. On either side, several hundred feet above the stream bottom, were mesas on which there were substantial additions to the town. Beyond, still higher, rose hills as steep as earth can lie, as inhospitable as nature can be, as torrid-looking and as nearly barren as is possible for land not actually sterilized.

We neared the first of the houses, a narrow one-story frame somewhat over a hundred feet long. Its shingle roof was extended two or three yards to form a shaded porch that gave the only relief from geometric harshness. The adjoining houses were identical, those on either side and those in the rear. In formal array of straight streets and alleys, intersecting, with one line and then another pinching out as the valley narrows, in orchard-like rows the buildings flooded indefinitely up the river-bed.

Some had been built with special walls to fit them for stores or offices, but for the most part they were the homes of miners, separated by cross partitions, each occupied by from four to six families. Their orderly progression was broken in the centre by a fenced-in plaza luxuriant with tall trees and with shrubbery that almost hid the bandstand. On one edge of the village was the school, on the other a church, a theatre, and the large company store. Facing the plaza was a two-story hotel—with a few such additions the warrens ran endlessly. Perhaps it is because only relatively young men can perform the work and only married men will that this settlement suggests so strongly a series of animal breeding pens. In each compartment—it seems as though there were no exceptions—is a male, a female, and a brood of young.

Santa Rosalía is the dirtiest, filthiest place I have ever seen. Thousands upon thousands of people huddle there without running water and without sewage. Water for domestic purposes is delivered from huge red bags swung upon burrows; the other is collected tri-weekly in open two wheeled carts. The stench of the place is nauseating, the death rate murderous, and disease so rampant that no careful man will as much as patronize a public barber. Mesquite in burning emits an odor almost indistinguishable from offal and, being virtually the only fuel, gives a finishing touch of horror.

On the southern mesa houses similar to those in the bottoms are occupied by quite a colony of the better paid Mexicans. The improvement in their surroundings well repays the long climb up the half perpendicular grade. There are among all the buildings none that are old. The highland addition is recent and in the valley are only replacements that have been constructed since a cloudburst, not many years ago, swept from the stream bed every vestige of man's handiwork. The northern plateau, however, dates back many years. It is the restricted headquarters of the French, the site of their offices and their homes. One American and half a dozen Mexican families—doctors and professional men— live there on sufferance. Even the Hotel Française is not open to the public; it demands an introduction as formal as a club card.

The French settlement is attractive, in a very simple way. The white and green company houses are generously spaced and no little effort has been made to force the rocky soil to support ornamental trees. In so far as local conditions permit a bit of France has been translated to these wastes. There is absent both the home atmosphere of England and the essential comforts of America which would have followed the Anglo-Saxon had it been he who had operated this immense and profitable mine for half a century. The frugality of France was a dominant note.

The Hotel Française, supported by the company and maintained only to care for visitors who have business or in whom it has an interest, is open neither to uncredited Mexicans nor to Americans. Little more than a boarded shack, without plumbing of any kind, it had four bedrooms upstairs and two large dining rooms on the ground floor. In charge was a voluble, excitable Basque, by a strange coincidence native of the very village from which Juan had come. He is one of the most interesting characters in Lower California. Could he be taught to do consciously before a camera what he does naturally when telling a story he would become famous on the screen.

An incident as simple as a passing automobile would be transformed by him into a drama so graphically expressed with hands and face and gesture that words became unnecessary. Any trifling event drove him to descriptive paroxysms. Hardly a meal did he serve that was not illuminated by his rapid-fire verbal pantomime. But he reached his climax in an apoplectic portrayal of the murder of Santa Rosalía's Chief of Police.

We came to the hotel two weeks after the event and Pancho was still boiling. Since his mate had formerly been the more or less temporary wife of the official, Pancho was step-father to two half-grown children and the personal element of the situation was very close to him. He could hardly await handshaking to unloose the torrent that took us to Santa Rosalía's underworld and the feud between the keepers of the up-town saloons and those of the restricted district. He showed us the living of the Chief of Police with the madam and the growing anger over unfair discrimination in the matter of liquor selling. He introduced us to the besotted husband of the brothel owner and he worked with the saloon-keepers on the emotions of the half-crazed moron until we could see them inciting and actually putting a revolver into the hands of the wastrel. Came the sneaking approach, the stealthy opening of a door, the cold-blooded shooting of a sleeping man, all pictured with such realism that we heard the vicious popping of the gun. An humble hotel-keeper is Pancho, but an artist of highest calibre.

The executive and technical heads of the Compagnie du Boleo are French. Intermarriage of the young European engineers with Mexicans cannot be prevented but, as far as possible, it is discouraged, for it is neither the wish of the staff nor the policy of the company that national identity be lost. With this end in view short annual vacations are not granted; they are replaced, at four or five year intervals, with long leaves accompanied by transportation to and from Paris. A studied social atmosphere is maintained; it finds expression on the tennis court, in horseback riding, and especially in formal Sunday picnics.

We were taken through the mines and the smelter, an interesting experience but in no way characteristic of Lower

California. On the other hand the relations between the officials of the company and those of the government and the laborers themselves constituted one of the most illuminating studies we made. The unskilled workmen, almost without exception, are Mexicans. They either do not like the work in the mine or are drifters by nature, for the hope of nearly all seems to be in some way to reach Mexicali and the United States.

Under these circumstances labor is one of the most serious problems with which the company has to contend. Lower California herself is of course hopelessly unable to supply man power in the needed numbers and the bulk of the replacements come from the west coast of the mainland. Recruiting agents work up and down that poverty-stricken region and ship across by the thousand men who certainly have no conception of what lies ahead of them. The result is a large proportion of mine hands who are sullen and dissatisfied.

The French acquisition of Santa Rosalía was a craftily planned political move and for that reason concessions have been granted which make the company immune from many of the petty annoyances inflicted on the gypsum miners of San Márcos. The Parisians, moreover, are not as hard to deal with as the typical American concessionaire demanding the last ounce of his pound of flesh. I do not pretend to understand the arrangement that has been arrived at between the company and the officials—such matters naturally are not a topic of general conversation—and I made no special effort to acquaint myself with the details, for they would be very changeable, but I do know that copper is mined in great amounts and that there is no surface friction. On the other hand the government is not a negligible shadow in the background. There is plenty of evidence that it is looking after its own interests and collecting every impost it can.

Into the threatened deadlock, not long ago, was thrown

a first class strike. The terms of settlement showed that the company was badly beaten. It retained its basis of payment by piece work but was compelled to grant to every laborer a guarantee of a minimum of two pesos and seventy-five centavos a day. An industrious man can make six pesos or more and a great many do. On the other hand there is an incredible proportion that lives on its two seventy-five— $1.20 in American money—and makes no pretense of earning that. Just another of those situations where no one profits, least of all the man who is getting something for nothing. The miners have so many just demands, there is so much that could be done to improve their status, mental and physical, that leadership which neglects substance for form and brings no real benefit is foolish almost to the point of wickedness.

Santa Rosalía mines copper over an area that spreads several miles on either side of town and consequently there have sprung up a number of branches and suburbs. The largest of these is La Providencia—more miles of wooden sheds and all the women of the town gathered about the first train in the morning to draw the day's supply of water from its tanks. There is Santa Agueda, a few miles up the cañon, where flowers are raised and fruit and vegetables. San Bruno is a dozen or two miles down the coast—it is the site of the company's farm, is called their country club, and is a favored spot for picnics and *paseos*. There are roads to Santa Agueda and Mulegé and San Ignacio. They cross cobblestone stream beds, they climb, mesa by mesa, a thousand feet or two, clinging to hillsides, and they stretch by the mile in narrow lanes where boulders and lava chunks have been piled in rows just far enough apart to allow a machine to pass. There are regions in Lower California more barren, more hostile, perhaps, and more difficult to explore, but no other point on the Peninsula equals the surroundings of Santa Rosalía in sheer, hopeless ugliness.

And of the people? With the laboring class we had our usual contacts only when we were going from house to house trying to buy cardinals. To some the birds meant nothing; to others they were household gods. One poor old soul epitomized a life drama with her refusal to sell. "My husband comes home for his siesta," she told us, gravely, "because he likes to listen to the singing of the bird. If it were not here he would come no more."

We rubbed shoulders with the miners and their families only in public, in the theatres, on the streets, and in the stores; we were so situated that we could contract no intimacies. We saw, on the whole, people somewhat more prosperous than those in the southern towns and there was evidence of a much larger proportion of the income being spent on clothing and on articles for the home. It was a never ending lesson to watch the shoppers in the company store. Often a hundred or more crowded at once beside the long counter—a much larger percentage of men than we would have had at home. Purchases were placed unwrapped in the big marketing baskets and were paid for in cash. Fresh vegetables were very cheap but were not freely bought—starches and meat comprised far too great a part of the diet of the people.

As would naturally be the case infant mortality in Santa Rosalía was heartsickening. The Partner protested and fought conditions with the local doctors. They freely admitted her criticisms, though I doubt if any of them had had any real training in baby hygiene, but one and all assured her that nothing could be done. These mothers raise their babies as they themselves were raised. The child is perpetually dirty and is forever exposed to disease, it eats more or less what and when it wants, or can, and as a result families of grown children are small in a Catholic country where birth control is not usual. If one of my friends loses her baby it is a tragedy—it should be. If a Mexican mother raises half of hers it is considered a blessing—I'd call it a miracle.

On one occasion or another we had spent quite a bit of time in Santa Rosalía, and largely in the French colony, it happened. Theirs is an exclusive little circle to which Americans are seldom admitted, partly for lack of interest on the part of the residents and partly because of the types that used to reach the mine. We had been fortunate from the start, being equipped with invaluable letters of introduction. The Partner's ability to contract friendships with any class of people with whom she is thrown was also a great help, and so we were absorbed into a culture fundamentally French but greatly modified by environment. We attended, and gave, social gatherings to which an invitation automatically included all the children, even to babies in arms. We learned to wait patiently for dinner guests who might be from one to three hours late because their excusing themselves to a chance caller simply could not be done. We tried to conform to their standards—I, at least, was very clumsy —and we learned to like them and to admire them. Never a complaint did I hear of hardship or loneliness—these people had come from a centre of high civilization to do certain work in the wilderness, and they were doing it well.

CHAPTER XXXIV

TORTUGA ISLAND

THERE were a number of details requiring attention in Santa Rosalía. For one thing Rogers was leaving. We had known from the outset that business would not permit him to finish the trip—in fact, he was already overdue in San Diego. It was, however, none the easier for us to see him go nor would we miss him the less because his departure was part of a prearranged schedule. A thorough gentleman, he had consistently contributed all he could to the pleasure and well-being of everyone aboard. Nothing more could be asked of a travelling companion.

We found the tanker *Argyll* on the point of sailing for San Pedro and her captain, an old-time friend, readily agreed to give Rogers passage. The *Argyll* had another mission to perform for us; we had practically exhausted our oil supply and she was to bring down twelve hundred gallons. It would take her eleven days to make the round trip; we had the alternative of awaiting her return or of running over to Guaymas to refuel. Originally we had planned to cross the Gulf but we received such contradictory reports regarding available supplies that in the end we declined to risk reaching Sonora with dry tanks which we might not be able to fill.

On San Márcos the company engineer told us definitely that no twenty-seven plus oil was to be had, while Garazar, the broker in Santa Rosalía, assured us we could buy all we wanted. The opinions of others, all of whom stated their beliefs as positive facts, were divided about half and half. This typical instance of the difficulty of obtaining reliable information exemplifies one of the principal annoyances of Gulf travel. We wanted to make every hour count and could do so only by planning far ahead and by dovetailing everywhere. Guesswork was not compatible with efficiency and yet we were hardly ever free from indecision; we found the utmost difficulty in being sure of even the simplest things.

No store seems to know what the next one carries, no community has accurate knowledge of itself, to say nothing of its neighbors. This in spite of the fact that mail and telegraphic communications are good and that there is a constant interchange of visitors. The causes of the confusion are many and go deep below the surface. The towns are far apart and over great areas there is almost no population, and so people are out of touch with each other. One complication that follows is the irregularity of commerce. Storekeepers are unreliable about replacing goods sold and their stock on hand is ordinarily so small that gaps constantly arise during the turnover.

Yet these little things do not account for the Mexican attitude. Fundamentally it is a matter of psychology, an absence of the fretting and hurry without which there cannot be the highest productivity. The poorer natives are fatalistic and take disappointments almost as matters of course. If their cantina has none of some desired article there is not the fussing that would cost an American merchant his trade. Instead is an apathetic resignation and a ready compliance with conditions. The people have not developed, either by training or through the power of example, appreciation of the value of exact knowledge or correct statement. They are easy-going and careless, they are apt to answer questions with courtesy or with the line of least resistance uppermost in their minds. Their intentions are good, and yet many an unpleasant experience follows a literal dependence on them for concrete facts.

The results of our enquiries was to keep us in a state of constant nervous tension. Certainty of what one can and cannot do may lead to many annoyances and disappointments, but at least it frees one from worry. Strain comes with forever having to make close decisions where one choice involves trouble or possibly danger and the other the abandonment of some really desirable undertaking. It requires time and patience to learn to reconcile one's self to conditions without, in the end, yielding to the lassitude of the country.

Though our supply was very low we were not entirely without fuel and so we planned to make a number of short excursions while awaiting the return of the *Argyll*. The first of these was to be to Tortuga Island. Conspicuous from the mesas of Santa Rosalía it lay stretched out twenty miles offshore, one of the most frequently seen and least visited islands in the Gulf. It was easy to catch the suggested turtle shape, the oval convex back and the extended head, that gave the island the name of Tortuga. The Turtle, about five miles by three, is comparatively low, its highest ridges barely reaching a thousand feet. It is a hard customer to tackle, for its sea-wall is virtually unbroken and its anchorages are poor and foul. Perhaps it is best known from being thoroughly infested with rattlesnakes.

The Partner remained in Santa Rosalía to visit friends made in former years. With Rogers also gone the *Least Petrel* seemed rather empty as she began her three-hour run. We plowed steadily through a rising sea with little or nothing to distract our attention until we were within less than a mile of the island. Then boobies began to come out to look us over. Singly, usually, they appeared on our bow, circled us two or three times, often within a hundred feet, and, their curiosity satisfied, returned to Tortuga. It is always interesting to watch them make their examinations; they stare with fixed intensity and keep their eyes steadfastly upon us as they go around and around. I wonder what reactions take place in their minds, what conclusions they draw, whether they regard us as living intruders or simply as another unaccountable manifestation of nature. It is noticeable that both breeding birds and last year's young share the interest.

Anchorage about Tortuga was especially difficult because we were riding a blow from the north and east. Such lee as there was we found on the southern end of the island and there we managed to land, leaving word with Captain to follow us if the wind shifted or went down. We were soon on top of the turtle's back in a country of gentle hills culminating in a long central ridge marked with cañons running at right angles on either side. On the western side the soil was soft underfoot—pure ash that held little vegetation. The eastern slope was more rocky and, for its greater part, was covered with cactus and brush. The feature of Tortuga is its sea-wall, high everywhere and along the southern sides mounting in palisades five and even seven hundred feet.

We made our way slowly, hunting for eggs and other specimens that might prove of interest. We felt the exhilaration that comes with easy walking on islands, the sense of adventure and the tense anticipation of surprise. For all we knew almost anything could be around the next corner. We noticed signs of rats and mice and later trapped some of the rodents, and we were intrigued by the little Black-throated Sparrows, which were here more numerous than any other land-birds we had seen on the trip. We found Duck Hawks and ravens nesting and we listed an unexpectedly large number of migrants. The snakes were our disappointment; we had hoped to collect a substantial series but were able to capture only three.

Tortuga is one of the outstanding breeding islands for

pelicans and boobies. The latter, especially the Blue-footed, have adopted the great southern wall. They have filled it to overflow, from tide-line to crest; every break, every ledge upon which they can lay, holds breeding birds. On the plateau above groups of left-overs, forced to accept less than their ideal, have crowded the edge, finding such comfort as they can in the proximity of the precipice below. The pelican colonies are far back from the water near the heads of the gorges on the eastern side. Inland, high on the slopes of the ridge, grow bushes large enough to hold nests. Here, in one cañon after another, the birds had congregated. They were wary, seldom allowing us to approach within a hundred yards. Flushed, their launching was awkward, their initial flight clumsy, but once in the air they were tireless in swinging circles about an intruder. Whenever our party became separated we could pick up the missing member by the revolving clouds of protesting pelicans.

Farther down the gullies the rocky bottoms had been preempted by colonies each consisting of a few dozen Blue-footed Boobies. As always, the gannets had scraped soft earth and had laid without further preparation. Some nests contained the usual complement of two chalky blue eggs —in a few there were three—others held naked black babies just hatched, ugly beyond words, sprawling and wriggling in protest at being left uncovered. More nearly matured young, able to stand or even walk, were heavily coated with a down that was long and immaculately white. Coal black legs and beaks and eyes gave them the appearance more of some toy-maker's art than of living creatures.

The walking on this eastern part of Tortuga was difficult. The ravine slopes, as we neared the water, became deeper and steeper and developed a covering of cracked stones and brush that increased in coarseness as the edge of the island was approached. Here Brewster Boobies and a few murrelets were nesting. The latter were not common but the former stretched intermittently for miles, choosing sites as close as possible to the precipitous sea-wall. We were beginning to understand their nesting psychology and could see that while ledges on insular cliffs were the first choice, the mentality of the bird did not draw a consistent distinction between the tops and the sides of precipices. The booby derived a degree of satisfaction, a sense of protection, from a near-by sea-wall even when there was no actual use and no direct gain in safety. The instinctive desire, easy to read, was the same for both races, with the all-important exception that the Brewster built a nest and the Blue-footed did not.

Every now and then, as we reached the crest of a ridge, the southern half of Tortuga spread in panorama. Through a swirl of circling birds we saw a sloping tableland with brush and cactus and sometimes a cardón. Brown and dusty, of course, and cut with cruel little arroyos. Yet it well fulfilled its mission in Nature's scheme of things, being sanctuary to an army of breeders that must be safe from prowling coyotes and cats and other vermin. It was one of the localities we had come to see; having looked upon it we were satisfied, even though it lacked the beauty of some of the other islands. It was vital, alive, accomplishing a purpose, and while it was of no direct value to man it was home to unnumbered mammals and birds and fishes.

My most interesting memory of Tortuga is of a pair of Duck Hawks on a mountain of sulphur. I flushed the male and, watching him, located the pothole in which I believed the eggs to be. Tony did some clever cliff work to edge his way around to the nesting cavity, only to find that the birds had not yet laid. So we amused ourselves studying the pinnacle. Well over a hundred feet was the sheer drop from the top to the waves at the foot, the face everywhere being lumpy and treacherous to the climber. It was sulphur in so nearly pure a state that when we held a match against the natural lumps we could make them burn. We actually set fire to the hill just to prove that it could be done and I have no doubt that the entire headland would have smouldered away had we been so wanton as not to have extinguished the blaze.

On our return to Santa Rosalía there awaited a message from the Partner telling us that she had gone on to San Ignacio and asking such of us as chose to do so to follow. I decided to go on the mail stage and to take Tony—the morale of the Easterners was ebbing so fast that a little break seemed wise. So it was arranged that, until the *Argyll* returned, they were to have the *Least Petrel* to use as they chose. There were, however, two one-day trips I wanted to take before we left. So I signed a lot of customs house papers and we set out for San Bruno.

It was a two hours' run along the coast in a fairly choppy sea. When we reached the company's little pier the waves were too high to permit our coming alongside but we had no difficulty in anchoring and in landing the dory on the beach. We crossed a quarter mile of dunes to reach a high one-story adobe that rambled into ells and wings under shade trees and palms. Alfalfa was the principal crop, milk and cheese the leading products. There were cornfields and orchards—all on a small scale—and there were many long rows of immense border trees that told of impressive age.

Birds were attracted in numbers to this garden spot— Vermilion Flycatchers, Hooded Orioles, Sparrow Hawks and Cactus Woodpeckers in glorious colors, and the more sombre Dwarf Cowbirds, Ground Doves and House Finches. There were a few wanderers migrating northward —Cooper Hawks, for instance, and Brewer Blackbirds. Where the desert came to the border of irrigated land mesquite and cactus were heavy and tall and were populated with San Lúcas Quail, Thrashers, Cactus Wren, Verdin, and a host of other desert dwellers. San Bruno was a very interesting and, to us, a profitable point of contact between truly arid life and birds that can profit by alfalfa fields.

Between San Bruno and Santa Rosalía lies a large mangrove-bordered lagoon. We did not land there partly because of the high sea and partly because, two years before, we had explored that region thoroughly. The little bay, known as San Lúcas, is formed by a narrow peninsula that extends several miles to the south. On the protected side is the fine white sand we had found in Concepción and along much of the border are mangroves. The most interesting of the birds were the Frazar Green Heron, the Mangrove Warbler, and the Belding Plover which, unlike its eastern counterpart, lays eggs with a pinkish tinge.

On the shore of San Lúcas Lagoon are two or three families living in huts under old palm trees. They are fisherfolk. They travel in an old dugout propelled by sail and paddle and probably keep a sharp lookout for a pearl oyster that may have escaped the general hunt. Once, in our canoe, we chanced to overhaul their heavy, clumsy craft, and what a surprise we gave them, the graceful thoroughbred racing a plow-horse. After we had drawn our canoe on the beach and were half a mile away they came over to where it lay and examined it, tested our paddles, even lifted it bodily to estimate its weight. Finding them still admiring it when we returned I invited them to launch it and give it a trial. Never have I seen children thrill so to a toy as did these simple people to our delicate craft.

The wide bench north of San Bruno includes and extends beyond San Lúcas cove, but long before we reach Santa Rosalía the hills have come back to the coast. There are a series of great arroyos cutting troughs hundreds of feet deep into the sides of the mesas. The greatest of these is Santa Agueda, a continuation of Santa Rosalía's cañon, which contains an oasis of no inconsiderable proportions. We persuaded Frank Davis to take off a day to drive us there. Our ostensible object was a duck shoot, though our enthusiasm was chiefly directed to collecting San Lúcas Black Phœbes and Goldman Yellow-throats and Brown Song Sparrows that haunt the fresh water.

Davis was the only American connected with the Compagnie du Boleo. His specialty is the diamond drill. He has prospected many square miles within the concession, running test-holes every few hundred yards to depths of nearly a thousand feet. He has been engaged in this work a good many years and has lived with his family at the Hotel Française so long as to have been absorbed into the French colony. He had done us many favors in the past and added one more to the list by leaving his crews to themselves and piling us into his light truck.

We drove directly inland, traversing the full length of Santa Rosalía to where the cañon narrows to a single street. On the outskirts we came to great flocks of buzzards and ravens, industrious and needed scavengers. Once out of town we climbed over a series of hills and ridges that really were as rocky and as barren as they had appeared from the boat. Their only avifauna seemed to be the lovely little verdins. After several miles of bumping over half buried cobbles we reached the beginnings of the irrigated tracts and from then until we arrived in Santa Agueda itself there were fields with flowers and vegetables, checkerboard patches that reached hungrily for all available soil.

The suburb consisted of a main street lined with a dozen houses and of scattered adobe huts in various stages of repair. Obviously the cloudburst that had swept away Santa Rosalía had not touched the pueblo. Its every aspect bespoke age. The cantina was just a bit larger than our experiences further south would have led us to expect, but otherwise was in every detail true to type. There was a suggestion of slightly more money here than in San Lúcas, for instance, a fleeting impression that came from the clothing worn and from items too trivial to affect the general atmosphere. Mud walls and thatched roofs and earthern floors, dusty streets and no shade, men and women and children and dogs and burros, no visible activity and no apparent suffering. We were in Mexico.

We drove two or three miles further to the fresh water pond where our hunt was to be held. We were successful in that we bagged a couple of dozen birds, mallards and blue-bills, shovellers and ruddies. Knowing fairly well what song-sters to look for and where to find them we had little diffi-culty in getting together the series we wanted. Having too good a time to leave we remained until it became so dark that we could no longer see our gun-sights. As Juan had probably gone to bed long before we reached Santa Rosalía we stayed in town for supper.

Hard as it is to believe, prohibition had been extended to include Santa Rosalía. No noble experiment here—the story we had, which may or may not be true, is that some visiting official close to the central government had become nettled at a saloon-keeper and had thereupon officially forbidden the sale of liquor throughout the municipality. The French refused to allow enforcement officers to come onto their mesa and so they were not affected, but down town the little round tables under the trees were gone. No more did the would-be boulevardiers sit beside foaming glasses to catch the flirting eyes of señoritas walking endlessly around the plaza. That always picturesque feature had ended. Driven from what had been a social institution we ate in a dirty back room where we were served with poor whiskey at double the old-time prices.

The liquor question at Santa Rosalía had become serious, for ourselves as well as for others. Gregory had reached the breaking point—his dread of the almost unknown coun-try to the north was driving him more and more to drink, which in turn was increasing the sickness that completed the vicious circle by adding to his fear. I fully expected that a collapse of some kind would come while we were in San Ignacio—he had already reached a state of intermittent drunkenness—and to tell the truth I had about ceased to care.

CHAPTER XXXV

TONY and I took our seats in the stage; it turned out to be one of the new Fords. As recently as 1928, when we last had been in San Ignacio, the mail was being brought in by burro-train, a three-day journey over winding mountain trails. The substitution of an automobile certainly was a mark of progress and for that reason worried us. We were afraid that San Ignacio, too, might have changed, might have lost her most priceless possessions, isolation and the absence of strangers.

I sat in front with the driver; the owner, Tony, and another passenger occupied the tonneau. The little machine was a realized dream to the mail carrier; it was a child of his hopes over which he hovered in constant guardianship. He had not learned to operate it and so it was necessary for him to hire a driver, but he made it a fixed rule to be present on every trip. A hundred times a year he took the tedious fifty-mile drive merely because he would trust no one with his car. The chauffeur, conscientious rather than skillful, piloted us with utmost care. Even on the shortest down grades he shut off ignition in the belief that he was saving gasolene.

We loaded ourselves and our baggage at the filling station in the plaza and after the usual and to be expected delays made our start. The final gesture was the buckling over the portly waist of the postman of a cartridge belt filled with lead bullets grimly exposed. There was no revolver, the heavy ornament merely serving as a badge of authority.

We crossed the village—of course there still remained errands requiring attention—and climbed the steep sides of the mesa. Our road ran beside a masonry retaining wall and unexpectedly passed over miniature railroad tracks and twisted until it brought us to the centre of the French colony. A broad avenue, though short, rough with half buried cobbles and ruts, faithfully sprinkled its full width, nominally shaded by stunted trees, it was bordered on either side by the white and green frame residences that stood, uncompromising, in their attempted gardens.

Past the Hotel Française, the shack whose wide verandas of unpainted and unfinished wood, offering relief from the sun, promised hospitality, and over a rickety bridge that spanned the great horizontal chimney, we came to a direction post, a conventional blue and white diamond officially signed by the "Auto Club of So. Cal." An arrow that pointed to Santa Rosalía, another that designated—what? It read San Ignacio, but did it mean just another village that had given itself over to catching stray tourist dollars or did it tell where lay what to us had always been and perhaps still remained the most enchanted spot in the world?

We slipped in between the buildings of the mine and came down to the shore. We followed the beach for several miles, crossing and recrossing the little railroad that brought ore from La Providencia. Almost without warning the road forked, we turned to the left and, leaving the level benches and the great river mouth, climbed abruptly to a height of six hundred feet. The added elevation brought no alleviation to the barrenness of the countryside. There were exceptions, of course, but the dominating character of the hills was loose rocks and dwarfed bushes that made no pretense of hiding sterility or nakedness. Below and above spread the baking sides and bottom of the furnace of the giants.

We ran along the crest of a ridge which narrowed until, in one place, there was barely width enough for the wheels

as on either side the almost perpendicular slopes fell to the
level of the sea. A mile farther came a drop on which no
two cars could hope to pass, where the excavated grade
fell abruptly to the largest river-bed we yet had seen. For
miles upstream we could follow the unbroken wave of grey
cobbles and boulders, an interminable level mass winding
among cliffs of inspiring splendor magnificent because of
sheer brutality of line and color. As we slid down and crossed
the well-named Cañon Inferno we realized that our first
attempt to scale La Giganta was just so much lost motion.

Then we started up, steadily, remorselessly, and climbed a
thousand feet before there came the first break in the steep
slant and the interminable curves. Past the pit mouths of the
mines, with the cobble bed falling ever farther and farther
below, with six or eight of the bends so sharp that only the
smallest of automobiles could take them without backing,
halfway to the top of the Sierra and still no respite from
heat or baking rocks. A splendid piece of engineering, this,
and a worthy tribute to Mexican technical skill and perseverance.

For several miles we drove across a rolling country, a
large twisting valley which we followed with frequent
detours over intervening ridges and hills. There was the
beginning of more vegetation, at first parallel bordering lines
of large mesquite on either side of dry stream beds, and
then patches of cholla, or stretches of mesquite mingled
with Palo Verde and Ironwood, and even white trunked
Palo Blanco in especially favored corners. To our right
rose the Tres Vírgenes, reaching the imposing height of
six thousand feet, their silhouettes showing through our
binoculars as a skyline of heavily massed Joshua trees. But
we were still hemmed with volcanic mountains and foothills.
Only on the valley floor itself did we escape the baking lava.

All too soon we arrived at the end of the plain. We found
ourselves again on a grade, steeper and more tortuous though

not quite so long as the one out of Cañon Inferno. Upwards steadily, and then we could see the pass two thousand feet above the sea, we reached the crest of Sierra de la Giganta and felt the wonderfully invigorating trade-wind blowing off the Pacific, a hundred miles away. Cooling and refreshing, it was our recompense for the hot, hard climb. In ten miles we had reached the summit and from then on could run downhill as far as we chose to go.

From Santa Rosalía to San Ignacio is fifty miles by road and in all that distance there are but two habitations. One lay behind us; it was a solitary hut in the valley. The other, still halfway to San Ignacio, consisted of three houses and was dignified with the name of La Esperanza. There was a windmill and a cement watering trough for the few cattle that could be supported by the mesquite and brush. We passed no other vehicles; only two make the trip with any regularity. There is the truck of Mindo and the stage which Para drives on the long grind from Tijuana to Santa Rosalía.

One cannot travel far from the mining centre along any road without encountering woodcutters' trains. These usually consist of from twenty to thirty burros in charge of a couple of men and a boy or two. All the equipment of the drovers is in plain view on the outgoing trains, a water keg, an axe, food, and blankets. A casual inventory makes one wonder, for surely, where there are no resources, people cannot camp with so little. Nevertheless they do, and they travel long distances to reach mesquite growths thick enough for their purposes. Santa Rosalía has already consumed the near-by thickets and all of the wood that is to be obtained easily, and has burned the clumps that once covered the scattered fertile spots. Now there remain long and tedious trips to surviving growths, yet hundreds of men continually toil and swelter to reach them.

Inward bound every burro carries a bundle of firewood

strapped on either side, his flanks protected by rawhides and padding. On top are distributed the camp gear, of little bulk by now and of almost no weight. The drovers trudge wearily, mile after mile, driving their unbridled donkeys and controlling them by gesture and voice. "Burro! burro!" is the shout of command, the second syllable long drawn out and accented to indicate meaning. "Ssh! ssh! ssh!" soft and sibilant and becoming progressively less audible is the order to halt, and a generous and hurried shoving is the common system of clearing the animals from the road when an automobile approaches.

The donkeys of their own accord step back onto the highway when the car has passed and resume the endless trudge, the drovers in the rear. Five centavos a stick does this wood bring in Santa Rosalía and seldom is money more onerously earned. The most pathetic of the pictures I have carried home from Lower California are of the trains of wood-laden burros, the starving and half dead animals that day after day slowly step off interminable miles and are followed by old men or young, often by fathers with sons that are still children. A sorry ensemble of discouragement.

We rode for hours through a country that, to the tourist, is empty, that to us, when in our own car, had held not a dozen people, but to which the amiable mail carrier was a veritable Pied Piper. As though by magic, at his approach figures appeared from the open desert, from the crossings of trails, or from the shades of cardónes. There were messages to be given, packages to be gathered or delivered, the news of the countryside to be exchanged. Great was the change from mail on burro-back to sacks in the tonneau of a Ford, but the minstrel of the desert who formerly had trudged from camp to hut, whose regular arrival once had been the goal and event of the week, whose coming had meant unsaddling, rest, and hospitality, today rode unchanged in his little automobile.

Tony and I learned quickly not to wait out the colloquies, but instead to walk down the road, searching the bushes for nests and specimens. Most frequently we found the homes of San Lúcas Cactus Wrens and Verdins, two unrelated races of birds that place their nests conspicuously in unprotected sites, frequently on the top of cholla. They obtain safety for eggs and young by weaving grass stalks into globular retorts with openings barely large enough to permit their own egress and exit. The normal clutch of Verdin eggs consists either of two or of three, as compared with double that number in the northern extension of the range. The wren practically never lays more than two, although in California four is normal and five not at all unusual.

Small clutches are universal among the birds of the desert portion of the Peninsula. There is a very widespread misapprehension as to the cause of this condition in that the reason generally assigned is limited food supply. It is the accepted belief that mothers lay few eggs because the parents cannot find enough nourishment to sustain any but the smallest of families. We saw in San Bartolomé Bay that starvation determines the number of birds and we know that, however fertile a region may be, the total of individuals of a species to be found within it will be the saturation point, the number which can obtain a living there.

It so happens that in places more favored by nature than San Ignacio there is a normally wide variation between the supply of food available during the breeding months and that to be had in the fall and winter. Where the spring increase is great large families are the rule; where the amount is constant parents are unable to feed many extra mouths. This, obviously, is true regardless of the total number of birds or the total amount of food. It is the ratio between the two factors, not the actual totals of either, that determines the size of broods. There are many races of birds that habitually lay two eggs under all conditions—certain genera of doves, for instance, and humming birds, vultures, nighthawks and poor wills. They do not weaken the explanation, however, but merely prove that sometimes heredity is paramount to environment. There is no question but that the average of small sets throughout the deserts of Lower California is due entirely to the fixity of food supply.

Time slipped by with disconcerting speed. It seemed as though Tony and I could hardly leave the car before we would hear the honk of the horn, though in reality the wayside conferences seldom lasted less than half an hour. We followed a shallow cañon and debouched onto a wide mesa covered with Elephant Trees. These peculiar growths are fitted for desert survival by the abnormal development of their root systems. A not unusual tree was six to ten feet high, with dark brown branches of fairly slender type, devoid of leaves and supporting only tiny buds. The twigs were long and thin, were more closely interwoven than those of an apple or a peach, and gave the bare plant something of a bushy effect.

If the main stem, usually but a few inches in diameter, is followed to the ground it will be found to join monster roots that suggest an elephant's trunk and have given the tree its name. Gnarled and rough, perhaps partly exposed, is a series of feeders that may reach a three-foot circumference, abnormalities whose coarseness enables them to extract a last vestige of moisture from soil that is theoretically desiccated. Near the top of the grade we found a forest of several thousand acres. This is not an altogether typical condition, for the trees often occur singly, sometimes most unexpectedly in crevices in rocks.

We kept working down the watershed and soon came to the lava mesas. These tablelands have the appearance of having once been covered with a three-foot blanket of red molten rock which has cooled and cracked into rough squares.

THE ROAD TO SAN IGNACIO

It seems but yesterday that the sheet was intact, for no soil has accumulated between the fragments. The broken edges are still so sharp that they can visually be fitted together again at the point of fracture. The coating formed by these great pieces runs up and down cañons and hillsides. It follows the contour of the countryside everywhere excepting in the valleys, which appear to have been scoured by intermittent cloudbursts. Perhaps to three-fourths of the area from the crest of the sierra to the edge of the coastal plains does this rocky covering give the touch of an earthly hell.

It is not wholly sterile, for between the boulders cardón and chaparral, cholla and mesquite, here and there, have managed to secure a foothold and to survive. The plants are not sufficiently numerous to relieve the monotonous nakedness of the brick-field and we were glad that our road avoided most of the uplands and followed the watercourses where life was more abundant and scenery more interesting. Thirty miles from Santa Rosalía we entered the largest plain we yet had seen. A broad cobbled stream bed was flanked widely on either side by sandy or even silty bottoms that yielded to the foot and only were half touched with desert growths. Ten miles farther we climbed onto a ridge covered with cracked rocks, we descended a narrow arroyo, we crossed a mesa of cinder splinters, and suddenly San Ignacio lay at our feet.

Down in the bottom of the river-bed, enclosed by walls of a hundred feet or more that rose to clinker strewn levels, hidden under a blanketing forest of palms through which appeared only the dome of the mission, extending to a small tule bordered lake on one side and encircled by infinite desert—this was our first view of the oasis. We passed an embankment thrown up to guard against possible cloudbursts. Beyond and over it we saw a typical arroyo, but at the base were half a dozen houses—the outpost of the "Otro Lado" of the pueblo. A few minutes more a stream appeared upon our right, and then a dozen houses on the hillside. We turned abruptly to the left, crossed the dam that made the reservoir, and buried ourselves deep in a tropical forest.

The first impressions were of river-bed vineyards on one side, a jungle of palms on the other, interlocking leaves overhead and a sandy road beneath our feet. Fences guarded the narrow lane, pickets of palm stalks or piles of boulders or even barbed wire, while here and there through the sheltering leaves came glimpses of huts of adobe staggering under thatched roofs. A by-road led into ours, another came where we forded the creek, a trellised vineyard appeared through the trees, the jungle was cleft by a narrow strip between two rows of imposing date and fan palms, we turned a last corner, and were actually in the village.

We followed the main street for two blocks and came to the home of Señora Leree, where we were welcomed with cordiality by everyone, including the Partner. We passed the guarded gate to enter a patio which has never ceased to bring to my mind the inspired description of Mohammed's paradise. In a neatly built ditch ran a small stream of water coming from under the wall and disappearing into a vineyard carried overhead on palm beams. Figs and pomegranates and potted plants made a garden as naïve as it was unconventional. Along the street side was a building one story high and one room wide. In this were to be our living quarters.

Across the sixty-foot patio, which was surrounded by tall walls of adobe, was an out-of-doors stove protected by an ambitious *ramada*. In the centre was a well, on the farther side were Señora Leree's adobe and a cane house in which her sister lived. The walls extended beyond these buildings to enclose what we would call a backyard. In it were kept a goat, a pig, a cow and calf, and sheds containing an assortment of various odds and ends accounted for the neatness of the patio itself. In the far corner were a

A STREET IN MULEGÉ

THE RABBIT WARRENS OF SANTA ROSALÍA

BLUE-FOOTED BOOBIES ON TORTUGA

huge oven and a latrine fringed with cane. How tired I did get kicking out that darned calf.

We were glad enough to go into our own room, to wash and rest. The building was a twenty by fifty foot rectangle of plain but well-made adobe bricks carried to a height of ten feet and pierced by a number of doors and windows. An unceiled gable roof with beams exposed, an outer layer of palm leaves geometrically arranged, like shingles, and a partition in the centre that rose only to the tops of the wall, completed the building. It was Señora Leree's abode when there were no visitors and here, as everywhere, she left the impression of her personality. Immaculately clean, open and airy, host by night to bats and by day to that sweetest of singers, the Cañon Wren, this was, of all spots in Mexico, most nearly our home.

In the evening we sauntered over to the Chinaman's for some of the native date brandy. His romance was the laughing stock of San Ignacio, for he had picked up in Santa Rosalía a woman from Mazatlan and had brought her to his home. For two months he had given everything he could to this sophisticated product of the cities who was making her way, as best she might, northwards to the border. One fine day the opportunity presented itself to accompany a traveller to Tijuana and, without so much as a word of good-by, she was gone. The Chinaman, poor soul, went into paroxysms of anger. He threw into the street everything left by her and, knowing we were interested in cardinals, brought us all her birds and sold them for practically nothing. Later he must have cooled off a bit, for he repented of his bargain and tried to get more money from us.

His cantina could not have been less than two hundred years old, for it had the thick walls of mission days and a counter of hand-hewn mesquite. The floor was of earth and the room dark and dingy. The only liquors he sold were home products, brandy from dates and wine from local grapes. Even so his stock was negligible; beer, soft drinks, and ice were items he never carried.

We were glad to step out into the evening, walk around the plaza, and return to our quarters. We pulled chairs to the grilles that served as front doors and soon lapsed into silence, watching and listening to a corner of our dream village. Slowly there stole over me the feeling that the scene upon which we were looking was an illusion, that nothing could seem so theatrical and yet be real. The opposite wall was near, the diagonal street was narrow, the toy stage of the puppets was blocked by Stygian darkness and illuminated with light that was spontaneous. Walls, doorways, corners, framed in black, were resplendent in a gleaming yellow glow free from the shimmering beams of white that tremble in daytime heat waves. Moonlight. No tints, no tones of color. No shaded borders. It was the full of the moon, the desert moon of the southland.

Overhead a balcony resting on an ebon rectangle, a serape across its rail and flower pots under its ceiling. Underfoot a dusty road streaked with ruts and edged with a yard-wide footpath, raised. On one side silhouetted trees and a straight line that glistened above the invisible frame of lighted doorways and windows. The other wall was unadorned adobe, a livid sheet of tan that disappeared at either end into a void. Out of the night not a murmur of air, only a gentle laugh or a whispered voice, and then there floated the stringed notes of Rancho Grande.

Across the lunar stage, slipping without gesture out of one shadow and into another, passed a figure, a long-skirted wide-hipped old woman with the carriage of a dragoon under a mantilla that draped from crown to waist. The spotlight shone empty one dramatic moment, then, coming unheralded and leaving without pause, walked two white-shirted men, girdled with sashes and crowned with high-peaked wide-brimmed sombreros of straw. They pass a child, a girl with the fringe of the black scarf of her sex meeting the hem of her knee-length frock. By one's or two's or three's other figures intermittently parade this bandbox of an arena which is a living pueblo.

It is San Ignacio, the Partner's pride and pet. She is the first American woman who has ever stopped here, so the natives tell her, and the only one ever to have visited. It is her village, to be praised whenever Mexico is mentioned, to be included when any trip is planned, to be dangled when coaxing is needed. It is the lodestone that drew the *Least Petrel* on its flight, and the Partner had brought no unwilling escorts to her Eden. She and I, with Tony, had been here before, had remained an entire spring, and all that any of us hoped for now was to find the unspoiled jewel we had left.

CHAPTER XXXVI

MISIÓN SAN IGNACIO

SUNDAY morning, and we were on a vacation. So without even a thought of getting up, we lay abed until well past eight o'clock. The Partner then supervised for each the cooking of his favorite breakfast, struggling to keep the dishes simple and the seasoning reasonable. Señora Leree brought from her own oven a basket of delicious bread and in return we could not do less than help swell the congregation at her early services. A few minutes before nine found us on our way to church.

We turned to the left for half a block to come out onto the plaza. About an acre had been fenced and given over to flowering plants, but the garden had not been very successful. It was venerable rather than flourishing and its open character, its lack of a bandstand, marked it as of unusual type. The practical feature was the comparatively wide cement walk, curbed and checkered in modern style, which surrounded it on four sides. This sidewalk was the attraction of the plaza, for on it gathered the young people of the village to promenade when the heat of the day was past. Men and women did not indulge in the pairings of an American crowd. The custom was for the girls to walk continuously in groups of two or three while the men were apt to be gathered in little knots by themselves, content to await reappearance on the next lap and to exchange provocative smiles.

Across the street and directly facing the plaza stood the Misión San Ignacio de Kadakaman. It was founded by

Padre Juan Bautista Luyando in 1728. That date is fifty years later than Loreto's, and forty-one earlier than the beginning of the first mission in Alta California. The figures represent more than nearly equal intervals of time; they separate epochs in the history of mission building.

The Padres learned the possible uses to which they could put adobe bricks at the very time that their resources were shrinking, and so, it being the only means by which they could satisfy their desire to expand, they developed the type of architecture familiar to those who have visited or studied the famous series of ruins along California's coast. Northward the governing motif is a semicircular arch supported on pillars—the arches always plain, the severity of the supports usually broken by caps. This construction particularly invited long narrow wings the width of a single room, fully or partially enclosed patios, and sweeping roofs that spread over shaded porticos, but it was also used for high vaulted chapels and other tall chambers.

In contrast with the later missions those of the early eighteenth century were great masonry edifices conceived in Spain and developed in Lower California into churches as nearly as possible in keeping with the traditions of the Society of Jesus. The one we looked upon is today the best preserved and the most pretentious in either of the Californias. It has been smiled upon by nature and favored by queens, its fate has been the least tragic of all its confrères, and a full half of its treasures are still within its walls. Since its construction there has not passed an interval during which it has not exerted a spiritual influence upon the people it overlooks.

Seen from the plaza it is a rectangle approximately ninety feet wide by eighty high, disregarding the tower and the finials. The walls are of masonry, large stones cut with precision, laid in mortar, and covered with plaster. The coating has weathered in places, especially in the upper portions, and in falling has partially exposed the labored work of its builders. Primitive tools, unskilled and unwilling hands—one cannot but marvel at the determination which drove it to completion.

A ground floor level is reached by a stone stairway leading to a generously large flagged terrace. The offset formed by the stairs is railed with a picket fence, the enclosure being filled with coarse garden bushes. The design of the front of the mission is of two sections superimposed upon each other. A series of six pilasters rises to an ambitious cornice and continues in design with a second very similar section. The façade is pierced by four bulls-eye windows with splayed jams showing the thickness of the walls, and there also is a rectangular upper-story window and four niches holding life-sized statues.

There is not much blank space on the façade, for ornamental trimmings have been added everywhere. At the time it was built the mission was surprisingly up to date, being an excellent example of the late Plateresque. The ornamentation between the finials apparently was a bit too extreme and probably about three horizontal feet of it have succumbed to time and have fallen. The tower, crowned by a bell-shaped roof and decorated with small finials and a cross, is not entirely appropriate. The main finials, too, while typical of the time miss being in complete harmony.

From a technical point of view there are faults to be found with the architecture, though the marvel is that they are so few. There is to be read, from the outlines of the structure, much of the history of its inspiration. It is not difficult to appreciate what the Padres had attempted to do nor to understand why they had partially failed. For one thing their plans were drawings on so small a scale that many details perforce were added from memory or in accordance with individual ideas. It is quite one thing to build in an atmosphere of artisans and artists and another to bring into being a complicated edifice in the heart of a desert.

The sequences of the influences that govern the architecture can best be traced by studying the façade. I have often come across the statement that in San Ignacio there survive Moorish tendencies, but a careful study fails to reveal any antecedents not purely European. From the Low Countries and from Italy the types can be traced to Spain and then directly to the City of Mexico and into Lower California.

To enter the church the lower half of the wooden doorways are swung in, with much creaking and groaning. They are a work of art, brought either from the City of Mexico or from Spain itself. Ponderous and deeply carved, fifteen feet to the top of the arch and nearly half as wide, the long wooden uprights and the massive panels have been very kindly dealt with by time. A touch of classical days remains in the Ionic imposts and the elaborate connecting arch.

A pause at the threshold to allow the eye to accustom itself to the change from outdoor glare to dim interior, and there comes the realization that the chapel and its fittings are free from the architectural defects of the exterior. Simple in outline and shaped like a cross the chamber, though only twenty-five feet wide, is five times that length and rises sixty feet to a series of spanning arches separating flattened vaults. The massed effect is harmony and great dignity and inspires reverence in those who enter.

Three panels first arrest attention. Two are at the ends of the wings, the other directly behind the altar, and each contains either seven or nine paintings dealing with the life of Christ, the crucifixion, and other religious subjects. Of the paintings two or three are modern—clearly replacements—but all the others are contemporaneous with or antecedent to the building of the mission. How easily could some gem, some unknown work of a master, lie neglected among

the twenty-odd pictures framed in the elaborately carved
wooden settings of the grey walls of San Ignacio.

Stone stairs lead to the choir and to the pulpit; banisters
are of carved wood in keeping with the altar rail. Other
stone stairs rise to the tower in which still hang the famous
bronze mission bells, cast in Spain it is said, by order of
the king, and which for two full centuries have filled the
valley with sweetly imperious peals. Neither pains nor
expense were spared to make this mission worthy; not even
has the use of gold been stinted. The panels that hold the
pictures are inlaid with it and are in a wonderful state of
preservation, and the chalice box, lined with the same metal,
is entirely intact.

A small cup of solid gold is in the mission, as are a few
tatters of the once gorgeous vestments. The ponderous silver
candlesticks are gone, however, and all but the one vessel
of precious metal. Fifteen or twenty years ago some horse-
men appeared in the village, declared that they had been sent
from the City of Mexico, and demanded, for the Museo
Nacional, all the mission relics. Were these men looters, stealing, or were they honest emissaries? No one in San Ignacio
knows—the people were helpless to protest and still mourn
the loss of their treasures.

The Mission grounds are liberal, apparently not having
been encroached upon, and are even today devoted to communal uses. In one of the wings school is kept, in the rear
is an orchard, and on the sides is reserved land onto which,
judging from the design of the façade, there originally were
intentions, or hopes, of extending the building in both directions. Services are held regularly on Sundays and Holy Days
—no mass by a priest, but prayers by the congregation itself,
led by Señora Leree.

Those who entered and actively took part in worship
were, almost without exception, women and girls. The men
who had accompanied their families usually remained just

outside the doorway, respectfully standing with heads uncovered, some indifferent, some following the ceremony intently. It was interesting to watch the paradox of men professing utter indifference and yet at no time approaching or even passing the doorway without some betrayal of reverence.

We all shared the impression, an intangible feeling we would be hard put to to prove, that the people of San Ignacio were more spiritual than others in Lower California, and we attributed their attitude to the shadow of the mission. Sundays seemed to have more meaning, both to those who went to church and to those who limited themselves to recreation. All morning long there reigned an atmosphere of rest and quiet with everyone wearing his best. For the men a fresh brightly colored shirt without coat or necktie was the rule. Vaqueros from the campo were in evidence, their costumes reminding us, though in greater degree, of Dolores Bay. There were families in groups, with the sexes usually separated, coming in from the outskirts in gala array. Music and quiet laughter and above all peace while the bells tolled and the long shadow drifted slowly from west to north. Afternoon and the spell was gone, drinking and carousing began; by that time Sunday had become nothing more than a day of relaxation.

The women were dressed according to their means. Almost alone Señora Mindo affected silk, either purchased by herself when she travelled to Tijuana with Para or sent to her by a mail order house in the States. Even the poorest seemed to have contrived to buy one of the half dozen patterns of cheap cotton goods that Mindo carried in stock. The older women wore black, sometimes relieved with white designs. The girls showed a preference for figured dimity or muslin in bright colors. Once upon a time we had met an itinerant peddler—an Italian—who sold men's shirts and trousers and a very inferior grade of dress length silks at prices two or three times those at home. Evidences of his salesmanship cropped out every Sunday in the mission, on the plaza, or upon the dusty streets.

Mantillas, always common, were universal on Holy Days. Even the smallest girls, usually in white muslin, wore long strips of cloth over their heads whenever they were out of doors or in the mission. The aftermath of church, of the singing of hymns and the saying of rosaries, carried through the week. There was hardly a corner of the pueblo from which the mission tower could not be seen, there was in the village no complete forgetfulness of God and his works, and the noble building, defying time and decay, is still a living inspiration to the people among whom it stands. In San Ignacio the shadows of the past are not wholly ephemeral.

CHAPTER XXXVII

SAN IGNACIO

It is a village of contrasts. Even its site is an anomaly. To the approaching traveller, until he actually finds himself overlooking a forest of palms, there is no premonition of the existence of the pueblo, no suggestion that within the horizon could there be anything to relieve the seared and desiccated landscape. Then, at his feet, filling the valley from side to side, nestling between high mesas of cracked lava rocks, he sees a jungle. It is sharply delimited in area, touching, but not encroaching upon, the flanking desert, and terminating at either end in the dry river-bed. To the east are boulders in a formation resembling glacial deposits, heavily overgrown with brush and mesquite and palo verde. To the west runs a series of shallow rock-bottomed ponds that are, in turn, reabsorbed into endless miles of gravel. One may enter or leave the oasis indefinitely and yet never lose the feeling of the suddenness of its coming or going.

The contrast is equally strong in the buildings; a masonry mission and homes of bamboo stalks. Between these extremes are adobes ranging from the most dilapidated to establishments as ambitious as that of Li Mindo. Diagonally across the street from our house stands the two-story building to which has been given a continental touch by the adding of a balcony porch. It overhangs the street, it has an unobstructed view in three directions, and is quite the pride of his establishment. The front of the ground floor is occupied by his *almacén,* a stereotyped Mexican store larger than one would expect to find in a village the size of San Ignacio. Yet along

299

one of its sides runs a combined orchard and garden and vineyard, cool and shady and trellised. The aspect is picturesque to the last detail, even to the toy fence and the cane gate that leads a little path into the street. A mystic opening, a ray that lights the outlines of the rear of houses, exposes the outdoor aspects of domesticity and reveals living people of two centuries ago.

Always contrasts. Above Mindo's the roadway is irregular and soon breaks against huts no two of which are alike. It dwindles into trails and blind leads at the foot of the hill upon whose almost unclimbable slopes a tier or two of huts have been splashed from the valley floor. Along one side runs the formidable wall of Señora Leree's enclosure, reaching to outskirts that are all the word implies. Yet the other end of that wall touches the block which represents the centre of town, the main street of business and concentration.

Again we come to Li Mindo. His patio is paved with cement and it is there that dances are held and, when not on the road, his truck is kept. The car is modern, of a heavy commercial type, and makes frequent trips to Santa Rosalía. I have not been able to learn the details of his transactions with his customers; I know only that all surplus produce, in being sold to the miners of the Compagnie du Boleo, passes through his hands. Mindo grows prosperous, gardeners remain poor, and I surmise that the old railroad barons knew few tricks they could have taught to this wily Chinaman.

As a storekeeper his methods were not so modern. He himself seldom appeared behind the counter, leaving the actual clerking to a native whom we promptly nicknamed "No Hay." She was without doubt the poorest salesman I have ever met; there was a directness and a finality about her methods that challenges comparison. Either she had the article wanted, in which case she put it on the counter, or else it was not in stock, and we heard the uncompromising "no hay." Never did she suggest a substitution or an importation by truck or stage; she was friendly enough but it seemed as though we could seldom half frame a request before there came the interruption: "no hay." I admit that we were often disgruntled by No Hay, that she ended too abruptly our attempts to buy, but after all she was an institution and part of the unspoiled environment.

What might be termed the business section, the long block that included Mindo's and ran to the street which the mission faced, was also a series of contrasts. Next door to the Chinaman's the pool-hall was located, a well patronized but rather incongruous institution, and beyond was the meat market, a combination of butcher-shop and family home. Across the narrow street a quadrangle, enclosed by four adobe walls, ran through to the plaza. In the community patio so formed was a lovely garden whose old olive and fig and palm trees rose high against the skyline. They intrigued with their age and their disregard for the passing of time and told of flowers and blossoms and beauties that had been lost.

The long wall was pierced by frequent doorways of which as many opened into occupied homes as into stores. Near one end of this block was a cantina, that of the romantic Chinaman, and at the diagonal corner another, that of a Mexican saloon-keeper. Sandwiched in between the residences were a number of shops—a barber, a grocer, and several places where were made and sold little articles as opportunity offered.

The central location did not drive away those whose homes stood wall to wall with saloons or with the barber shop incessantly filled with a group of gossiping idlers. The thick walls and the custom which relegated inmates to the rear of dwellings cut off the noise of arriving pack-trains by day and of singing and carousal by night. Conversely commer-

cialism strayed into what with us would be purely residential
sections. On the street on which the mission stood, half a
block away, was the rambling adobe that gave hotel service
of a sort to Para's passengers. Across the plaza, running
towards and up the cañon, were several blocks half filled
with grey huts, but among them was a Chinese grocery,
the telephone and postoffice, and two or three nondescripts
which might be considered either as homes or stores. Not
peculiar to San Ignacio, these contrasts, but nowhere else
quite so strongly emphasized.

The section which might be termed the built-up portion
is but a small part of the village. The pueblos we had visited earlier on our trip had impressed us by being very compact; they were characterized by a sharp demarcation
between town and desert. To a large extent that condition
was due to the scarcity of water, though many other causes
contributed to the desire of the people to be close to each
other. San Ignacio is an extreme example of the opposite
type. Houses are scattered for a couple of miles wherever
water can be brought to tillable land. Hidden under palms
or exposed upon hillsides the scattered village, its houses
well apart, includes the entire grove and extends, in every
direction, a little beyond the edges.

From the reservoir meander three arterial ditches carrying streams of water to tiny farms. The oldest flume, probably the one built and used by the Padres, skirts the foot of
the hills to the south. On either side, along the greater part
of its length, grow immense date palms whose leaves, inter-
weaving near the top, arch to form a tunnel for the passage
of water. A footpath jumps from side to side or deploys
around giant stumps as it winds its way for a couple of miles
under a sylvan vault, cool and refreshing. Halfway to its
source the stream begins to run under a series of abutting
figs which, growing less densely than the palms, expose a
series of small but well cared-for vineyards. For the last half

mile the ditch, lying under an inhospitable mountainside, works its way among brush and boulders—at one spot it is even tunnelled.

The central flow starts at the dam and follows the natural course of the river. Beginning in a willow thicket, the home of goldfinches and chats and Brown Song Sparrows, it soon enters virtually impenetrable stands of sugar cane and bamboo. Its wanderings often lead it across sterile fields of boulders, but even so, little of its water is lost. At irregular intervals diverting trenches run to truck gardens, to fig and pomegranate and olive orchards, and especially to one of the numerous neat little vineyards. The water spreads, sometimes at random, sometimes under careful handling, to fields and to the palm jungle, it gathers itself together in tule patches, haunts of the Goldman Yellow-throat, and it finally comes to an end in a series of shallow rock-bottomed pools far below the village.

The third branch traces the northern edge of the valley and separates the small colony of houses distinguished from the village proper by the appellation "Otro Lada." There are a dozen or more adobes in ragged formation on a bench above the valley bed, with a road of their own twice crossing the stream and winding in and out among the cholla. Apparently some of the larger mesquites have been spared because of the shade they give to an otherwise unsheltered settlement. There is little or no correlation, no conscious effort to connect the sites of the huts with the comfort that comes with protection, and not the slightest effort is made to plant ornamental trees to relieve the glare of the half tropic sun and bring a measure of comfort to the heat-ridden people.

Below the running water lies a continuation of jungle and also of cleared fields given over to grapes and onions, peppers and tomatoes. Scattered throughout the forest, covered and hidden by its tall and luxuriant growths, are huts of adobe or of simple cane, roofed with palm leaves that usually extend into *ramadas*. It is very noticeable that while the houses in the more thickly built-up sections are urban in character those that are detached, that are the centres of little homesteads, retain the primitive characteristics of rancherias.

The enduring charm of San Ignacio is to be found, not in a diagrammatic catalogue of its components, but in the spirit of its people. I am homeward bound from a day afield and come to a little half isolated hut of cane. It has no door, but across the entrance is strung a piece of fibrous rope—as purposeful and as effective as the portals of a bank vault. I peer inside to find a single room, almost bare, and yet its earthern floor is swept clean, its few furnishings are neatly placed where they belong. Because I am in San Ignacio I know I have seen more than a primitive abode; I can picture a family of real intelligence calling this its home.

They will be people who have never possessed nor yet who have never felt want. They will be kindly to each other and to their neighbors, for they will not have been embittered by disappointments nor exhausted by striving. They will have neither appreciable knowledge of nor interest in the outside world, and will yet be tolerant to an extent that passes understanding. They will be content and happy, with all their simple lives, for they will be doing as their neighbors are doing and fulfilling their destinies as did the grandparents of their grandparents.

By this I do not mean that all individuality will have been lost. Many who were born and raised here have been too ambitious to remain, have drifted to Mexicali or Tijuana or California. A few fish half the year in Port San Bartolomé and farm at home the other six months. Others dig copper on the coast, but that work is too repugnant for most to endure for any length of time. There are some who, after testing the life of the great cities, have been unhappy and have returned. None of those who left had taken San Ignacio

SAN IGNACIO

MISIÓN SAN IGNACIO DE KADAKAMAN

SEÑORA LEREE AND HER GRANDDAUGHTER

with them; they had to meet and adjust themselves to uncontrollable new conditions. And none of those who had come back had brought anything from their exiles. Every habit or thought that may have been acquired in other communities was dropped and forgotten when the palm jungle was reëntered.

To look back upon San Ignacio is to think of music—music and moonlight. Stringed instruments and song and dance. The spirit of the living and of six generations of their forefathers became to us, in time, the customary sounds of the night. Scarcely ever was it wholly stilled, after the day's work was done. From next door or from far-away homes among the palms would come the notes of single players or of vocalists, or of groups combined, untrained but expressive of national love and talent for music.

There was a four piece orchestra of two violins and two guitars which was greatly in demand. It was perhaps most frequently employed by some gay young buck who had come in from a distant rancheria to hold a celebration. He may have sold a steer or two or have had some other stroke of good luck, or possibly may have saved his pittance of wages for one grand night. There would be drinking, sometimes to excess, and there would be many visits to pay, but the dominating note always was music. They sang, these happy carefree peons, to the accompaniment of the band, they laughed and they listened to its airs, and they drank till their pockets were empty. After that, well, what is money for except to be spent?

Many were the uses to which that orchestra was put. A few convivial souls, and music was wanted; no gathering was complete without stringed harmony. A beau did not send flowers or buy opera tickets; instead he hired musicians to serenade the object of his regard. Any pretext or none at all, and there would be singing, drinking, and an orchestra. Yesterday has gone, tomorrow has not come, life is the present moment only and its purpose is pleasure. No regrets, no dreams, nothing is worth while but happiness.

As a corollary to the love of music were the frequent dances, but the native *bailes* were hedged about with custom and convention until they bore little resemblance to an Anglo-Saxon gathering. Most noticeable were the chaperones. Every girl sat by her dueña until asked for a dance; the moment the music stopped she returned to her seat. There was no such thing as sitting out or even being in the company of a partner during intermissions, and as for a couple leaving the little room, it simply was not done. The perennial stringed band, of course, furnished the music, but the usually languorous melodies were speeded, the tempo became fast and the steps dizzy whirlings at high speed. A furious pace and then quiet resting with others of the same sex.

There was always date brandy and native wine in abundance, but to the credit of these people it should be noted that it was touched only by the men and the oldest of the women. Young matrons were conspicuously absent at all dances— either they were about to have babies or were recovering or were kept at home by household duties. There is no provision in their domestic economy for anyone to care for the young while the mothers go out for an evening and so custom decrees that they shall remain at home. That does not mean, however, that the husbands stay by the fireside. A typical gathering includes the younger men, whether married or not, and all the girls, together with a sprinkling of older couples.

Tony enjoyed these dances, for he was very welcome and easily made friends. There is a charming naïveté about girls as carefully chaperoned as are these; they frankly throw all responsibility upon their elders and express themselves with very little repression. The men were cordial, too, and convivial, and prided themselves on their intimacy with "Rubio," and so he acquired an understanding of the people which I greatly envied. He was young and San Ignacio reacted upon his idealism even more than upon that of the Partner and myself. He had been there for one season before us, he had induced us to make our first visit, and nowhere is he as happy as in this little village. His romanticism is well expressed by a remark for which we have often teased him. "If ever I am married," he said, "it is here I will spend my honeymoon."

The Partner enjoyed every phase of San Ignacio which appealed to Tony and to me, and also several features from which we were barred. She never tired of what we called her tea-parties, when women came ostensibly to trade with Señora Leree but actually to visit and gossip indefinitely in the patio. The hours they could spend talking of nothing— but we are drifting away from Lower California and towards the eternal feminine. There were the many times that the Partner, scouting through the village for nests, would come upon the home of one of these friendly callers and would accept the invitation to sit in the humble hut and exchange the news of the day. Her knowledge of Spanish was limited and so conversation had to be aided by gestures, something in which these people are especially adept. But neither freedom of speech nor community of interests proved to be necessary prerequisites to sociability.

We must not forget the little Yaqui girl, ten years of shyness and timidity. She passed our house two or three times a day and always looked through the grille to see if the Partner were home. For a long time she could not summon the courage to speak but eventually she nerved herself to coo, *"Adios, Señora."* After the first time she never failed to give the greeting. Hers was a musical note, sweet and low and superbly attractive. *"Adios, Señora."* It became almost a part of our lives. In some way she learned that the Partner was fond of flowers and many a little handful, from garden or hillside, slipped through the railings of our door. She could not be coaxed to carry her friendship farther, to linger and talk, or even to consider coming inside. Her rashest act was an occasion on which she told Tony, *"La Señora es muy bonita."*

"Tell her so," he said. "She will be glad to have you."

But the limit had been passed. She fled, frightened, and could not find courage to carry the matter further.

My closest contacts came through a group of boys whom I had trained to hunt eggs. In time they learned their lesson; a nest untouched and undisturbed was worth fifty centavos to me, but if collected by the boys themselves brought nothing. I gathered together the best of those who had worked for me two years before, and they ranged far and wide through the brush, in gardens among the palms, in the thickets and the tules, into vineyards and orchards and houses themselves. Every morning about breakfast time it was the custom of the fortunate to assemble in the street in front of our house and greet me with the call, *"Nido, Señor."*

We would start out, the whole gang together, and one after another they took me to what they had found. San Lúcas Orioles, San Lúcas Black Phœbes, San Lúcas Linnet, Costa Humming Birds and Vermilion Flycatchers, in addition to two species of doves, were our most common takes, but every now and then something rare and unexpected came to the surface. I learned much of the characters of Mexican boys and found them not at all unlike our own, the principal difference being that these children had been raised under little discipline and almost no restraint. They easily tired of orderly work and tried to fool me by placing nests in convenient trees or by building up sets with the eggs of more than one bird. It was a game in which they had no chance and I rapidly weeded out those who were not dependable, until, in the end, I had half a dozen as nice as one could find anywhere.

To them I owe much of my enjoyment of San Ignacio.

They took me on many a long hard tramp but they also led
me to cozy, attractive, out-of-the-way places that otherwise
I would have missed. We went through gardens and houses,
we found the pools and the deepest recesses of the jungle,
we explored the mesas and the potholes in cañon walls, we
waded in the ponds and climbed the cardónes. When we had
finished there was not a rancheria uninspected nor a family
with whom we were unacquainted.

After a firm footing of friendship and understanding had
been established these jaunts became matters of pure pleasure,
whether eggs were found or not. I miss those happy days
under the palms or in the cholla, climbing mesquite or drinking water with quaint ceremony in the shade of a *ramada*,
stepping aside for a burro-train or exchanging pleasant greet-
ings with anyone who passed. I would give much to wake
some morning and hear a soft, drawling, half intimidated
voice crooning:

"Nido, Señor, nido y huevos."

CHAPTER XXXVIII

THE ARBITER OF SAN IGNACIO

It grew upon us, as we became more and more intimate with the villagers, that, even in their poverty and simplicity, social traditions and distinctions were as strongly drawn here as in any spot in the United States. There were families which, for two centuries, had passed from generation to generation not merely their holdings, but also the prestige of their origins. Little had been introduced into San Ignacio since the days of the Padres; life had flowed as serenely and as unaffectedly as though the pueblo were an island isolated from the world. Few had the ambition or ability to better themselves or their children and not many born to it failed to meet the simple requirements of the so-called upper class.

In the pyramided social strata there was one figure who, unchallenged, dominated her neighbors. Señora Leree had been our friend since the spring evening two years ago when she had taken into her home a small party of travellers too tired to make camp. She had turned over to us her own house and had helped prepare our supper. For the ensuing four months we spent the greater part of our time under her roof and all the while there developed the mutual understanding that had had such an auspicious beginning. From the first night she had taken the Partner under her wing and had begun to exert the gentle pressure by virtue of which she ruled.

Of course there were two sides to the matter. The prestige of entertaining La Americana was not to be overlooked, especially when automobile rides were considered. On one pretext or another Señora Leree would contrive to be taken out, and the errands that called her to Otro Lado and the number of people whom she must see and talk to from the tonneau, were surprising. These drives, simple as they were, gave her unlimited pleasure, and yet there was not the slightest suggestion of presuming—she was shy and diffident in spite of her force.

On the other hand, she did try to guide the Partner's errant footsteps and found her visitor quite a handful to manage, as many others before her have done. There was the matter of clothes. The Partner did not have the moral courage to wear shorts in San Ignacio, but Señora Leree could not reconcile herself to the use even of riding breeches. In the evenings or on the days she did not go afield the Partner usually slipped on a simple dress, and her hostess' smile of approval was always benign and motherly. Awful tales came from La Presa when Tony and I took the Partner swimming, but I am sure our chatelaine believed none of them. The real trouble revolved around stockings.

"Are these Americanos rich or are they poor?" was the village gossip constantly brought to our patio. One clique insisted on unlimited wealth—we owned a car and a boat and had a bag full of silver pesos. The majority vote was for poverty, for the Partner wore no stockings, *probecita,* and of course there could be no reason other than that she could not afford them. Señora Leree tried courageously to reduce by one the things for which she must apologize, to persuade the Partner to put on stockings just to show that she owned some, but unfortunately all had been left on the *Least Petrel.* Then our hostess tried to explain American customs to her townspeople, but century old prejudices were hard to overcome.

There was the matter of people; the Partner was far too democratic and required constant advice on the degree of cordiality she should bestow. It would not do at all to be

equally friendly with everyone. For instance there was
Señora Mindo. The Chinaman's wife represented about all
the wealth in the village, but Señora Leree would concede
her no social position. This not because of being married to
a Mongolian, not at all, but because of antecedents. The line
between the permissible and the forbidden was very finely
drawn. Señora Leree was perfectly willing to accompany
the Partner to the Mindo house to attend the larger functions, when fifteen or twenty people gathered to listen to
the phonograph, or twice that number attended a dance or
possibly assembled to watch a pair of itinerant actors. But
to go upstairs to the living room or to sit sociably on the
balcony, that could not be considered.

I'm afraid Señora Leree was a bit intolerant. After our
first visit I had sent her an enlarged photograph of the
Mission, a picture on which I rather prided myself. When
we spoke of it on the present trip to San Ignacio we did not
meet with the cordial thanks we had anticipated. In fact it
soon developed that she was anything but pleased. I had set
up my camera and had waited patiently until figures appeared grouped as I wanted them in the foreground.
Unfortunately none of the three men who chanced to pass
met with the lady's approval. Why had I not selected some
of the prominent characters of the town instead of these
worse than nobodies? To this day she has not been pla-
cated on that point.

Her townspeople were either peons or else members of
the upper class—there were no intermediates. The line of
demarcation was most closely drawn at the dances, for
those who were eligible to attend the better *bailes* did not
mix with the peasants and, conversely, the latter were barred
from the more aristocratic functions. I firmly believe that
the Partner and Tony and I broke all precedents by feeling
free to attend either. The greatest difference between the
two classes of dances lay in the fact that the simpler ones

were held in adobes while Mindo's large cement floor was always in demand for the others. At the Chinaman's better clothes were worn, there was more formality and restraint, but the conventions were the same at both and were equally well observed.

Color was a matter which Señora Leree regarded as of utmost importance. She helped prove the Spencerian theory that standards of beauty are local and variable, for to her the one and only measure was the shade of the skin. Features, figures, the vivacity of youth were as nothing when compared with complexions. Her point of view, since she herself is decidedly of the darker type, would be the more remarkable were it not that she merely reflects a national idea. There are, of course, many pronounced blondes in Mexico, but there were none in San Ignacio and to us all the people were merely a group of dark-skinned natives. Not to her, however. She drew gradations so fine that only a trained eye could follow and step by step she interpreted them and charged them with meaning. Unconsciously she was drawing inspiration from the Conquistadores and the more swarthy Indians.

The Partner who, by the way, is a brunette, had amused herself ever since leaving home by following the current fad of acquiring a tan. She had taken advantage of many free hours to lie in the sun in a bathing suit, and by the time we reached San Ignacio she was brown as a berry. She told, no, she bragged to her hostess of what she had been doing and of the success which had followed her efforts. When Señora Leree was finally made to understand the purport of the words, when it was proven that a young woman would deliberately darken her skin, the Mexican was flabbergasted—there is no better word. Nothing we had seen, no quaint customs that had surprised and amused us, no traits we had looked on with condescension, could be compared with the effect upon Señora Leree of the criminal folly of reversing sane and respectable custom and wantonly making one's self darker than one had been created.

At one time or another nearly every woman and child in the village came into our patio. Señora Leree presided over a clearing house of all manner of odds and ends of which chickens and vegetables were the most consistent imports and the generally accepted return was bread. We learned little of what transpired on these occasions, for both parties to the transactions were reticent to the point of furtiveness, but we were in too close contact spread over too long a period of time not to sense that more than simple trading was taking place. In her own way Señora Leree was holding levees; she always exacted a certain amount of homage for she was jealous of the position she had established and demanded that it be duly recognized. It was in the patio that she gave the advice or made the suggestions which to all intents and purposes were decrees. She so far excelled her associates in knowledge, experience, and hard common sense that it was not difficult for her to lead them into doing what she wanted, especially since she adhered to a delicate sense of justice. Few there were who could afford to or who wished in any way to give offense.

Her charities were extensive in proportion to her means. By our standards she would be judged a poor woman struggling for existence, but in San Ignacio she was one of the favored few. So to her came the sick and those in trouble, and though, of course, she could not play the Lady Bountiful, yet there was much she could and did to relieve distress. Materially she would have been helpless did a pittance not go so far. Spiritually she was leader both in mundane and religious affairs. There can be no measure of the good that was done to the people through her kindnesses, while at the same time she acted as guide to a community that had no ordained priest. As a matter of course into her keeping fell the keys of the Mission. She led in the hymn singing and in as much of the service as is permitted the layman. If ever there was a labor of love it was her care and devotion to the old building.

Before Tony and I came up from Santa Rosalía the Partner had need of a Mason jar. She could find none; such a receptacle was treasure trove in San Ignacio. Señora Leree, on condition that it be returned when I arrived, contrived to borrow the only one in town. Unfortunately the owner discovered that in it was being preserved a snake and great was the outcry and lamentation. The jar was an heirloom, a prided possession, and now it could never again be used. Since money would not compensate for its loss nor could it by any means be replaced the situation became too delicate and complicated for us to handle. So we took our troubles to our guardian who, with patience, tact, and an understanding of how to deal with the more primitive mind, exchanged a peso and all was peace and harmony. We had her inborn diplomacy to thank for smoothing down many an involuntary breach and she won our admiration with her uniform successes.

Out of the multitude of her lines of influence the one that stands preëminent, in my mind, is Señora Leree's possession of yeast. She alone in San Ignacio knew the secret and technique of its perpetuation and the culture she maintained with painstaking care had come down at least from her grandparents. Bread, we observed, is an acquired taste, for the older people preferred tortillas and it was only the younger generation that had developed an appreciation of leavening. If there were listed those who had left the patio holding between forefinger and thumb a pinch of the magic dough a good start would have been made on the roll-call of her feudal retainers. Whether the yeast was traded or whether it was given it always was more potent in the court than in the oven.

Señora Leree was guardian of the gate. Whenever she

could so contrive her work she kept a vigilant eye on the only street adit to the patio. Few entered without her consent and none, I dare say, without her immediate cognizance. She was a reliable watch dog for us, especially for the Partner, and weeded out, with unrelaxing vigilance, those whom she thought might cause annoyance. She was our adviser in a country where the duties of dueña are taken seriously and where customs are rigidly observed. She played her triple rôle, of hostess, of friend, and of mentor, without once, in all the time we knew her, striking a false note, the wise little woman who never disclosed the steel that lay beneath her urbanity.

Her community bakings, when the big adobe oven in the yard was fired and fed mesquite and palms until its great interior glowed, were red letter days for the neighbors. They trooped in with baskets or molded dough, they waited their turn to push aside the door and slide their raw bread into the hot chamber, and to draw out the finished product, light, fluffy, and covered with a rich brown crust. It was a mixture of two eras, of two civilizations—full length dresses and mantillas and Indian stolidness on one hand, science and invention on the other, a high priestess presiding at a ritual and an everyday social gathering with unlimited time and opportunity for talk.

In spite of her settled habits of thought the Mexican was willing to learn and to adopt the few things in our mode of life which appealed to her. I have in mind as simple a matter as meat. One day the Partner went to the butcher, intent on securing sweetbreads for the table, and took Señora Leree with her. The Partner asked for the delicacies she wanted and then the trouble began. The combined knowledge of these people in two languages was insufficient even to make a start. The Partner is persistent, as may have been noted, and she made that poor butcher go through everything until they finally arrived at the waste heap. The sweetbreads were found and the meat seller gave all that were wanted—he wouldn't accept money for anything as valueless as that. So they afterwards appeared with regularity on our table and I noticed it was not long before they became part of the routine diet on the other side of the patio.

Señora Leree's big event during the time we had spent with her had occurred two years before, on the morning of the horse-race. The match was scheduled for sun-up, before the heat of the day, and so all the details of preliminary work had been completed the night before. Two parallel courses, about three furlongs in length, had been cleared of brush and marked with horizontal stalks of bamboo fastened to short stakes. Of the two horses entered one had come up from the coast and one from an outlying ranch in the neighborhood. Each owner had brought his family on horseback, and there had drifted in other mounted, unfamiliar groups that had made their way by trail from hidden corners which are reached by no roads. These outsiders were the most primitive people we had met, especially the women. The latter wore full length skirts and, in stock-saddles, rode sideways by putting one foot in the stirrup and hooking the other knee over the horn. They were self-conscious and thoroughly ill at ease in the environment of the large city.

We were up at daylight, the Partner and Señora Leree in their best bib and tucker in the tonneau, Tony and I on the front seat of the old Cadillac. We followed the road that runs under the palms and between the stone fences until it reaches the clearing on the other side of the reservoir. We were in the centre of a milling holiday throng, for this was Mexico's big day, the Cinco de Mayo. Mostly afoot, with some on burros or mules or horses, with dark-skinned occupants bulging from three overflowing Fords, the procession made its way under the fairy canopy.

317

Triumphant, with every imagined air of the grande dame, Señora Leree looked down from the heights, speaking to this reveller and that and making sure that none should fail to notice her.

As a sporting event the race itself would hardly be popular at a modern track. The running start required that the two horses should cross the first line on even terms, a condition that resulted in their being called back time after time until I, at least, had lost all interest in the event. Every few minutes they would break away, only to return, and for two hours the tedious process was repeated. To the natives all this was part of the game and so far from showing signs of restlessness they gave themselves over to sociability and to meeting the men from the campo. The two hours were anything but wasted on the Arbiter of San Ignacio. No royal box has ever brought more real pleasure than did the back of that battered old car. When we speak of her, the Partner and I, our thoughts usually revert to the time when the fine old woman, as thrilled as a debutante, enjoyed the hour to which she was most deservedly entitled.

CHAPTER XXXIX

INTO THAT SILENT SEA

THERE came the day, all too soon, when word was tele-
phoned from the coast that we must go back to Santa Rosalía. The *Argyll* was to arrive the next evening and we had
promised to be ready to receive our oil as soon as it could
be unloaded. So we hired the mail stage to take us down,
stipulating that the entire day be spent on the drive and
that we be allowed to hunt to our hearts' content along the
roadside. We were up early and before breakfast had
packed stuff into the Ford until it looked like a camper's
car. We were under way without loss of time, but even so
found that San Ignacio had wakened before we did.

The Partner received a remarkable ovation. Nearly every
woman in the village came to our door or waited for us
along the road, and many of the men and boys were in evidence. The orchestra of violins and guitars serenaded her,
their repertoire including all her old favorites, especially
the oft-repeated Rancho Grande. Such a patient gathering
it was, of quiet people who made no demonstration, who
merely watched in silence or with, at most, a soft *"Adios."*
The Partner deserved the tribute. She had been interested
in these villagers, had done much for them, and her remarkable faculty of winning friendships and giving her
own in return had been at its best. A patrician had met San
Ignacio on a basis that at least approached equality and in
return had been appreciated.

Eight miles from town found us in a wide valley with a
gently sloping floor. The covering was breast-high brush,
thick, but so spaced that walking was not difficult if care

were taken in dodging the scattered patches of cholla. The taller growths, Joshua Trees and cardónes, were not common, but they sufficed to break the monotony of the plain that stretched away on every side to the lava-covered hills. We were in the favored habitats of thrashers and wrens and gnat-catchers, of Crested Flycatchers and Gilded Flickers, of Cactus and of Ladder-backed Woodpeckers. We spent a couple of hours flung far afield, and it is remarkable how much country one can cover in that length of time. While we did add a few sets of interest we did not succeed in finding eggs of any of the birds of prey, which were what we particularly wanted. The smaller owls and falcons were in holes in the cardónes, well hidden, while Caracara and Harris Hawk spread over so much territory that discovering one of their nests would have been a rare accident.

Driving a few miles further we crossed a creek-bed, small and dry and heavily lined with mesquite. Here we took eggs of phainopepla and found cardinal nests, and walked up and down stream for miles in search of Xantus Jays. These birds lay two, sometimes three eggs in a little cup of hair or fine weed held in place by a ring of thorns. They seek out the heart of the ironwood tree, the densest, thorniest, most unbending growth in the whole lower country. No one who objects to scratched cheeks or bleeding hands should try to collect their sets, but when the Partner, after miles of hunting, flushed her blue quarry, nothing could stop her from going after the nest. She had wormed her way almost to where she could reach it when the thorns got the better of her. It was diabolical, the way they laid themselves flat on her head, her body, and her limbs and dug in with every movement she made. Tony and I tried to help, but by the time we reached her she was stubborn and refused assistance. Not having any better sense we sat down on the bank and laughed. Out of the quivering tree came a variety of movements and sounds, of which I most distinctly remember: "This is no country to which a man ought to take any woman."

However, she found eggs and collected them, and as they are especially rare she was soon restored to her old-time enthusiasm. We drove on halfway to our destination and camped for lunch under spreading mesquites in the Valle des Tres Vírgenes. This was the prettiest spot on the drive; there was plenty of shade, the walking was easy, and the minor collecting good. After eating and resting we tramped up the valley, hunting its full length and width. We had marked many places to which we wanted to go, for this had once been our favorite hunting ground. We located most of our old acquaintances—some were building, some had young, but a few flushed from eggs with which we were greatly pleased. The bird-lover in a city who notices that every spring a certain pair of breeders comes to his garden, to the tree or at least to the corner used in previous seasons, will understand the theory on which we worked.

It is a habit with nearly every bird, migratory or resident, to select for breeding a site close to the one used the year before. The instinctive desire to duplicate former conditions is carried so far that it is not at all unusual for two or even three nests to be superimposed upon each other. Often a single tree will contain half a dozen old structures in progressive stages of decay and it is normal to find a neighboring series scattered through half a dozen similar shrubs. These groups can safely be assumed to be the work done by one pair over a series of years. The wreck of a thrasher nest in a cholla, for instance, is evidence not only that other old nests and probably one that is occupied are to be found in the immediate vicinity, but also that the situations of all will be very much alike. The variation is far wider in racial instincts than in those of the individual.

Taking advantage of previous surveys we put in a very pleasant afternoon, devoting all the time that was left us to this one spot. When the sun began to drop close to the horizon we drove, without stopping, into Santa Rosalía. We went directly aboard the *Least Petrel,* to find that much had occurred while we had been in San Ignacio. For one thing the Easterners were gone. In our absence they had given up work entirely, preferring, apparently, to prove that prohibition was no more successful in Santa Rosalía than at home. They finally abandoned the trip, caught one of the small passenger vessels bound for Guaymas, and returned home by rail.

Such a move on their part was inevitable and should have been anticipated—perhaps it was. The line from Santa Rosalía to Guaymas represents the end of what might be considered the occupied portion of the Gulf. To the north lie waters that are entered at rare intervals and only by vessels called on special missions. After leaving the copper mine we were to be virtually alone in a great arm of the ocean and the thought that, in case of trouble, we would be out of contact with mankind and unable to call in help had become unbearable to the two deserters. Their reactions to the earlier and lesser loneliness had not given much hope that they would muster courage to cross the final barrier.

Their having been conquered by Lower California was not in itself surprising, but the extent to which they had been broken was eloquent of the power of the country. I know men by the hundred who are afraid to take a trip like ours—at least three have gone with me to the edge of the wilderness only to rush back in panic. There is something appalling to certain types of mind in the mere size of the uninhabited void, in straying so far from the herd. The men referred to were not of the out-of-doors type, campers or hunters or travellers. City trained, when put to the test they were frightened and ran away—nothing more was involved.

Peter and Gregory, however, were experienced and they

resisted; when they broke, the snap was more serious and far reaching. They illustrate the power of the Lower Country over men who have no business being there, men who are not gentlemen either by instinct or breeding, who have neither courage nor poise nor standards to which to adhere, who cannot gracefully admit that the fault lies within themselves and who, in yielding, act dishonorably. Baja California does not make such men, she does not distort admirable or even passable characters into people no one can respect, but she is unmerciful in dissolving the veneer.

The details of what had been done are of minor importance. If the conduct of one man were to be extenuated on the ground of weakness there still are no allowances to be urged for the other. An obsession of fear, fear of the country and the Gulf and the boat, of uncharted rocks, of breakdowns where there are no other ships, and, at the end, of the terrible bore of the Colorado River. An attempt to make the trip so disagreeable that it would perforce be terminated. A betrayal of the interests of those who had spent considerable sums of money to make a scientific survey of these waters. Minor breaches, small in themselves but cumulatively impressive. Lack of common politeness, for instance, and the civil and considerate treatment of one man by his fellow. Consistent, pointless lying. Repeatedly broken promises. Dishonesty in money matters. Wanton repudiation of agreements. The loss of morale was thorough, for stories came from Sonora of a continuation that shattered the friendship and respect of a consulate. Gregory and Peter were gone and had best be forgotten. They contrived, between them, to break most all of the commandments—except the sixth. Perhaps the saddest commentary lies in the fact that, coming as strangers, after months of association such as ours, not a soul aboard the *Least Petrel* had a regret over their departure.

With a smaller party and lightened responsibilities we spent the late afternoon in final preparations for sailing. In the evening, at the Hotel Française, we gave a farewell dinner in return for courtesies that had been extended to us. The meal was served in many courses and in a style betwixt French and Mexican. Almost none of our guests spoke English and many either French or Spanish only. Conversation was difficult to maintain, but those who could, helped. We opened a few bottles of champagne, told of our travels and experiences, and exchanged many labored compliments. The unspoken spirit carried the evening, though I realized, as never before, the stupidity of there being more than one language. With a group of men at least half of whom held doctor's degrees, we were able to discuss only the most trivial banalities.

It was not long after midnight, the hour scheduled for sailing, that we returned to the *Least Petrel*. A storm was blowing from the north—Charley regaled us with stories of watching little ships coming in from the open Gulf, and if any rolled half as much as he said they did, Santa Rosalía harbor was a snug little place for us to wait. Our decision was wise, for the wind increased and soon boats were drifting all over the bay. The *Least Petrel* dragged her anchor so badly that no less than three times did we have to start her engine, and buck back, under power, to our berth.

With sunrise the wind went down and it was not long before the outer waters were smooth enough to allow us to start. In the Gulf there is no swell even after a hurricane; the sea becomes smooth almost as soon as the gale is spent, and so we had a very pleasant day for the beginning of what we considered the last leg of our long trip. It was with mingled emotions that we slipped through the gateway of the bulwarked harbor and turned our bow to the north. The most romantic and the most desolate part of all our journey lay ahead—as also did our homes.

We watched the fading of mountains that were dismal to look upon unless one's imagination could see the rancherias and the oases. Distance did not relieve the cruelty of the hills of Santa Rosalía, the town became more and more a cloud of smoke hiding the unpleasantnesses and the ugliness, but blotting out none of the memories of happy care-free days. We passed the outskirts, so well known from the auto road, we left behind all visible habitation—we were Wedding Guests no longer, but a group of Ancient Mariners.

CHAPTER XL

LAS TRES VÍRGENES are three conspicuous mountains cresting the great Sierra. They stand fifteen miles inland, the highest with an elevation of sixty-five hundred feet, and serve as landmarks for boats and burro-trains through all this central part of Lower California. They are heavily covered with Joshua Trees—at least that is the impression my binoculars gave—and, on their higher slopes, support an abundance of deer. Geographically they mark the beginning of the end of Sierra de la Giganta, for beyond them the great range begins to flatten and the long San Lúcas Faunal Area to disintegrate.

Coming down from Imperial Valley and the Delta is an extension of the influence of the Colorado Desert and River. Across from the Pacific Vizcaíno skirts the Lost Plains and makes contact with the Gulf. It was our immediate purpose to follow the shoreline and to determine, as far as possible, the melting points of these three districts. Our task would be simple were the demarcation fixed and definite; unfortunately the regions blend into each other long before they become typical. The most we can hope to say of any place for the next hundred miles is that one in particular of the three faunal areas predominates rather than occurs in pure form.

Santa Ana Bay was our first point of call. Twenty-five miles north of Santa Rosalía, it is a slight indentation about three and a half miles wide. From the sand and cobble beach the water deepens so rapidly that satisfactory anchoring is difficult. Ordinarily the topography of the sea is similar to that of the adjoining coast, deep bottoms are adjacent to bluffs and long shoals extend from more nearly level land. But at Santa Ana Bay we met a contradiction, for, in spite of the abrupt drop under the Gulf, the terrain is nearly level. It was the first flat, open country we had seen since picking up la Giganta, and though rough and brokenly rugged, though marked with steep hills hardly less dreary than those of Santa Rosalía, still there was a long stretch of rolling desert between the beach and the now distant Sierras.

Through the plain came an immense river-bed, its width indicative of an extensive drainage basin in the interior. It had gouged out a proportionate arroyo that spread a mile or more in either direction, to the sharp slopes coming down from the mesa. As we worked our way up and across the depression there came home to me as never before a realization of the age of the volcanic associations in which we were doing our hunting. There is just one way in which it was possible for this valley to have been created. Rains and cloudbursts draining into flowing channels have cut out the soil and have carried it into the Gulf. Theoretically we can imagine a primal stream finding its way over the broken land and establishing a definite course. Then we picture the route being diverted, the stream becoming clogged by obstructions brought down by itself, by the caving of undermined banks, or by the deposit of silt. A shuttlecock on a loom, the river swung to and fro, from one side to the other, as it repeatedly was thrown from its natural position of lowest level.

It is written in the sands and on the rocks that many, many times, more often than one dare compute, the river has made the full crossing, and the number of centuries of actual flow required for a single traverse is a matter to be guessed with courage. The resultant must be multiplied by a thousand or two, for I doubt if in the last hundred years, or in any hundred years for an indefinite time in the past, there have been twenty days of appreciable flow. Nothing is to be gained by attempting to compute actual figures; the first step would throw us back into conditions of which we know nothing. Furthermore no mathematical expression could portray the element time in any form geographically comparable to a walk across the valley. Just another of the countless examples of the fact that the less the rainfall the more the country is marked, and the case of Santa Ana Bay is extreme in both respects.

The birds we collected did not furnish proof that we were as yet beyond the Cape Faunal Area and so, when dinner was over and the day's work done, we left for San Carlos Bay. A matter of two or three hours and yet, of all the nights I have spent on the Gulf, this short run stands out as the most sublime. It was another of the theatrical effects that so frequently had been staged, one which reached its heights through the motif of simplicity. Pure black and white—night and phosphorescence. The trim furrows turned by the bow glowed in a brilliant mass of incandescence and the waves in the wake, spreading V shaped, danced to extinction in space, maintaining to the last the thinning, lengthening silver crest.

At right angles and timed to meet us head-on a monster silver form, a sunken Zeppelin, rushed to our destruction. No time to check our headway, no chance to change our course, but we did not strike the whale. His the speed and his the decision, and there had passed another thrill though, reason tells me, no serious peril. Near-by and far away played schools of animals larger than our boat, wraiths potentially able to destroy us with a gesture, and yet through whom we must serenely sail, powerless to make a saving turn. We watched the ghostly spheriods, singly, paired, or in groups as they went about their occasions or came to the surface to blow. We, as men, by birth rulers of the world, passed through by the grace of the silvery forms, and at the mercy of their slightest whim. And always the feathered cushion at our bow, the mocking, beckoning crests astern.

Out of the night, churning to white their contacts with the water, came troubadours who, in the light they themselves were making, proved to be porpoises. They played with us a game that lasted half the run; like puppies taken for a walk they rushed us, they threatened, and then swung circles, again to come alongside abaft the beam. Pinwheels of cold fire, they were to starboard or to port or on both sides at once, excepting when absorbed into the glare of some larger monstrosity, whale or sunfish, manta or shark. Moths drawn to the flame of a candle, playfellows coaxing us to join, acrobatic escorts of honor, they slowed their speed to meet ours and to give us company.

That there were fish in the Northern Gulf was no surprise, but never before had we realized their numbers nor the prodigality with which they were distributed. We sailed on an infinite blackboard smeared with fuzzy X-ray outlines—not a minnow was too small, not a swordfish too fast, not a turtle too frozen to tell of its presence and of what it was doing. I am no stranger to tropic phosphorescence, nor have I been carried away by a phenomenon that, no matter how glorious, is yet commonly to be found. The virgin life in these warm northern waters, in this untouched aqueous Eden, where currents merely flow and ebb and do not emerge, is not to be likened even to the wonder spots on ordinary routes of travel. The Partner and I, until the anchor fell by Trinidad Island, sat atop the glory-hole, enthralled, fearful lest even our voices break the spell of the most wonderful of all evenings.

San Carlos Bay by daylight offers much the same perspective as we had seen the day before at Santa Ana. The coastal lowlands are wide and stretch back to mountains so far away that details are not distinguishable. There is the inevitable drainage basin, half valley and half ancient stream bed. The growth is the growth of the desert, head-high thorny bushes of many species far outnumbering the cacti. Excepting where steep slopes marked the edge of the arroyo the broad littoral was nearly homogeneous. The footing may have been more sandy in the bottoms and more heavily flaked with cracked stones on the slashed mesas or the rolling hills, but neither vegetation nor animal life showed material variation between the contours. We saw deer tracks and kicked up jack-rabbits and identified our old-time bird friends as often in one association as in the other.

The influence of Vizcaíno was now making itself felt at the expense of San Lúcas, but there still was no indication of the proximity of the Colorado. More than on the mainland of the Peninsula we found our interest centering on the bay itself and on its islands. San Carlos is comparatively shallow, in marked contrast with Santa Ana, and contains three small outcroppings of rock on which we landed. By one of these—Isla de la Trinidad—we were anchored. The name is imposing for a flat emergence nowhere more than six feet high and little over a hundred feet long. It is circled with a beach ring of coarse cobbles above which is a guano covered conglomerate, a paradise for nesting birds. Here we found a breeding colony of Elegant Tern, one of the two known from the Gulf side of Lower California, and, in lesser numbers, Western and Heerman Gulls and Frazar Oystercatchers.

Five pairs of the oystercatchers nest in the small circle, but even so their eggs are hard to find. The birds pick a suitable location among the pebbles, one from which they can watch in many directions for the approach of enemies, and proceed to line a shallow basin about a foot in diameter. The finished work is a neat bit of tiling; the materials used are thin flat pebbles or broken bits of clam shell the size of a half dollar. Here two, sometimes three eggs are placed, dull grey and spotted, their protective coloration rendering them almost invisible. As long as the parents are satisfied that their eggs have not been seen they remain quiet, simulating indifference in a most convincing manner. Once it becomes apparent, however, that the nest is discovered they make the day hideous with their noise and their attempts to distract attention. Poor things, not one set in five they lay escapes the ever watchful gulls and ravens.

We spent a second night in San Carlos and then made a leisurely daylight run up the coast past a series of headlands, San Juan Bautista, San Miguel and Santa Teresa. It was not until we had rounded the latter that we came to a country which we decided to work, though later we regretted that we had not made at least one intermediate stop. The weather was against us, however, for the water, though not really rough, would have made an offshore anchorage uncomfortable and this stretch of coast contains no intervening harbor.

Santa Teresa Bay lies south of a cape of the same name and just beyond, around San Gabriel Point, is San Francisquito. The two harbors are separated only by a narrow neck and we made use of both, moving from one whenever the shifting winds drove us to the other. Here we spent several days under fairly comfortable conditions, carrying out a rather minute study of avifaunal forms. We were again in the associations of the Vizcaíno Desert, as was indicated by the birds we were taking, for the San Lúcas traits were disappearing and still we could find no sustained traces of the influence of the Colorado. One matter of distribution made a great impression upon us; the fact that the line of demarcation is not fixed as between the various genera. We might find the point at which the San Lúcas gave way to the San Fernando Flicker fifty miles from where the San Lúcas Thrasher was replaced by the Mearns. Divisional points will

331

have to be established separately for nearly every race; our work could not go further than to disclose this necessity.

On the shore of Santa Teresa Bay is an hacienda occupied by a Mexican family who run a few cattle, care for shipments from a mine in the interior, and supply water and wine to casual boats. The establishment is far from prosperous and little has been done to free it from the clinging desert. It is of interest chiefly because of being the only visible habitation along the coast from Santa Rosalía to the head of the Gulf at San Felipe. High up in the valleys and in the mountains, scattered at cruel intervals, are a few peon huts of rancherias. I've been told of them and have seen traces of trails leading down to the sea, but with the exceptions mentioned, the littoral of Lower California's side of the northern half of the Gulf, together with all its islands, is uninhabited desert wilderness.

We killed a buck at this station and the venison was a delicious relief from the constant diet of beef and the goat meat to which we were occasionally reduced. This was the only deer seen on the trip, in spite of our having run across footprints almost everywhere except on the islands. Antelope and Bighorn as well as deer, the latter especially, are still numerically abundant in Lower California, but as our experience shows, are not to be picked up incidentally. The large-animal population per square mile is so small that big game can be successfully hunted only by engaging an experienced guide and by packing with a burro-train into favored places. Even then long days and hard work under punishing conditions are needed to produce trophies. The hunting on the Peninsula cannot be compared with that to be found in certain parts of the United States.

I have lived along the border years enough to see a paradise of game birds melt away before the development of Southern California and the introduction of the automobile. Twenty-five years ago in the Tijuana Valley there were flocks of quail that numbered ten thousand birds and more, while in the foothills and along the streams herds of deer feeding with cattle were not an uncommon sight. Today there are a few isolated spots where quail are abundant but their very existence proves them to be unknown to hunters. Mourning Doves, not very highly regarded, seem to be holding their own, but of the ducks that once darkened the lakes of Sierra San Pedro there remain but spectres of the former hosts. Ruddies and Lesser Scaups, in greatly diminished numbers, still migrate to the oases and the fresh water lagoon as far as the Cape, but birds enough for a meal are as much as are now to be expected. Hunting and shooting are still to be had, but, to the old timers, the size of the bag no longer seems compensation for the labor involved.

When we left the twin harbors it was to cross Sal Si Puedes Channel. I am amused at the name, for the pilot who christened the strait "Get out if you can" must have had an unpleasant experience. In this part of the Gulf the tides are beginning to reach their great height and the currents to become correspondingly strong. The racing waters are diverted between islands and mainland and develop added speed as they pour through the funnel. I have frequently seen Sal Si Puedes under conditions which readily allow me to sympathize with the discoverer. It just doesn't seem right for water to go crazy without warning or wind; I have a vivid appreciation of the feelings of the old-time pilot who felt he was not being treated fairly.

We had a pleasant crossing to the San Lorenzo Islands. The group is a long and narrow volcanic uplift cut into three unequal parts to which are added a number of outlying rocks in themselves almost worthy of being designated as islands, and named. By far the largest of the group is the southern member—nearly ten miles long, seldom over one in width, and reaching a height of sixteen hundred feet. As may well be imagined it is almost a knife blade and its edges drop unbroken into the sea. Even then they continue downwards and soundings of two thousand feet are to be found within less than a mile of the shore.

There are a few ravines but most of the drainage runs directly into the Gulf. The slopes support almost no vegetation and, though the arroyo bottoms contain low stands of brush and breaks in the declivities give root-holds to cacti and thorns, the mass of the island lies within two bare, corrugated slopes. Paradoxically spits of cobble, half a dozen or more, run out from the base at the southern tip and at right angles to the western side and there are, in places, narrow terraces of gravel between the sea-walls and the water. We hunted along both these formations for Western Gulls and Frazar Oystercatchers, meeting with indifferent success, and then turned our attention to the higher portions, the little cañons and the slides.

San Lorenzo can and must be explored, but the task proved to be too great for us to undertake. Geologically, and I believe time will show biologically also, this island is more closely akin to San Estéban, in Sonora, than it is to the nearby peninsula. The life on San Estéban is typically mainland, as disclosed by its Verdins, its Palmer Thrashers, and other forms unknown in Lower California. One of my unfinished tasks is to determine definitely whether or not any of the true mainland forms have jumped successively to Tiburón, to San Estéban, and on to San Lorenzo. When I start to climb those hills, win or lose, I will have earned a lot of sympathy.

We coasted slowly along the western side of the principal island until finally we came to its end and to the boat passage which separates it from North Island. We did not risk taking the *Least Petrel* through the opening, using the outboard and dory instead. We saw the nest of the only pair of Bald Eagles known still to exist on the Gulf and came to a country which, though soft in comparison with what we had been watching, would anywhere else be designated as little less than a series of vertical cliffs. The sun was down by the time we were aboard again, our collecting baskets nearly empty. All of us felt that we had opened a book to be read, one to which we had been unable either to devote the necessary time or bring the required knowledge.

We spent the whole of the next day exploring the two remaining islands. They became progressively less precipitous and more heavily covered with soft ash. Indeed the more northerly of the three, officially but not in general acceptance named Sal Si Puedes Island, was little more than a sterile capping of brown dust covered with a coating of guano. There were signs of a formerly enormous bird population there—history can be read for a long time in the past throughout this arid country—but a strenuous ten hours resulted in no discoveries of real moment. We all were tired, worn out and glad of an opportunity to indulge in a long, unbroken sleep before passing on to one of the outstanding climaxes of our wanderings.

CHAPTER XLI

OUT from behind San Lorenzo at daylight we headed directly for a low island of conglomerate. The morning broke auspiciously on this day of our great gamble; of our visit to the most changeable, most fickle, and most inconsistent of all the islands. Raza is at once a name with which to conjure and a source of breaking disappointments. Six times in the past I had landed upon her and on each occasion she had displayed a differing temperament. I have seen her the centre of a polished mirror and I have watched her quiver under huge waves that spewed spoondrift from headland to crest. There is always the possibility of not being able to make a landing at all. There might be no safe anchorage; there might even be no beach whose breakers would allow to pass and to drag up the dory.

Another risk we assumed involved the dates on which the birds would begin to lay. I visited here on the 17th of April in 1925 and again on the same day in 1928. On the first occasion both tern and gull eggs were plentiful and fresh, on the second one of the birds had not yet laid and the nests of the other contained either eggs that were heavily incubated or else newly hatched young. Then the market collectors may have garnered the entire crop, leaving nothing for us. Four times I have found, harbored by the island, little flotillas of three or four tiny sailboats filled with eggs to be sold as food in Santa Rosalía.

We watched Raza develop from a bare line into a thing of substance, from a blur into an irregular guano-covered

336

A DAUGHTER OF THE NEOPHYTES

A RANCHERIA

OUTWARD BOUND

flat. As we speculated on the fate that Fortune would have in store for us today we were winning the first throw of the dice. The weather was perfect, and when that term is applied to the Gulf of California it means conditions that cannot be surpassed anywhere in the world. Neither tide nor current was making itself noticeable, no breath of wind was breaking the glassy surface that on every side reached the horizon, no cloud nor haze was adulterating the unstrained sunlight.

If this beauty of setting were not hers alone, if it were shared with the encircling islands, Raza at least was the hub from which it radiated. To east and southeast lay three islands in Sonora. Tiburón, mystic and indistinct, shut off all but the mainland's highest hills, San Estéban rose in the foreground, tall and circular, half cone and half cylinder, appearing as a monstrosity of ash and lava, while the dim outlines of Isla Pedro Mártir were shaded from villainous slopes into a deceptive softness of contour.

Still the panorama. Due south the open Gulf and then the long string of the San Lorenzo group and beyond it the rugged hills of the Peninsula, backing San Rafael Bay. North of west was silhouetted nearby Raza Rock and then Partida, almost lost against the end of the great Isla Ángel de la Guardia. There is open water to the northwest, not much, not enough seriously to break the circle of this miniature fairyland. A planetary system isolated in a heaven of its own—the outside world distant and vague as unknown stars. On all sides protrude the deliminating reddish brown slopes, each characteristic in shape and color, each paying tribute to the central spot that is least pretentious of them all. Incomparable with any other type of scenery, its evanescent beauty at the whim of every vagrant breeze and shifting current, the Kingdom of Raza is a glory to be caught when it flashes, not a fixture eternally available.

If there be neither sail nor dugout to break the silver sheet there is yet the life and movement that not only elevates the scene beyond one of cold beauty but, at times, relegates the superb background into the setting of a museum habitat group. Fish and birds, as far as the eye can see, as far as binoculars can follow details, have taken over for themselves these charmed waters. Directly below our keel, scarcely above the anchor, are sluggish bass of an indeterminate number of species, swimming in and out of the kelp, visible in two or three fathoms of the crystal clearness. Crawfish and minnows and the weird marine life of a tropic sea.

Breaking the surface at intervals are fins of silent monsters, near-by or far away, floating idly in the warmth of sunlight or pressing in haste, pursued and pursuing. Ever and again a flying-fish leaps from the depths to shoot through fifty yards of open air—not the foot-long exocœtidæ of the Pacific, but tiny aviators scarcely larger than a humming bird. We traced school after school of small fry by the clouds of birds that circled over them and by the fast moving ripples of the carnivorous fish that were swimming in hot pursuit.

We were in an aviary. Birds were overhead in the air, they were skimming or flying just above the water, but by far most commonly they were resting on the surface. They gave the final touch of enchantment to a scene that through a long spring day held us enthralled. Black spots flecked the surface, singly, in pairs, or in flocks that might be small or might be numbered by the hundred. If years of ornithological study held no other reward they were repaid by our being able to recognize all the various species, to understand what they were attempting to do, and to follow the means by which they were accomplishing their purposes. Nowhere crowded, so great was the space they occupied, yet as distance drove them more and more into the background the swimming birds blended into each other until a thin black ring edged the horizon.

Like swallows over a mill pond thousands of petrel darted

338

in and out, their erratic flight seldom taking them more than a few feet above the water. Slow moving freight trains, Brown Pelicans on mathematically straight lines bound from one point to another lessened air resistance, for they have no predatory enemies, by flying within a foot of the water. Faster moving black cormorants, less sedate and less orderly, imitating their cousins, and then the air express, half a dozen species of ducks shooting by and trusting to speed for safety. Gulls and terns of many kinds, resident and migratory, errantly wandering, patiently resting, or conscientiously fishing, were the most conspicuous contributors to life and movement.

All of these birds were at times to be seen on the water, but there they were far outnumbered by divers and phalaropes. Eared Grebes were the most abundant of all, occurring in small compact flocks every few furlongs. They were in migration to northern breeding grounds and, though not paired, their nuptial plumage was fully developed. Sometimes, at our approach, they dived in unison, emerging at intervals scattered over a surprising area. More often they tried to swim away from the boat, and if that proved impossible they would take to the wing, beating the water for a hundred feet before they acquired sufficient speed to launch themselves into the air. Murrelets were often seen in family groups of four; at our approach all would sometimes dive but often the parents would fly, circling the boat while the babies, too young to follow, found safety under the surface.

The number of phalaropes that swam about in little flocks was a constant source of surprise, for these shore birds had thousands of miles to go and their breeding dates were not far away. They are most interesting when reversal of sex duties is considered. The male is by far the less ornamental, he builds the nest, incubates the eggs, and cares for the young. The spoiled lady lays—a duty she cannot well avoid—but with that her responsibilities come to an end.

An illuminating study is the relation between sexes as disclosed generally by instinctive divisions of the labor of incubation and house-keeping. Every conceivable time schedule has been arranged, the extreme local examples being the phalarope on one hand and the humming birds on the other. There are instances where both birds incubate, of exchanges made with the accuracy of time tables or indifferently and according to whim. With Goldfinches the female alone carries building material, though her unladen mate bears her company. A pair of ravens, flying side by side, go to the nesting site with their bills equally filled, and, of course, there are many males who do all the construction. Among hares the sire is not allowed to see his own young or know where they are hidden, but the father of a litter of foxes assumes the chief responsibility for their upbringing.

Nowhere better than in these open surroundings where mass observation is possible can a picture of mental processes be obtained. We can see the most intimate details of domestic arrangements and especially the portion of the burden that each sex assumes. We can reassure ourselves that however wide the difference in animals as a whole the individual component members of any given species conduct themselves along virtually identical lines. We can note the exceptions and weigh their values; some are meaningless idiosyncrasies, some so elemental that they indicate divergent inheritances. We can follow the marriage relations from the simplest to the most complicated forms of life and arrive, with satisfactory conviction, at the basic conclusion that in them all heritage has determined the details. We can go so far in the field that there is no question in our minds but that, as in all other forms of animal life, the relations between a man and his wife as regards the part each plays in the family unit, is fixed, not by custom or training or prearrangements, but absolutely at the dictates of instinct.

In appreciation of our hopes and in recognition of the

preëminence Raza occupied in our travels, Lady Luck held with us as we stepped ashore into a breeding colony of Heerman Gulls. From the lowlands just above the sea-wall there flowed over the hummocks and swept across the level valleys and climbed the highest ridges, which are only a hundred feet above the sea, an unbroken series of nests. They were seldom more than a few yards apart and little of the island was left uncovered. We made an endeavor to estimate their number and two hundred thousand breeding pairs was the lowest figure at which any of us arrived.

The nests themselves are little more than shallow saucers scooped where the earth is soft. Twigs either surround them as flimsy halos or else lightly line the little dishes. Two or three eggs constitute a clutch—we did not find a set of four which we were willing to accept as the work of one bird. Disregarding abnormalities, there was no great variation in the coloring of the sets. The basic shades ranged from light to dark grey, the markings from small to heavy blotchings, and our work was to look the clutches over in an endeavor to secure representatives of as many combinations as possible. The birds are dark, almost black, with white heads and brilliantly colored bills and feet, and are, as gulls go, medium in size. The downy young show an endless variation in color and the juveniles, for the first season or two, do not develop the white head.

An interesting example of a step in the process of evolution was noticed on the wing feathers of a few of the birds, of perhaps one in a thousand. Normally all the primaries are black; the sports have from one to three or four of these quills pure white. It seems strange that such a peculiarity should not either be entirely bred out of the flock or else be spread uniformly among all the members. We have no correlation to tell us what the irregularity means—whether it is a disappearance or a nascent development. Its importance does not lie in the condition itself, for all through biology there are minor variations within species. But nowhere else as on Raza, I feel sure, is there such an opportunity to study the subject in the field, for no other spot combines both the ready recognition and the number of living specimens that can so easily be examined in life.

It is always fascinating to wander through a breeding colony of Heerman Gulls. They flush as soon as we come in sight, but instead of flying away stand beside the nests and scold with their harsh, raucous cry. They circle about an intruder when he reaches the colony, threaten to strike without doing so, and make themselves offensive in every possible way. If a colony be disturbed these gulls, unlike the Western, do not attack and eat each other's eggs; all outdoors seems to be engaged in the one process of driving off the common enemy.

I like best to watch them in repose. Half a dozen valleys that at one time had been lagoon beds and are now flat and bare, excepting for occasional touches of sage or salicornia, are packed with sitting birds. Their nests are so shallow that, at a little distance, the gulls on eggs are not distinguishable from those on the ground. Occasionally the mate stands beside the brooding parent, or, if among the hills, upon a near-by rock; more often he is with the flock down on the cobble beach hunting minnows, perhaps slaking his thirst by drinking salt water. Peace and quiet in the colony come in short interludes, for almost any motion serves to start a fight. Singly or in flocks there is always movement to and from the shore, and, moreover, the Duck Hawk must be remembered.

Every hour or two the thousands of birds in a valley suddenly desert their nests and, in as compact formation as they can fly, stream out to the Gulf. It is surely a case of devil take the hindmost, for the falcon will strike only the last bird in the swarm pouring down the ravine. Some instinct warns the hawk not to allow himself to be ganged, which is perhaps just as well in the case of these gulls. They are almost as large as their enemy and, moreover, are prodigious

342

fighters. I have seen more than one of them struck to earth only to struggle back to safety, but I also have seen thousands of plucked skeletons marking unsuccessful attempts to escape.

The crowning glory of Raza is its colonies of Elegant Terns. The birds, rather large for the genus, are white, except for the pearl mantle, the gorgeous jet black cap, and the brilliant reddish bill and legs. Alone of all their family they assume, in breeding plumage, a pinkish tinge upon the breast. This is readily visible up to fifty or a hundred feet and serves as a mark of positive identification. They breed, as far as known, only on islands of Lower California or in the Gulf, and a majority of them have chosen Raza. The number on that island varies greatly from year to year. I have seen as few as two thousand and as many as ten.

The eggs are laid as closely together as the birds can sit without touching each other—the purpose of this congestion being to leave no room for the arch enemy, the Heerman Gull, to walk through the colony. In order to breed in this close formation the terns first go to an island where they cannot be molested by predatory mammals, and then find a comparatively level piece of soft ground in which they can scoop their tiny saucers. Such sites, of course, are rare, but Raza offers them in abundance.

Starting a colony is a difficult and delicate proceeding, often involving the loss of tens of thousands of eggs and involving months of time. Let us say that the first night of the season twenty birds lay. That is not nearly enough, for in the morning the Heerman Gulls will tramp round the edges of the sitting birds, shoulder them aside, and proceed to eat every one of their eggs. I have seen a gull slip his bill, from behind, under a sitting tern and pull out the egg without the bereaved parent being aware of the loss. The method of eating usually employed is for the robber to pick up the egg after thrusting his upper mandible through the shell, and then to throw back his head and literally drink the contents.

The second night is a repetition, and the third and the fourth, but all the time the number of laying terns is increasing. As a four foot ribbon seems to be about all the gulls can account for in twenty-four hours in time a nucleus is formed, and if it widens eight feet during the night and shrinks only half that much the next day a colony will have been established. Only the peripheral birds are ordinarily molested and so, in time, the core grows to a circle having a diameter of from thirty to sixty feet.

As a going concern the tern colony is a curiosity. I have slept several nights within twenty feet of the edge of one and have amused myself during the moonlight and at dawn watching the nefarious gulls working round and round the circle like prison guards on duty. Spaced a yard or so apart, with frequent replacements, they march solemnly, soldiers on parade, ever alert for the slightest opening to step in and snatch. Throughout the entire period of incubation their vigilance is maintained, so when hatching time comes the centre of the colony will contain babies while the fringe still consists of embryos in the early stages of development.

The terns themselves are among the most noisy and nervous of birds. All night and all day, at fifteen or twenty minute intervals, a sitting colony will rise with a great racket and in panicky excitement, hover for a few moments, and then drop back on the eggs. Occasionally the movement is accompanied by an influx of mates who have been fishing on the spits or in shallows just covered by the tide. When the mixture occurs an opportunity is offered to exchange the duty of hatching, but apparently the procedure usually is wholly meaningless. Its outstanding trait lies in the fact that thousands of birds simultaneously drop upon their nests with no confusion. The act is as mechanically perfect as though each individual had a predetermined route and destination and slid into place along a prepared chute.

Obviously on the return if there were a medley, if birds

were running about looking for their nests, two or three
trying for the same egg and therefore leaving others exposed,
the alert Heerman Gulls would step in and raid the colony.
Markings on the shells hold the key to the secret, for the
eggs of no two Elegant Terns are alike. In series in cabinet
drawers these eggshells make the most beautiful display in
oölogy, with ground colors of white and blue and drab and
red, with dots and scrawls and blotches, some immaculate
and some a mass of twisting lines. The Royal Terns that
colonize with the Elegant lay a much larger and easily
distinguishable egg, but theirs too, though in lesser degree,
run through wide variations. It is always dangerous to try
to separate cause from effect in oölogy, but it appears certain, in the case before us, that the tern colony, as a going
concern, demands that each bird be able to recognize her own
egg with speed and certainty. Either the shells have been
adapted to the purpose or the birds have built the solution
of their life problems about the variegated eggs.

From the time the young hatch until they are able to protect themselves from gulls, parental labor and anxiety assume
constantly increasing proportions. In the earliest stages of
development, babies remain in the nest under the protection
of the bodies of the adults. It is not long, however, before
the desire to wander becomes too strong to be suppressed.
The youngsters then gather into flocks and, since they cannot be huddled, become potential prey to every large scavenger that flies in the Gulf. The parents meet the situation
by forming themselves into a dashing, screaming vortex
through which no enemy dares to pass. Day and night, for
weeks on end, the old birds maintain ceaselessly their ardu-
ous vigil. In all the wide realm of biology few mothers reproduce their kind with the sorrow and under the strain that
falls to the lot of the Elegant Sea-Swallow.

The terns give the impression of always being confused.
They seem to be in a perpetual mental fog; there is no break

345

in their spasmodic tension, nothing in their conduct that is either leisurely or deliberate. Rattled and brainless, their minds appear weak to the point of representing the minimum of avian mentality. They cause me to wonder why evolution has been so inconsistent as to have created such beautiful things and then to have endowed them with so little intelligence. The thought opens the entire field of animal psychology.

To an anatomist the brain is not a specialty to be considered apart from other physical mechanisms of the body. In step with glands and muscles and bones it has evolved and, like any characteristic, is subject to the laws of variable inheritance. I am inclined to believe that it is the least staple of hereditary manifestations and that the individuals of any given race vary more in mentality than in any other quality. Be that as it may in any given species—a flock of Elegant Terns serves as an excellent example—there will be a certain number of individuals decidedly above and also a number definitely below the mental average of the whole. In either case the abnormality is a detriment and normally will disappear.

Stupidity and super-intelligence result alike in departures from racial customs. One means an inability to conform, the other an unwillingness to do so. Added brain power implies at least a certain degree of original conduct; in no other way can it be expressed. Established usages, however, are not to be ignored with impunity. Every existing species is living proof that it has arrived at a workable basis by virtue of which it has being and the power of perpetuation. It seems safe to add that every status is vastly complicated and has been reached through eons of trial and error—with ghastly prices paid for mistakes and impracticable experimentations.

When it is remembered, and appreciated, that the continuation of every genus is at best precarious and is kept by competition on the borderland between survival and extinction, it is not difficult to realize that any variation necessarily must be hazardous. The initiation of a novel line of conduct by an individual to whom it seems beneficial is almost certain to end in disaster. Life is such a maze of complications and contains so many obscure essentials which must dovetail into each other and be rigidly observed, that no animal mind, unless aided by accident, could conceive and carry out an improvement. Something at once vital and too deeply hidden to be anticipated in all ordinary cases will destroy the owner, or progeny, of an abnormal mind.

The conclusion is clear that every racial group has arrived at that state of mental development which best fits it to endure. In the case of the Elegant Terns the power to think is very low, with the Duck Hawks very high, and the reason for the difference is not far to seek. The necessity for making decisions. Hunter or hunted, prey stupid or clever, enemies resourceful or mechanical—mental development and the necessity for individuality of conduct necessarily parallel each other.

Sketched in barest outline are my reasons for believing that I understand why Elegant Terns have so little sense and why none of them either stand appreciably above or fall far below the average of the flock. The theory, if sound, should not be affected by levels. It should apply with equal force to other races either of lesser or of greater development. It does not admit of any distinction other than of degree between the mind of one animal and that of another. It sweeps aside all the mysticism that has been allowed to surround the function of the human mind. It disregards a mass of unsupportable and unwarranted hypotheses which have as excuse for acceptance only that they flatter. It denies to mankind a reasoning power peculiar either in source or in quality. It tells that in degree only does the brain of the turtle that floats beyond Raza's beach differ from that of the scientist who studies him from the shore.

347

CHAPTER XLII

RAZA ROCK is an isolated boulder a mile northwest of the mother island. It stands seventy-five feet above the water, an irregular pyramid whose sides, though climbable, are dizzily steep. A bare and wind-swept and polished monument of solid stone, it is a geological incongruity in this land of volcanic uplifts whose usual concomitants are conglomerate and sandstone strata.

We spent several hours on the lonely sentinel in a concentrated hunt for eggs. A pair of ravens occupied a little crevice near the top. I took two sets of Craveri Murrelet, and half a dozen pairs of Yellow-legged Gulls were nesting on the lower benches. Having recorded these facts we had accomplished our purpose, which was to add to the known breeding points of these birds.

Three or four more miles of travel brought us to two small islands arranged in a design similar to the Turkish star and crescent. We slipped into a berth directly between the islands, in the shadow of their three peaks, where we were perfectly protected against all gales except those from northeast or southwest. It was not only a comfortable anchorage but one which was free from worries; we knew of a delightful little bay to which we could run in the unlikely event of being disturbed by a storm. The two islands together are known as Isla Partida and as such have earned a niche in the ornithological hall of fame through harboring breeding colonies of Least Petrels. Before we began our studies in the Gulf the rare little birds had elsewhere been

348

known to nest only on Los San Benitos in the Pacific. Partida is still regarded as the metropolis of the race.

After months of wandering our boat, in this most out-of-the-way corner of the world, reached the home of the fairies for whom she had been named. The Least Petrels are the smallest of the birds that migrate by water from the upper end of the Gulf around Cape San Lúcas to the border near San Diego. Our *Least Petrel* is one of the lesser, if not actually the tiniest, of the craft that undertake the same pilgrimage. The flight of the birds is haphazard, midway between bat and swallow, a dart with sudden swerving towards anything which promises food. Thousands of miles of open seas are covered, the real objective always hidden by apparent aimlessness. In much the same way was the route of the boat determined—its course erratic, always dictated by momentary exigencies, and yet, in the end, reaching its destinations.

If these parallels did not make our choice of the name inevitable, there was an appropriate and sufficient reason in our fondness for the petrels themselves. They are the most gentle and harmless of all water-birds, the personification of the softer aspects of life. They show none of the greediness or pugnacity of shore-birds grubbing in the muck, none of the fierce desire of hunters of meat or fish. Timid and diffident and self-effacing they scarcely struggle if handled, and yet, when harrying the ocean far from the sight of land, they express the epitome of unrestrained freedom. Their lot in life is hard—helpless against enemies and doomed to follow the up and down heaves of heavy swells, to work hardest when prolonged storms threaten them with starvation, they are yet the harbingers of goodwill and kindness and, as such, were our unchallenged favorites.

Isla Partida consists of volcanic ash mixed with strata of sandstone. It is comparatively low, nowhere exceeding four hundred feet, and is correspondingly easy to climb and explore. Its vegetation, true desert in type, is heavier than anything we had encountered since leaving the Cape Region, but it was not high nor difficult to penetrate. The most fascinating feature of the island's physical geography is the western shoreline with its lovely miniature harbor and its long headlands. Here is another example of the endless series of contrasts to be found in this strange land. The bay suggests peace and comfort—nothing could appear more serene—but battered sea-walls and polished cliffs tell of the fierce northerners that seasonally bombard it with monster waves.

Over quite an extent of the eastern side of the main island and along the western beach of the smaller one the undermining of the stratified sandstone has resulted in the accumulation of great piles of talus. The brown fragments are slabs, seldom more than two feet long and usually only an inch or so in thickness. In more or less disorderly formation they run from the water edge to junction with the sea-wall, an irregular slope ten to thirty feet high. They are soft and yellow and wholly unattractive; nevertheless we spent two days of hard work excavating them.

Everyone on the boat except Captain, who was above such folly, dug himself a little trench, throwing the rocks out by hand. Even Juan and the Partner caught the fever and soon could be seen standing waist deep, excited by their Easter hunt. As soon as the surface covering had been removed signs of life began to appear, and when a depth of two feet had been reached the removal of any flagstone might disclose a bat or a petrel on an egg. The Partner didn't like the little mammals; they reminded her too much of mice slinking downwards into the talus. But she was determined to and very nearly did take her share of Least Petrel eggs.

In the aggregate our party, working on both islands, took nineteen. We did so through the exposure of a many storied tenement house in which floors consisted of a few square inches of weathered sand and doorways of narrow crevices, devious, perhaps, but not quite closed. With great care we cleared the larger slabs so that no small stone would slip down when they were removed and then we lifted them bodily so that nothing beneath would be crushed. Usually we found below only more rough stones or possibly an empty roosting place, but sometimes there would be a mean-looking fish-eating bat, occasionally a Black or a Least Petrel sitting, or an exposed egg whose parent had escaped. No nesting material was brought in by any of the breeders and nothing was done to improve the sites that nature had made. There was acre upon acre of talus, congested with these three forms of life to greater depths than we could reach, an impregnable citadel that will ensure the perpetuation of the inhabitants for a future longer than mankind can foresee.

There are two species of petrels in the Gulf—the Least and the Black. The latter is about three times the size of the former; otherwise, except in the hand, the two are indistinguishable. In the Gulf they nest in mixed colonies wherever found, the larger birds laying about a week before the smaller. This intermingling of species is a very interesting trait of Petrels. I have examined many of their colonies in Western America and have yet to find one in which there are not nesting simultaneously at least two genera of the birds.

We lost two petrels before we learned that the bird we lifted from the nest should be allowed to crawl back into the rock crevices and not be thrown into the air. The first few escaped to open water, but one, rattled by the gulls, rose too high. A streak of grey, speeding like an arrow from a bow, shot over the island, pointed directly at the little waif. Petrels, as we used to watch them from the boat, had given us the impression of being prodigiously fast, and I was anticipating an exciting chase. But the Duck Hawk overhauled this one as though it were standing still, as though it were just fluttering and making no effort to escape. I still felt no apprehension for I remembered the bat-like twisting flight, but the falcon flashed by and, in passing, stuck out his talon and grabbed as though with a hand. The ebon quarry was granted no time in which even to start a dodging movement.

The Duck Hawk had not been unobserved. No sooner had he made his catch than his mate, screaming, rose from her nestlings and made directly for him. He surrendered the prey to her by the simple method of letting it go. The petrel started to fly away, unharmed, and was again picked up as though it were waiting, suspended. The incident was the most graphic illustration of relative speeds that has ever come under my observation.

The curiosity of Western Gulls, to the number of a dozen or more, had attracted them to where we were working, and, with apparent indifference, they had flown around every petrel we released. To us this seemed a casual matter until the flock finally succeeded in surrounding one of the little birds. They were able, through excellent team play, to keep it confined, one and then another striking with wings until they finally brought it down. A life needlessly lost through the ignorance of outsiders.

Isla Partida had yielded her few specimens so grudgingly that we had not had much time for sightseeing. The Partner and I spent one hour tramping along the crest and another down by the rocky beaches exploring a dusty field of soft, sterile ash. We found the aëries of the Duck Hawk and of an Osprey, each with young almost ready to fly, an Oystercatchers with two eggs, and a Yellow-legged Gull nest that had been abandoned. We watched the birds and the marine life among the breakers or, from the heights, studied fish and lobsters swimming in the transparent water.

Our pleasure came from relaxation and the sense of ad-

LA PROVIDENCIA

EASTWARD OVER THE RIDGE OF SIERRA SAN PEDRO MÁRTIR

A BREEDING COLONY OF ELEGANT TERN

venture. Always, on these little islands, our knowledge that we were alone insured a freedom to enjoy and discuss that comes only where there is no chance of being seen or overheard. We followed the waves that rolled down from the north and broke gently against the reefs and the rocks of the shore; we were content merely to watch and admire. The sense of privacy, of enjoying something all our own, was strong upon us the last afternoon we spent upon that thoroughly delightful island. The unspoken thought was in both our minds that not many such hours lay between us and home.

We had worked harder than we realized and when, in the morning, the time came to weigh anchor we all were tired and more than satisfied to rest and do some sight-seeing. So as we came to White Rock and studied its harsh lines we easily persuaded ourselves that it had nothing new to offer. A hundred and seventy foot monument, a tough looking customer with steep sides and a whitish covering of guano, it is one of the chain that comes down from the north to end with the San Lorenzo Group. We studied it through our glasses and then laid our course, a little north of west, to carry us across Ballenas Channel into Ángeles Bay.

To starboard rose the famous Isla Ángel de la Guardia, the longest, the highest, and, excepting Tiburón, the largest of all the islands of western Mexico. From the southern tip to Sail Rock is forty-eight miles, but the island is so narrow that its width averages less than one sixth of that figure. Down the centre for the full length runs a ridge that is a mountain range. A height officially measured at 4315 feet is reached on the northern end, and, after dropping to two thousand or less in crossing the narrow central isthmus, the peaks rise again to over three thousand feet. In appearance the ensemble is not unlike an enlarged reproduction of San Diego or Santa Cruz Islands.

In the northeastern corner lies a quite pretentious valley through which a temporary stream runs immediately after rains. Perhaps this is the foundation of the stories and legends that make of this island a site of romance second only to Tiburón. Rumors and tales of flowing water and weird occupants circulate all over the Gulf and even find their way into print. It is no pleasure to destroy a pretty story, no matter how fantastic, and there certainly would be satisfaction in finding an oasis in these incredibly inimical surroundings. The hard fact remains, however, that La Guardia is a desert, uninhabited and unwatered. With the exception mentioned long high ridges extend in a single line from end to end, their sides dropping directly into the Gulf. There are neither foothills nor benches nor valleys, and the slopes of the high sea-walls have no hiding places where secrets can be treasured.

Between the western side of the island and the Peninsula itself lies Ballenas Channel, as nasty and as temperamental a stretch of water as one could wish to escape. Currents and tides and winds; there are times when they are dormant or when they neutralize each other, but more often than not they are at cross-purposes. Then the waves become unnatural in outline and viciousness, they lift themselves and drop faster than water should move, they assume shapes too nearly knife-like. The rise and fall of the tides is approaching fifteen feet, currents run as high as two or three knots an hour, and eighty-mile winds tear down from the Delta or up from the open south. If it were not that this stretch is characterized with the finest bays in the Gulf I doubt if many vessels would pass the island on the landward side.

San Rafael Bay, on the Peninsula, is fifteen miles of open roadstead, well protected from south and west. Las Ánimas is simply a deep indentation protected on three sides. Ten miles to its north, around a thirty-five hundred foot mountain spur, lies Ángeles Bay, the most famous north of Guaymas. We ran in, late in the afternoon, feeling our way carefully through a group of fifteen little islands that combine to give the harbor perfect protection in all weathers. It is the drydock of the Gulf. Here, at least twice a year, come the small power boats from Santa Rosalía or Guaymas to have their bottoms scraped and painted. Safety, a fine sand beach, and an amply sufficient difference between high and low tides, are the factors that bring boats here to be run ashore. They are beached, worked upon, and as well cared for as though they were on regular marine ways.

Ángeles Bay is supplied with water from wells dug in the river sands. Its present rather dangerous entrances could be made safe and easily negotiable by the placing of a few well-placed buoys. One of the finest harbors on the whole west coast, and yet lost to commerce because there is nothing produced in its back-country. As we entered we saw the familiar ash piles and guano-covered rocks and when we anchored it was beside one of the endless volcanic hills that, arid and stony and hot, stretch away to the Cape. Mesas and valleys and laval peaks, of critical importance to the scientist, held no other allure for man. Only near the beaches were there signs of human visitation; nowhere were there traces of occupancy.

The wind apparently had settled down to one of its interminable exhibitions and we were well pleased that by the end of the third day there came a lessening which encouraged us to leave. The air was hot and so dust-laden we almost choked for lack of free breath, and, as we were too short handed to accomplish much, we all found it a great relief again to be on the water. While on the way out we stopped to explore an islet just south of Smith Island, and were surprised to find an iguana, a harmless lizard two feet long. These reptiles are common on the southern

355

islands of the Gulf, but this is the only specimen I have seen in this northwest corner. For some reason its presence nettled me—perhaps at times I am not wholly true to the desert—and the contrast between what Ángeles Bay might have been, had it had a chance, and the repulsive iguana that it actually did yield, was too much for my temperament.

When we passed Smith Island and entered Ballenas Channel we found that the strait, too, was in anything but a pleasant humor. Pitching and rolling we passed beside the grandest mountain scenery of our voyage. We were in a water-filled cañon of tremendous depth, with peaks rising in the air four or five thousand feet on either side. Those on the Peninsula were slightly the taller but the mountains of the island were, within my experience, unequalled for towering grandeur. Near Humbug Bay four thousand feet is reached at an average ascent of thirty percent from the sea—of sixteen hundred feet to the mile.

In spite of our discomfort I couldn't help smiling when I thought of the plight of the old sailor who first entered Humbug Bay. He must have been caught in Ballenas Channel on some such day as ours, perhaps on one much worse, and, coasting Isla Ángel de la Guardia for a refuge, came to this beautiful, peaceful haven. Of course he ran in and, looking for a place to anchor, dropped the lead. It doesn't matter how much line he carried; no one in those days had enough to reach this bottom. He probably tried and tried before he gave up and again went out into storm. Let us hope he reached Ángeles Bay or Puerto Refugio.

As we came opposite the northern tip of La Guardia, with Sail Rock conspicuously beside us, I cast longing glances at the most perfect of all the insular harbors. A substantial reef running out from the large island is flanked on one side by Mejia and on the other by Granite Islands. Twin harbors are formed that not only are protected at all times but permit of easy passage from one to the other.

After leaving Ángeles Bay we had added two score miles to the hundreds that had slipped behind since we had rounded the Cape, and I was ready to call that a day's work. Captain, however, insisted that after we left the channel not only would the currents disappear but the sea itself would go down with the tide. He wanted to make an overnight run—there was nothing to be seen after we passed Bluff Point—and I agreed to his plans. The governing motive was not so much confidence in his prognostications as a desire to wake in the morning at San Luís—my first and greatest favorite among the islands in the Sea of Cortéz.

CHAPTER XLIII

CAPTAIN proved himself an overly optimistic prophet. The Gulf did not become calmer; if anything the size of the waves increased. Sometime during the night he yielded to the battering we were taking and ran for the shelter of Gonzaga Bay. Daylight found us peacefully at anchor, the storm broken, the sea rapidly subsiding. Before us lay a vista of low mesas and small hills, an unattractive desert which barely escaped being a waste. In emphatic contrast to the crowding walls of Sierra de la Giganta this was a nearly level plain. It looked dry and hot and big, it promised unpleasant walking and mirages and distorting heat waves. Nevertheless it aroused our curiosity and, though there was no longer anything to prevent our running over to the islands, we decided to gamble a day, exploring. We were encouraged to do so because many of the high-lights of our trip had come from circumstances just as fortuitous as our having taken refuge under Willard's Point.

As soon as we had landed Tony and Charley disappeared in search of specimens, but the long day's walk, to the Partner and me, was a study of the conditions which mission builders had dared to face and had hoped to conquer. We made our way into their country by going up the bed of the ancient river that drains into Gonzaga Bay, for in that arroyo was one of the sites the Padres had selected. We covered only half of the twelve miles to the ruins, but even so approached closely enough to reach surroundings virtually identical with those of the mission and so were

358

able to appreciate the hardships that had been endured. We wandered from cactus patch to mesquite tree, always alert for nests, but our absorption in ornithology did not conflict with an even greater interest in our environment.

The Mission of Calamujuet was old, dating back to 1766. The church and its complement of buildings were adobe bricks, dug and shaped on the spot and dried in the sun— there was always plenty of that. The needed timbers were hand hewn in the mountains above and laboriously packed down to the cañon. Irrigation ditches were dug, fruits and vegetables planted, neophytes assembled by the giving of food, and the usual curriculum established.

Eighteen months elapsed before the hopeless adventure was abandoned. Such water as was to be had was so strongly impregnated with alkali that it killed the half-grown crops, and naturally the Indians were not inclined to be docile unless they were fed. It was not failure that impressed us; we saw the landscape just as it had appeared to Arnes and Diaz and, being more practical than they, realized that there never had been any means by which a mission population could have been supported. We paid our tribute to fortitude and devotion rather than to judgment.

North of Gonzaga Bay and in a more mountainous country had been built the Mission of Santa Maria. Father Arnes founded it in 1767, just prior to the expulsion of the Jesuits. We could not actually see the site, still we did place it sufficiently well to assure ourselves that altitude had not brought it any material benefits. Santa Maria and Calamujuet had faced equal hardships under almost identical conditions, and had succumbed as soon as outside help had been withheld. Wasted was the incredible labor of construction and wasted too, I fear, was the even greater travail of bringing Christ's teachings to the aborigines. Wholly gone are the tribes which, the mission records show, once counted their numbers by the thousand.

We carried canteens and light lunches, the Partner and I, and put in nine hours tramping under the desert sun. We had thought ourselves quite inured to the hardship, yet we suffered more than a little from the heat and the glare. We crossed the valley and climbed to the mesa, resting, when we must, under the shade of mesquite, slowly working our way through brush and over mounds of volcanic rocks to tops of little hills. From them we surveyed the country we had crossed and the land that lay ahead, only to find unending repetition. We still saw the desert that we had followed for a thousand miles, but this portion was more arid and more sandy than Vizcaíno, more open and more lightly clad than the Cape Region, more widely flung and more nearly level than the base of La Giganta.

By every test the wind-swept, sand-covered barrens that shaded in between the oases of the south and the stark nakedness of the north were twice as gruesome and horrible as the baking fields on which Salvatierra and his comrades had won, or at least had earned, immortality. Loreto and Mulegé and Commondú had possibilities, but here the arroyos that ran back from the sea to be lost in the angular hills drained watersheds too small for living streams and the moisture stored in their gravels was too briny to be usable. Sand had so far replaced silt that even tillable soil had little fertility and the jungle-like growths of the more favored sections were here represented by isolated plants clinging to hummocks their own roots had made.

In this desolation had halted the march of the Jesuits. Writers of histories and of memoirs give us, in detail, chronicles of the missions and their founders, tales of tragedies and triumphs. But no written word has ever reproduced the scene of the enactments, even though the struggles of the Padres were with Nature rather than with man. The first explorers found a race of people into whom had been bred resistance to the country. The natives had been able to exist, to take a living from a land that did not have tangible resources for men of other stocks. Even with them the margin had been precarious and survival had been governed by the fundamental law of saturation that had controlled the birds of San Bartolomé Bay.

When the missionaries came with an offering of food to these ever hungry people, contacts were easy and submission to baptisms was not too great a price. Annals of the early days number converts by the hundred, by the thousand in favored valleys, as the promise of food drew untamed people from far and near. Yet the region which we, the Partner and I, were studying, was now bereft of all signs of human life. The Europeans, because they could not economically endure, withdrew to Mexico or to Spain upon the cessation of subsidies, but the disappearance of natives cannot so simply be explained. Many died from the scourge of Old World diseases, a few, a very few, remain, and the rest are gone because, seemingly, after the softening influence of mission diet they could no longer combat their former hardships.

Another day had passed and shadows were lengthening as we started back to the *Least Petrel*. We sensed a walking over an old battlefield, and the possession, possibly the sole possession, of the secret of the defeat and rout of the human by the physical element. No need for us to read heavy books or study ancient archives or listen to reports of accumulating details. No account of the contest could so thoroughly expound or be either as graphic or as convincing as the tantalizing panorama that extended eastward to the mountains and indefinitely to the north and south. We had been spoken to by the unconquerable.

Next morning, before sunrise, we were on the open Gulf again, headed for San Luís Island. As we approached, Captain avoided the long reef that comes out from the southwestern corner and swung into a comfortable anchorage just north of the spit. All arrangements for landing had been made while we were crossing from the mainland, so but a few moments elapsed between the shutting off of the engine and our starting with the out-board for the shore. A pair of Oystercatchers greeted us; their nest, which we were unable to find, was near the landing. Western Gulls, Blue Herons, and Reddish Egrets, Osprey, Ravens and Prairie Falcons, protesting, formed the reception committee, and these old favorites gave, if not a welcome, at least a feeling of homecoming.

The beach is of black lava. That rock also permeates the island, constantly forcing its way through the coating of ash to emerge as low outcroppings or pinnacles. These points of vantage are eagerly sought by Ospreys; we found some thirty-odd occupied nests, all containing young nearly ready to fly. A fringe of a stubborn bush that is halfway between sage and salicornia borders the western side of the island and has been taken over by a colony of Brown Pelicans. The breeding birds, massed for a mile or more along a strip several hundred yards wide, constitute the largest colony of their kind that I have ever found. Nests of coarse twigs, poorly constructed, are preferably placed on the tops of the bushes, but late comers are compelled to accept the lower branches or even content themselves with the ground. Mixed in at random are a small number of Reddish Egrets, dainty birds of whom one would expect better things than home-building in anything as foul and nauseating as a pelican colony.

Beyond the bushes San Luís assumes the aspect which, from my first visit years before, had endeared this island to me as the gem of the Gulf. It is neither monotonously level nor too abrupt for comfort. One can wander over it everywhere with pleasure and comfort; there is compensation for the scarcity of vegetation in the corresponding ease of walking. Underfoot crusted ash and pebbles replace the cracked lava blocks and the great cinders that make intolerable so many of the other islands. There are endless little gullies to explore and one never tires of the view from vantage points. Perhaps the attraction is the lagoon, changing daily from a mud basin to an altogether charming lake, perhaps one or more of the other islands which, flotilla like, spread northward for eight or nine miles.

Bird life is by no means the least of the fascinations of San Luís. Much ornithological history has had its source in discoveries made by the successive small expeditions I have brought here during the past five years. Distributional knowledge has been extended by the finding of record breeding grounds of murrelets, boobies, and petrels. New races have been named, as the Yellow-legged Gull and the Lower California Reddish Egret. The end has not been reached, yet ornithology does not occupy the position of prime importance in this archipelago that it does, for instance, on Raza and Ildefonso. There are too many counter attractions.

On the seaward side of San Luís is a smaller island of pure sandstone. Without a beach and with no discoverable break in the circular cliff, it rises abruptly from the water, taller than a large building. The walls have been polished by the elements until their sanded surfaces almost glisten. We abandoned as hopeless any effort to reach the fairly level top, consoling ourselves with the assurance that there was really no reason why any such attempt should be made. We assuaged our curiosity by circling in the *Least Petrel,* marvelling the while at the geological formation, the most unexpected and the most paradoxical in the Gulf.

There are, in the group, three islands smaller than San Luís, which, like it, are of volcanic ash and lava. They are steeper and have no level areas in any way comparable to those of the mother isle. They might be dismissed as being merely three protruding peaks, but each has an individuality, each has something personal by which to be remembered. One that Tony and I climbed had a sharply inclined face of impalpable dust so soft and yielding that we sank deeper than our ankles. We each left a trail no less distinct than had we been crossing a field of virgin snow, marks so clear that they were conspicuous even from the boat.

On another island of the group Duck Hawks nested, and we unexpectedly flushed, from an almost impenetrable thicket, a flock of a dozen breeding Great Blue Herons. Wild birds were these, rising when we first appeared on their skyline, to disappear until they could return to their nests under cover of the night. Long before evening hungry gulls had sought out and stolen every egg. Then there was the island of rattlesnakes, chubby short reptiles with a penchant for climbing onto boulders and sunning themselves, coiled, while all other living creatures found comfort only in the shade. It is one of our regrets that we failed to secure specimens of these isolated reptiles.

There are features which, of minor import in themselves, aggregate to affect the atmosphere of the whole archipelago. The whales, for instance, that play about the islands in schools. They seemed desirous of adopting the *Least Petrel* as a fellow, so assiduous were they in swimming under her and around her, blowing alongside or hurling themselves clear of the water. There were the lazy turtles that, when all was quiet, could be seen sleeping through the early summer sunshine, with only the head exposed above the unrippled surface. The ocean floors sometimes allowed us an unexpected glimpse and showed us a wealth of fishes and plants and primitive life which we, in our ignorance, could not understand. All we could grasp from our fleeting glances was evidence that fully half the wonders of the Gulf lie beneath the tidal levels.

We found particularly interesting a large rock which

we christened Gnat Island because of the swarms of pests that pursued us the moment we set our foot upon it. The tiny insects followed us into the dory when we left, they remained upon our hats and clothing as we climbed over the rail of the *Least Petrel,* and, though not reinforced by the main body, they retained a semblance of their hold in spite of a generous use of insecticide. There followed us too, from the rock, a flock of thirty or forty Man-o'-war or Frigate Birds that, though not breeding, have here established an apparently permanent colony. At least I have never visited Gnat Island when they were not present.

San Luís is the spot to which my mind reverts when the complications of civilized life become oppressive. I picture a little shack in one of the sheltered ravines; a hut with walls to break the wind and a roof to provide shade and, if I were to remain long enough, to shed a possible rain. In these surroundings could be found freedom in an absolute sense. No slavery to time, no obligations, no interruptions, even potential, nothing to dwarf mental perspective or interfere with concentration. The most perfect of sanctuaries, this, granted the sufficiency of the desert.

The conception is bizarre only to those not of the fraternity. The Order of Cactus Eaters, however, is large; it numbers its real or would-be members by the thousands and tens of thousands and draws them from every walk of life. An urban dweller who apparently has never slept under the stars may possess, for sage and sand, an enthusiasm greater than my own. More than once have I found myself, when trying to explain the fascination of the desert, talking to a man who himself was listening to a call as strong as any felt by sailor or mountaineer, artist or explorer or delver into the mysteries of science. At the other extreme are tramps, hoboes if you will, afoot or in battered cars, living in an orbit which ends where verdure begins. They may not practice self-analysis, may not be conscious of the spell, but they do know when happiness goes and when it returns.

Prospector and tourist, hunter, naturalist and engineer —the attraction cannot be emptiness, the polar icefields are vastly larger, nor yet scenery, most of us are familiar with the High Sierras, nor even sweeping width of landscape, the prairies, in part, are still open. Rather is it a combination of these elements with simplicity and flexibility. A panorama of wonders, neither hemmed in nor crowded, vegetation not so overpowering that detail is lost, animal life not so abundant that individuality is gone, and yet both present in numbers sufficient always to be interesting. An isolated, unexpected flower in contrast with a great field of unbroken color. A landscape whose composition changes with every hour and is transformed with every footstep. A whole-souled sense of participation devoid of a spectator's detachment. Why, why has the man who is content only when buried in a city so little understanding that he cannot grant intellectual equality to those who regard a purely metropolitan existence as a wasted life?

Of course I know that corporeally I can never indulge my fancy, nor would I choose to do so if I could. There are too many complications in this world. But there is nothing to prevent spiritual projections as often as the whim occurs. These, I find, nearly always involve San Luís. So I take such pleasure as I can in my imagined home and add real happiness whenever I make a visit.

CHAPTER XLIV

CONSAG ROCK

NORTHBOUND on an all-day run, we had left the San Luís Archipelago early in the morning. A fairly heavy sea, squarely on our bows, was causing the *Least Petrel* to pitch and buck with jerks that would have made us very uncomfortable, had we not, by this time, become well hardened. The cause of the unpleasant disturbance was a conflict between the tremendous tides of this region and the racing local currents. The offshore wind certainly could not account for the waves; it barely brought white caps to their crests.

The beauty of the Gulf was gone. Her charms, as always, had disappeared when the weather frowned and we were left in a truly colorless world. A monotone, spreading over the receding islands and dulling the near-by coastal plain, reached the paralleling mountains and was broken only at their summit by hovering clouds from the distant Pacific. So sombre and inhospitable was the lap that was leading us to our last port in the Gulf that, even before leaving this whimsical sea, our fairyland was being taken from us. At least so it seemed to me, but I couldn't have been cheerful in any event; we were nearing the end of our trip and I did not want to go home.

We had by this time reached a point opposite El Rosario and the foothills of Sierra San Pedro Mártir. Again we saw, outlined against the sky, the hog-back that ran north into dimness and towered nearly two miles above us. Once more we picked out the pyramidal sides of La Providencia, as there came into our view one of the marvels of the world. There is no unit by which to measure the greatness of Lower California's famous mountain; it can no more be gauged by the Grand Cañon or the Yosemite or the Canadian Rockies than they can be compared with each other. Sierra San Pedro Mártir has no counterpart.

Arizona's glory is a soft formation, cut and colored and inspired. California's is a jewel of carving and waterfalls and tree-framed pictures. Alberta shows what can be done with rocks and ice and lakes, while Lower California holds the masterpiece of Satan himself. Boulders. A cubic yard or the size of a house or of an immense building. Rusted and faded and weatherbeaten, they lie neither in beds of flowers nor on shelves of conglomerate. They are piled upon each other, they rest on those below, they support those above, they form spurs that coalesce into ridges, they aggregate great hills, and, in the end, they are San Pedro itself.

Hollows, half leached and half filled with debris. Square miles where the structure has collapsed, skinning and mutilating the precipices against which it once had leaned. Vortices of boulders, deep hell holes without mouths. Senseless, wanton piles conspicuous in their ego but, in the last analysis, contributing nothing. Cañons whose sides are tiled with boulders, whose narrow gutters are traced with inadequate lines of sand and are mile-stoned with lonely, hardy shrubs. And then a ledge or perhaps a plain, for even in her agony must San Pedro pause as, in a few miles, she drops from La Providencia to the level of the sea.

Ever a landscape of rough and rounded stones. Monsters, they cover the floors of valleys, they coat almost perpendicular slopes. Through the ages rays of the white-hot sun, caught, much of the time, where no wind can check mounting temperature, have been concentrated on the reptilia until the landscape resembles something it often approximates, the clinkered walls of a furnace. On the Mountain

Springs Grade between San Diego and El Centro a miniature sample of San Pedro has been seen by an army of
motorists. If curiosity should impel one of them to leave
the highway and find a spot where no human earmarks
come into the vista, if his imagination could conceive an
awfulness ten times greater than the view that would be
spread before him, then he might be able to picture to himself the mountain that has but one side.

When there are no dust-storms the air is clear and dry
in the northern corner of the Gulf. The eye can gauge
only extremes of distance because, within the first few
miles, near-by and far-away objects are equally distinct.
So the spurs and ridges that carry the clinging scales appear
to have but two dimensions, to be without thickness. The
illusion goes further; there seems to be no space between
the successive layers of serried walls. The man who stands
upon an eminence from which he can see one hilltop after
another rising in series can readily feel that he is not in
the mountains at all, that he is on a stage surrounded by
curtains of painted canvas. One must almost fight the
illusion that a stereopticon is projecting cardboard walls.

All day, with the sierra on our port, we plugged along,
paralleling a country that is little known. The spectacular
slopes are even more difficult to explore than they are to
reach. Towards mid-afternoon the mountain began to slip
away from us, drawing further and further inland from
the coast as there developed a great intervening plain. An
emergence from the Gulf mixed with sediment brought
down by storm water, scarcely less horrifying than its sire,
it was flat and bare, hot and big.

Of course there was vegetation of a sort, and mammals
and birds, but they were not visible from the *Least Petrel*.
All we could see was a field of swales and hummocks and
lines across dirty brown barrens where dry river-beds
debouched onto the plains. The largest of the unused water

369

channels reached the Gulf where a little volcanic promontory, together with the shoreline, forms a crescent known as San Felipe Bay.

Captain was taking soundings while we were still a mile offshore. The gentle fall of the plains continues unbroken from the foothills, across the beach, and along the bottom of the Gulf. So unusual care becomes necessary in selecting an anchorage. Unless there be plenty of water under the keel and unless due allowance be made for the tremendous fall in the tide, ebb might find the *Least Petrel* lying on her side, a considerable distance inland. Even with our precautions we were almost caught by the change which takes place every twelve hours. We had become so accustomed to fixity in seascapes that we were hardly prepared for San Felipe's daily alternation between a seacoast port and an inland town. If in the morning the Gulf lapped the edges of the desert, nightfall would disclose great fields of sand stretching an incredible distance to the east. There would still be canoes drawn on the beach above the flood line and large flocks of water-birds, gulls and terns and migrants, would remain in evidence as they diligently searched for careless aquatiles that might have become stranded, but all the while there would be no sea.

We went ashore, Captain and I to attend to business, the others to wander over the desert. We were faced with the necessity of finding a competent fisherman to pilot us through the mouth of the Colorado River. Shifting channels and sand-bars nullify the value of sailing directions and we were too well aware of the danger involved to risk a passage unaided. So we went into the town. Our first impression was lasting; here was a foreign note, the people were not Lower Californians.

Their huts and customs showed them to be mainland Mexicans from the lagoons of Sonora and Sinaloa and Nyarit. The distinguishing earmark was a simplicity even greater than that commonly found on the Peninsula. The houses were smaller and, on the average, contained appreciably fewer chattels than those we had seen farther south. Presumably good money was being earned but it was not reflected either by the clothing worn nor in the purchase of household necessities, to say nothing of comforts. The ancestral standard of living was too deeply ingrained to have been easily changed. Nationalistic traits were still dominant as shown, for instance, by the inclusion in the camp of the families of the workers. The wife was there and the children and the dependent relatives that settle on nearly every Mexican who is making wages.

Walking through the one street, if it can so far be dignified, we saw about a dozen structures that were little more than lean-tos. Mesquite stakes had been driven in the ground and joined by cross rafters. Walls and roofs alike were thatched with sage or arrowweed or any convenient brush. With openings left for doorways the house was complete. Stones for crushing grain were much in evidence, as were strings of peppers, and mixed packs of dogs and babies. And of course the usual dust and sand that is the concomitant of earthern floors.

Our reception by the fisher-folks was amusing. If there were envy of us who relatively had so much or if there were any unwillingness to permit our wandering among the homes, there was no surface indication of such feelings. On the contrary we seemed to furnish a welcome break in the monotony and to be the cause of a most naïve display of curiosity. Everywhere we went we were keenly watched, every movement we made was closely followed. There was nothing casual about the way the people looked at us, no concealment, no sidelong glances. Men, women, and children faced us squarely and, after the manner of their kind, gazed openly, standing motionless in their absorption until we seemed to be in a museum of wax figures. This national habit always disconcerts me; I am not accustomed to such frank staring and do not feel at ease under it.

San Felipe is a camp, not a permanent settlement. Its occupants have but one field of labor. They catch fish in the Gulf and load the harvest onto trucks, to be iced and hurried to the fresh meat markets of Los Angeles. Several of the men, as was to be expected, were familiar with the Colorado and all had respect for its treacherous burro. There was no difficulty in finding guides competent to pilot us and we were fortunate in that the best of these was willing to go. That matter settled, I joined Tony and the Partner in exploring the immediately surrounding country.

We were now definitely in the Colorado Desert Faunal Area, a region which centres about the Imperial Valley and works north up the Colorado River and east along the Gila. San Felipe is as far south as the district has been definitely proven to extend; the line of contact with Vizcaíno not having as yet been fully established. For the first time on the trip we were surrounded by bird forms familiar in Southeastern California and adjacent parts of Nevada and Arizona. Northern Cactus Wrens were here, Leconte Thrashers, Texas Nighthawks, Frosted Poor Wills, Arizona Verdins, Plumbeous Gnatcatchers, White-rumped Shrikes—the list would be lengthy if it were completed.

The most easily recognizable of the birds which do not wander far below San Felipe is the Western Gambel Quail. This species might be described as a California Quail which has faded until half the pigmentation is gone. Over all of Lower California except the northeastern corner are to be found one of three sub-species of California Quail. The distribution follows zonal boundaries and is indifferent in spreading from mountains to littoral. The Gambel includes the entire Delta Region in its range, but its real habitat is the Colorado Desert.

There exists, of course, a substantial reason why one

form cannot survive north of Vizcaíno and why the other race is unable to invade the southern area. Simple multiplication of individuals and the limitations of food supply compel this as well as all other forms of life to struggle against artificial boundaries and to extend ranges to the utmost available limits. A transformation of physical conditions has taken place between Vizcaíno and the Colorado, in each field there is lacking something which exists in the other, and yet painstaking study does not give even a suspicion of what that something may be. It might be food, or enemies, or possibly seasonal dates—the most I can say is that I lean towards the latter hypothesis.

Having an insatiable curiosity to know not only what but also why I am not at all satisfied to accept the unexplained fact that neither of these genera of quail can live in the other's territory. I know that the condition is not an accidental happening and yet I cannot put my finger on an even plausible solution of the question. Climate or vegetation or some phase of the life problem—the answer is too deeply hidden in biological complications. The various deserts look alike and feel alike—and as long as I am compelled to dismiss the subject with that unsatisfactory statement I realize that our ornithological work has fallen far short of its purpose.

At sunrise of the second day we turned directly east and commenced a three-hour run to Consag Rock. The half submerged white sepulchre rose slowly from the line of curvature and steadily grew in size and clarity of detail as we plowed our way across a field of glass. Yes, the Gulf had deigned to smile upon us on this, our last morning, and though she could here show no such glories as at Raza, she did frame Consag in a setting that approached artistic perfection.

The single motif, a white double domed cylinder, with nothing extraneous to distract the eye. A silver plaque upon which to rest the subject, and then a replica as the mirrored island, pointing downward, showed a counterfeit scarcely less distinct than its original. While the pilot was finding our anchorage we were looking upward at this strange Old Man of the Sea. It was so utterly out of place. What was an island doing out here in the middle of the Gulf? If there had to be one why was it not of sand, of silt, like the shores and borders that encircled it? Lastly, if we must have it of rock why should it be sedimentary, when the whole countryside is volcanic? No, Consag simply does not fit into the scheme of things.

If I have spoken of the Peninsula as being old what shall I say of this venerable pillar? It reeks with age, it cries aloud survivorship from an era beside which other cycles are momentary, it totters and trembles in hoary senility, this hold-over from the past. Its shrunken sides are scaled with fragments on the verge of falling, its top is a loose jumble, its every aspect spells decay. I stood on the tongue of boulders that runs westward from its base and fired my rifle at a pothole near the top, to flush a Duck Hawk's mate. The pandemonium that followed sent us all down the spit, running for our lives. The impact of the bullet loosened rocks that, in their fall, started others, and fan-wise the avalanche spread until it seemed as though the island would disintegrate. When the commotion subsided and the roar of the cataract was dulled, the lower half of Consag was hidden from view behind a responding cloud of opaque dust.

The rock is three hundred feet high. I know it has been climbed by three men, for I have seen Clyde Field, Nelson Carpenter, and my elder son perform the feat. That others have done so I doubt; that no one under my control will ever do so again I am sure. Before I realized the risks incurred a gold mine of avifaunal records had been established. On the top were found eggs of the Brewster Booby and of the Least and the Black Petrels. Circumstantially we proved the breeding here of Duck Hawks, Craveri Murrelets, and Red-billed Tropic Birds. Of these all but the falcon and the larger petrel are northern records which we established, and we had found on Consag Lower California's only breeding ground of Tropic Birds.

Tropic Birds, in systematism, are grouped with the pelicans and cormorants, frigate-birds and boobies, simply because the order includes all aves which have webbing joining four toes instead of the conventional three. In reality Tropic Birds resemble nothing else in the world and should have been placed in an order of their own. In the local race the straight tern-like bill is yellow in the juvenile stage, red in the adult. The plumage is white, laced with black etchings. Feet are so weak that the birds cannot launch themselves from level ground. The most conspicuous attribute are two tail feathers, elongated to a generous yard, that stream behind whenever the owners are in flight. The birds are about as large as a good-sized chicken.

Booby-like they had come out to examine us when the *Least Petrel* first approached their homes. They flew with frantically rapid strokes, exhibiting wings seemingly inadequate. As we neared our anchorage they continued the circular flight but were no longer near us, for they had commenced to climb. Higher they went, and higher; we lost all conception of their altitude as they dwindled into miniatures against the sky. There, to the number of several dozen, they gathered in protest against our intrusion, swinging endlessly through the hours on unmoving wings. We, looking up into the heavens, saw a halo worthy of Father Consag. Against the blue vault the ephemeral wraiths had no substance—delicately etched, they were fairy fish which we watched from the bottom of the pool. A thought appropriately poetic came to Linnæus when he christened the family "Followers of the Sun."

THE FLIGHT OF THE *LEAST PETREL*

In their homes these Tropic Birds are anything but angelic. They crawl into cavities among the rocks, insisting on complete concealment, and there, with no further preparation, they lay a single reddish egg. Motionless they sit, in perfect quiet, with a malevolent black eye the only sign of life, until either some intruder sees them or they believe he has. Then pandemonium breaks loose and the Fourth of July at its loudest comes streaming from the cave. Sharp staccato of clashing mandibles vies with the screams of a tortured soul and bold indeed is the robber who dares break through such a berserker defense.

We had come to Consag to take bearings for the passage of the mouth of the Colorado; we landed in order to check, as far as we could from the base, notes made on previous visits. On going ashore we disturbed the repose of hundreds upon hundreds of sea lions that had been sunning themselves upon the cobble spit. They took to the water at our approach and, from a distance of a few hundred feet on either side, made our stay hideous with their yappings. Whatever interest one may develop in these brutes as individuals and however cute their babies may be, in a herd they are repulsive creatures.

It's always so in the Gulf, that mixing bowl of fairies and ghouls, where the fascinating can never be separated from the ugly nor the charming from the uncouth. One moment an ethereal Tropic Bird, the next a slimy, worm-like shape. Speculating on contrasts Consag and the Gulf fairly drove my mind to the greatest separation of all, the difference between life and death. None of the Peninsula seems young, Sierra de la Giganta staggers with its evidence of age, but nothing I have seen, in the whole world no place of which I have heard, gives such a feeling of reversion to an inconceivable past as does this decaying rock. Other geological formations are progressing, at least are changing; Consag is absolutely dead. Time can do

376

no more than crumble the skeleton and dissipate it into space. Resurrection has ceased to be a possibility.

In antithesis there is the Gulf. For nearly two thousand miles we had travelled through an isolated region of teeming life, of life that killed and was killed, that came and functioned and died in rhythmic succession. It might be compared in futility to the tides, or to the alternate rise and fall of a continent, for it is a definite, continuing process without purpose and without goal. Yesterday's individuals are gone, tomorrow's are on the way, the rarity of past years now is abundant and next season will be waning, a race becomes extinct while a new genus comes into existence, and still there is maintained the ceaseless repetition which may have had a beginning but certainly has no end.

If life be considered in terms of size there are the whales that played with us at San Luís, the giant who now is blowing half a mile away. If numbers be the criterion thoughts might run from the cormorants of Magdalena and the gulls of Raza to the shrimps that for twenty miles reddened the waters of San Carlos? Numbers. Who dares try to calculate the aggregate of individuals that brought us a springtime of phosphorescent nights? Even were that done a start would not have been made, for beyond all known and suspected forms lie strata after strata that increase in geometrical progression to infinity.

More impressive than magnitude, greater than the miracle of numbers, is the element of time. The individual body has been likened to a machine. It consumes fuel and evolves energy, conforming in every way to the laws of chemistry and physics. The conception is satisfactory, but it does not begin to go far enough. If we conceive an engine charged with the latent ability to develop seed we can account for a new generation. Perhaps a mechanical contrivance could produce a germ which in turn could produce another—living bodies are wonderful things. If that much is conceded any definite number of generations become possible, but even so the facts of life are not explained.

We know that there are as many potential generations before the son as before the sire. That is to say we can be sure that if or when life ceases to exist upon this earth the end will not have come about through a collapse of the reproductive system. We are dealing with infinity and no machine can reproduce itself through an infinite number of generations. That can be done only by an underlying mechanism which in itself is a perpetuity.

Satisfying my mind and apparently meeting the severest of field tests is an explanation which I give as a matter of opinion and without any present effort to prove. I believe that at the absolute zero temperature there would, theoretically, be no movement within the atom and that the ultimate particle of matter would be wholly disassociated from energy in every form. I believe that the only manifestation of energy and the only possible relationship between ultimate particles is their movement with regard to each other. If from such a beginning inorganic atoms are assembled it is understandable that a different combination of particles and motions could produce life.

This conception demands that the life atom be able, under certain circumstances, to impart its peculiarities of motion to other and adjacent atoms, nascent or in being. From this point the reasoning is not difficult. Rather strangely it demonstrates that the force of gravity is not instantaneous and that life is at least potential on all other celestial bodies. More to the point, it satisfies the requirement that life can be transmitted through an infinity of time.

CHAPTER XLV

EL RÍO COLORADO

WE had left the Gulf. An uneventful overnight run brought us to Montague Island and to an anchorage in which we awaited a favorable tide. The "burro" was no longer something in the hazy future; it had become an immediate venture on which even now we were embarked. Behind us lay Gore Island, a two mile marsh subject to regular overflow. Across the river was the Sonora shore, bordered by a five hundred yard strip of soft mud consisting of tidal flats held in place by Bermuda grass and salicornia. Behind, far in the distance, rose the mesas of the Great Desert that, to us, was marked only by sporadic hills.

Montague Island is six miles long, almost level, and so little above high water that logs and débris brought down by the river are apt to be found upon it anywhere. It is a solid bed of Bermuda grass—the name is used to describe appearance—cut only by infrequent drainage channels. Lower California, now no longer a peninsula, stretched beyond, a vista of mud flats rising to an edge of grass that drew a line across the face of the Cocopah Mountains.

It was here, five years ago, that Clyde Field, Griffing Bancroft, Jr., and I discovered the eggs of the Large-Billed Sparrow. For half a century the migration of this bird had puzzled ornithologists, as well it might, for even today nothing is known of the route. About Thanksgiving time the sparrow appears in large numbers in the marshes of San Diego Bay, from which it spreads northerly along

379

the Pacific Coast. Throughout the winter it remains in California, yet in March it begins to appear on the edges of the Delta and by April its nesting is in full swing. Do the birds make an overland crossing? If so how and where? Or do they take the long coastal trip? It seems hardly possible that they could do either without our having somewhere come across them.

We had the morning at our disposal, for the ebb would continue many hours, so we went ashore and tramped ourselves weary on Montague Island. The Partner has a special talent for finding eggs of Marsh Sparrows, but today neither she nor any of us were lucky. It was far too late in the season; old nests and young on the wing were all we saw. We had hopes, for the date was right, of coming in contact with Yuma Rails, birds so rare that their breeding grounds are unknown and only three specimens have been preserved in museums. We didn't find a feather or a track or any evidence of the presence of the rail—I did pick up an old nest, but it might have been carried down by floods—still we hunted till the Mexican flag appeared upon the mast of the *Least Petrel*.

Our pilot was recalling us. He didn't know just when the tide would turn and was playing safe. The mouth of the Colorado is not a place in which to take chances; no equally frequented waterway in the world drowns so large a percentage of those who make the trip. We went aboard and, for almost the last time, the Partner and I perched on the hatch of the glory-hole. And because the marvels that were about to take place around us would largely be hidden I described to her, who was making her first trip, the appearance of the bore when seen from the front instead of from above.

Several times I have stood on the bank near La Bomba waiting for the wave to come. The Colorado then would be, comparatively, a narrow river, the mud flats of lower Cali-

fornia reaching for those of Sonora across a negligible ribbon. Eastward were salicornia fields so nearly level with the
eye that they could scarcely be seen, westward was a black,
grassless flat sweeping, smooth as a floor and almost as
sterile, to the foot of the Cocopah Mountains. At our feet
nothing but mud, soft and slimy wherever exposed by the
ebb. The landscape was a half mile, or a mile, of muck harboring sickly-blue crabs.

From the south came a murmur that insistently made
itself heard above the wind and the noises of the desert. The
sound became distinguishable but not recognizable—it was
unlike anything we had ever heard. It most closely approxi-
mated the roar of a breaker when striking, but the ocean's
challenge rises in quick crescendo to a climax, and halts; in
the voice of the Colorado was perhaps the same tone, but
there were no pauses, no interludes. For half an hour we
listened to the wonder sound which varied only in constantly
becoming louder, and then, from around the curve, like a
triumphant army sweeping to victory, came a great crescent
of white.

A half mile long, as I remember, one end rested on California's shore and the other, lagging as friction held it back,
touched the salicornia of Sonora. The flats disappeared like
grass in a fire, the magic white line passed, transforming mud
to a glorious river. The parade came on, it reached our feet,
and we looked down upon two free sheets of water, one a
man's height above the other. Spellbound though we were
we seized our opportunity to examine the marvel. It is not
a wave in any sense, however much it may suggest a breaker.
It is simply the crumbling wall between two levels, the slack
being taken up too fast to permit of an incline.

On past us who had watched it from La Bomba had
travelled this sudden change from low tide to high, and, even
as I described the burro, the age-old forces that had caused
the previous transfigurations were gathering about the *Least*

Petrel. Ceasing to tug, she rode at ease on her anchor chains. José told us the tide was changing, Charley turned compressed air into his engine, Tony, Juan, and I hoisted the anchor, and we were under way, pointing up the river.

The start and the first stages of our run were disappointingly normal. It was not long, however, before it became apparent that we were moving rapidly, and that in spite of the motor barely giving us steerage way. As the river narrowed our speed increased, we began to hear the noise of the bore, and almost before we realized our position the river banks were rushing past us, twenty, twenty-five miles an hour. There was the roar of falling water, the angry slap against walls of silt, and the crash of great blocks of earth falling into the stream.

Our pilot made a miscalculation—perhaps he was showing off a little—and found himself too near the face of the burro. So we had to tack back and forth across the river, killing time. We took a good drenching; especially Tony, who was allowed no let up in working the lead. We were soon safe again, back on our course, enjoying the thrill of the wildest ride of our lives. Mile after mile of unchanging scenery, of unceasing crash, until we rushed around the last bend and four little shacks appeared upon the shore.

With flags flying and the whistle tooting we shot past La Bomba and then swung back, to make our berth against the current. No anchoring here—we tossed two hawsers ashore and were made fast, our sides resting upon the bank. A short plank was extended and we stepped ashore to meet officials of customs and immigration. The automobile we had ordered was waiting—had been for several days—and there remained of our trip only the fifty-mile drive to Mexicali and the four-hour run to San Diego and home. The Flight of the *Least Petrel* had come to an end.

We were delayed but a short time in La Bomba. Leaving everything aboard until we could send a truck, saying good-

382

by to Captain, who remained with the boat, we piled into the car and started for the Sierra Pinta. La Bomba itself is merely an outpost consisting of a few frame houses, homes of officials. One of the shacks I remembered particularly; it was the noisiest place in which I had ever spent a night. It was sheathed with gasolene cans that had been cut and flattened but were not nailed tightly enough to prevent their sliding under pressure. A true desert gale, blowing insistently day after day, had shaken them with a rattle and a bang and a creak that gave no rest and made sleep impossible. Our first few miles, until we cut the San Felipe road, was across a crusted flat which was barely hard enough to carry our weight. There was no established route—every driver made his way as best he could according to the dictates of his own fancies, dodging as seemed safest, drifts and hollows and hummocks of brush. The land is subject to an intermittent overflow which periodically makes it impassable, sweeps it clean of vegetation and dust, and leaves many a treacherous spot to be avoided.

The Sierra Pinta is a highly developed example of the peculiar range formation so familiar in Southern Arizona. Running north and south, long and narrow and high, it is a detached volcanic uplift rising abruptly from level plains. These mountains have not the boulder formation so conspicuous on San Pedro nor are they at all like the brush-flecked islands of the Cape Region. In appearance they are solid rock, yellowish-tan walls of baking sterility, and yet they conceal enough vegetation to have become favored haunts of Mountain Sheep.

We followed closely the edge of the artificial silhouette and presently came to the immense depression between Laguna Salada and the Hardy River. The lake-bed, now dry, catches the overflow that drains from a thousand square miles of the flat we had touched on leaving La Bomba. The flow is away from the river; when the banks are broken the water, instead of returning, finds its way into the laguna. Unusual conditions have produced an evanescent inland sea twenty miles long, deep when spring floods are exceptionally high, dry whenever evaporation is greater than the inpour.

For twenty miles, as we passed the great gap in the hills and until we came to the Cocopah Mountains, we were on overflow land that had blocked a railroad and makes independable travel by motor. On the northern side we entered abruptly into an area of willows, saplings with occasional venerable trees. They marked the end of the saltwater influence and the beginning of the incredibly fertile Delta. The stretch from the Cocopah Mountains to Sonora, from the Gulf to the edges of Imperial Valley, is a heterogeneous mixture of marsh and desert and jungle, the determinant always being water.

Where the sea is dominant plant life is confined to forms which can resist brine, so the tidal flats support only such growths as salicornia, the so-called Bermuda grass, and scattering salt-bushes. Where the land is dry, whether extraneous to the influence of the Colorado or as islands, small and large, the unending desert seizes its opportunity, and adds to its domain of sage and briar and cactus.

The differences in elevation may, usually do, involve but a few feet. Yet between the extremes lies the last frontier of Imperial Valley and the scene of one of mankind's most romantic victories over nature. A mighty continental river has been dammed and diverted, has been carried through the Bee River to Volcano Lake and via the Hardy to the Gulf. It has been tapped by a series of immense main canals, its muddy flow has been spread over half a million acres, and America's greatest truck and dairy area has sprung into being.

In California the land that has been reclaimed had so long lain dry that, when the pioneers came, they found only desert. In Mexico perhaps one half the present farming acreage was, until recently, willow associations of the Delta. Salvaged, the jungle became an integral, indistinguishable portion of the major system, but the subjugation, the clearing, draining, levelling of swamps and thickets and tributaries, is one of the West's famous achievements. A river harnessed to obey, cement dams and waterworks with foundations resting on silt, lakes and canals coming or going at the word of command, an effective though unruly Slave of the Lamp.

Four distinct zones cover the northeastern section of Lower California. Between the Cocopah Mountains and the Sonora line are the Gulf Swamps, the fertile Delta, the Colorado Desert, unreclaimed, and the irrigated plantations. Of these the first two comprise by far the greater part, though the last is still capable of indefinite enlargement at the expense of the others. Its are the romance of youth and the dreams of hope; so different the Peninsula, with little behind and less ahead.

Our road took us along the eastern edge of the Delta, so close to the desert that we alternated from one association to the other. We dropped into corners of willow-bottoms, saplings or trees or rank growths of wild mustard. We passed a few homes of the almost extinct Cocopah Indians, a race of tall men and large women whose mental development is not in keeping with their physiques. They live as families rather than in tribes, these remnants of the many thousands who once found sustenance on the western shores of the Colorado. Their huts, completely under Mexican influence, have retained hardly a trace of aboriginal design. They are placed on small knolls where they are above the high-water line and where the wind, if it will, can disperse the summer mosquitoes. Lonely and dreary, widely separated from each other and relieved by no gardens or fields, they excite sympathy for the primitive race that has paid its all for the agricultural development of the Valley.

Past El Major where only the width of our tracks separates the mountains from the river, and then onto higher levels above the ancient beach line to the Colorado Desert at its worst, to unlimited sands of stunted brush and ocotillo, and at last to Black Butte and Volcano Lake. A mountain of glassy black blocks stands detached. It harbors at its feet the intermittent lake, full or dry at the dictates of engineers. On the opposite side is an incline, a greyish desert, and along the southern edge wraiths of steam mark the little geysers known as the Mud Volcanoes. Skirting Black Butte on the north **is** an immense canal, deep enough to float the *Least Petrel,* wide enough to turn her. It is the main source of supply for the water that gives life to the great valley.

From the northeast corner of Lower California, from the cluster of saloons and brothels about the border gate at Algodones, comes a war-time trench. Without a No Man's Land, crowded by the sand-hills and the high desert to the north, the cultivated area comes full tilt to the last levee. Cotton-fields and alfalfa and stock, houses of tenant-farmers and huts of peons with the untamed enemy country always below. When we drove on to the wooden bridge at Black Butte the crossing of its timbers carried us from the domination of Nature to the dictatorship of man.

CHAPTER XLVI

MEXICALI

COTTON is King. Over an area measured by hundreds of square miles desert has given way to plantations, to neatly furrowed rows and fenced fields and subsidiary ditches. A network of cross roads has replaced virgin thickets of mesquite and briar and cactus. The landscape is now an unbroken plain that may stretch to distant cinder hills half submerged by the horizon but more probably will terminate in border rows of cottonwood or poplar or eucalyptus. The foreground, massed bushes sparkling with bursting balls of white, is varied sometimes with an alfalfa field, sometimes with a little frame farmhouse.

At Black Butte we had entered a terrain that slopes downward from south to north. The tilt is so gradual that it is inappreciable to the eye, it is, in fact, less than one foot in a thousand. It continues without cessation for a hundred miles, eventually ending in the Salton Sea, a briny lake two hundred and seventy-five feet below the level of the ocean. Once an accidental body of water, Salton is now the drainage basin of the Garden of the Desert. On this topographical condition is based the entire engineering structure of the valley's irrigation system.

The Mexican part of Imperial Valley is simply an extralimital continuation of California's development. The principles involved are the same on both sides of the line and water is carried in a common series of main canals. Political

387

separation, as compared with other places along the border, here is hardly noticeable. The outstanding difference in the agricultural status of the two sections lies in the fact that in the United States there is wide diversification—lettuce, alfalfa, melons, cotton, grapefruit, dairies—while in Mexico cotton predominates almost to the point of exclusion. This is an economic condition due to such factors as contracts, concessions, and enormous individual landholdings.

For twenty-five or thirty miles we drove through cultivated fields whose productivity is wholly dependent on an unfailing supply of irrigation water. Rain, far from being an asset, is dreaded by the farmers. Scenically the ride was not attractive; it soon became monotonous to us who so long had lived in an atmosphere of constant change. The reclaimed country was depressing. It retained all the hardships of the equally arid southland, yet the compensations were gone. One cannot but have sympathy for those who make a living in these surroundings. Distressing temperatures, silt that works its way into every crevice of house and machinery, frequent three-day windstorms with choking clouds of sand, mosquitoes and the vicissitudes of farming. Those who grapple with Fortune in this valley certainly fulfill the mandatory biblical requirements.

As we approached from the south Mexicali first advised us of her presence when we saw her water tank. A huge metal cylinder has been mounted on a steel tower and is held high in the air to produce pressure in the mains. Rising above the trees it served as our introduction to the town; but for it we would have passed without warning from farming lands into the streets of the territorial metropolis. In spite of the sign-post, after running up the slope from the bridge over New River, we found ourselves abruptly in the city.

Our first impression of Mexicali was of a place out of step with anything else we had seen on our trip, of a town wholly unlike other Mexican cities, of a border hodge-podge of unassimilated units. Primarily it is a commercial centre supported by fifteen or twenty thousand people who live and work in the reclaimed area. It is also a political capital and a provider of entertainment. At its worst it has pitiful Chinese and native quarters, at its best pretentious government buildings, a splendid school system, and mechanical plants of the latest type. Most of the latter, of course, devolve about cotton, the gin being one of the largest in the world. The buildings devoted to education would be a credit to any city of equal size, the primary grades being well housed and the high school deservedly a source of great local pride. The paved streets also belie much that has been said of Territorial governors.

Officialdom lives and moves on the eastern fringe. The *palacio* has gathered about itself large and ambitious homes, as well as others which are more simple, and the quarters of executives who handle an immense business lie on this edge of the town. Adjoining is the Chinese section which, until recently, contained half of the contributing population. Several thousand coolies remain, though the greater portion of the old-time horde has been driven out by adverse legislation which sought, successfully, to supplant Oriental with Mexican labor. The Asiatics, crowding narrow alleys and tenement rooms, have brought with them their age-old culture. They lead their lives apart, finding more in common with Negroes and Hindus than with either Americans or Mexicans. Exclusiveness reaches the point of a gambling hall to which white men are not admitted.

The Mexican quarter is in the southwest corner, along the deep gash of New River. Here is Old Mexico, not Lower California. Little houses and stores and stands from which trinkets and food stuffs are sold in the streets and the always pitifully tiny stocks from which the peon must make his choice. Blending into this native section are two streets filled

389

with Mexican saloons; half a dozen of the cantinas have brothels in the rear. Mexico handles prostitution by recognizing it as inevitable, by making it as sordid as anything can be, by regulating it, and keeping it within restricted areas. Which may or may not be the better way—that is a matter of opinion.

The small district that extends from the border south to and just beyond the railroad tracks holds a number of ornate saloons, a really first class restaurant, and the Owl, a gambling hall that maintains a standard of respectability. It is to these few blocks that Americans come from all over the Valley to eat and drink, to play and dance, in an atmosphere free from legislated puritanism. There is here neither the stage settings nor the artificiality of Tijuana, nor, it might be added, the Americanization of the western resorts. Mexicali's tourist trade is negligible, she deals with residents of the Valley towns, and in consequence her offerings are more real. To many, perhaps, they will seem by comparison to be therefore less neatly and attractively presented. To me the atmosphere of genuineness more than offsets the loss of stage effects.

We finished our business and remained below the border for dinner. Mexicali by night is a city of men. The narrow sidewalks are crowded with an indiscriminate mixture of races, lighted shop windows alternate with cantinas, restaurants with street counters over which are sold Chinese lottery tickets, swinging doorways of dance halls with places of business, serious or frivolous, but there are almost no women on the streets or in the stores. Quiet and orderly as always, noticeably without surface evidence of viciousness, happy and care-free in shirt-sleeves and overalls, rarely in tweeds, the crowd is at once picturesque and disappointing. A flash from India in a tall, lean, turbaned Hindu, backwash of China in a group of coolies, young America, skylarking, serious Spanish types, condescending, peons from Tepic or

Sinaloa, wondering, the spirit of old-time mining camps, flickering, Mexicali, masculine in thought and in fact, has yet to develop a character of her own.

Nine o'clock was nearing, the border was about to be closed, so we pressed on with the stream that was working towards the international fence. Afoot and in cars they were passing two sets of federal officials, and almost before we realized what it meant, we were caught in the current. We reached the line and, passing through the gate, ceased to be Argonauts. We were at once absorbed into the body politic of our nation as merely a half dozen units of the hundred odd million. Our trip had developed from an experience into a memory.

We had done the things we had come to do and they have been recorded. There remains to be added a discussion of the completed writing; the idealistic goal has not been abandoned. If the reader is to formulate original ideas he must know where implicit trust may be placed and where qualifications are to be made. He should look upon our story not as a tale of adventure but as a completed photograph to be examined and discussed, for in the end, if he is to arrive at the conclusions which would have been his had he made our journey, he must depend upon his personal judgment of accuracy and scope. With the object of aiding, not of influencing, I am appending a few of my own thoughts.

The broadest generalization seems to be the question as to whether or not the picture is representative. If we had chosen another route, if our itinerary had taken us to a different series of places, would we have had a background materially differing from the one we are examining? The assurance that can be given on this point is surprisingly favorable. We touched at all the principal centres, Tijuana, Ensenada, San José del Cabo, La Paz, Loreto, Mulegé, San Ignacio, Santa Rosalía and Mexicali. On the other hand we missed the pueblo of Todos Santos and virtually all the inland settlements. The latter, however, are of minor importance. At one time or another I have been in nearly all and, though a picturesque aspect is usually to be found, they offer nothing to modify our conceptions of Mexican life.

It may be that the time devoted to the various towns was inadequately short, but against that it must be remembered that to seven of the nine places mentioned we did not go as strangers. Had we done so neither several days nor several weeks would have revealed much that did not appear upon the surface. The people of the southern republic are friendly and polite but they are extremely shy and have in high degree the reserve which, the world over, accompanies formality. Sensitiveness is a national trait, as is also an almost timid reluctance on their part to being placed in a position in which they might be patronized or ridiculed by Americans.

The question of the thoroughness with which we saw the various towns is clearly less a matter of time than of luck in breaking through the crust and in reaching the stratum of college trained men and convent bred women who have little interest in foreigners. Ask any critic of Mexico about the women of the aristocratic class who have received him into their homes and the answer should be an index of his familiarity with the country. We were very fortunate on this trip in picking up old threads of friendships and so of being able to discuss contemporaneous matters with educated people who, trusting us, talked frankly. Of course months spent in each village would still have left much to be learned and yet, I believe, would not have changed any of our conclusions. As far as the towns are concerned the picture, though necessarily fragmentary, should be satisfactory.

In our contacts with the open spaces our survey was less thorough. For every anchorage made a hundred were passed and it may be presumptuous to judge the entire country

OCOTILLO ON THE COLORADO DESERT

PASSING THROUGH THE GATE WE CEASED TO BE ARGONAUTS

MEMORIES

from the few places we saw. My reaction is suggested by the parallel of an engineer taking samples from a mine. Were his first selections judicious his assays should show little change if, as a check, he took a second and independent series of specimens. So, if we had gone to Black Warrior Lagoon instead of Scammon's, to Guadalupe Island instead of San Benito, to Cape San Lázaro instead of Magdalena Bay, to San Antonio instead of San Lúcas, to Puerto Refugio instead of Ángeles Bay, to El Golfo instead of San Felipe, if we had stopped at every river mouth and had landed on every island, we still would not have materially changed the picture. Lower California is a country of zones, the Northwest Corner, the Sierra San Pedro Mártir, the Littoral, the Coastal Plains, the Vizcaíno Desert, the Central Desert, the Oases, the Victoria Mountains, the Cape Region, the Gulf Coast, the Colorado, the Islands. We have sampled each of these distinctive areas too thoroughly to attach significance to the part of the ledge from which we took our ore.

Then there is the matter of people. Lower Californians, far from being a type, lead lives of personal freedom which allows them to develop unusual individualism. Nevertheless I feel that our opinions would not have been modified by an entirely distinct set of officials, townspeople, and ranchers; substitutes would still have been struggling against the same fixed economic conditions. One outstanding lesson the territory teaches is that physical geography is master. Another group would not have had distinct inheritances nor a differing nationalistic point of view and, averaged, would very closely approximate the men we met. It seems safe to assume that, however much the individuals of the Peninsula may differ from each other, the mass psychology of a first representation would be nearly identical with that of a second.

The subject matter is recorded as I saw it and, of course, was not done mechanically. I have unavoidably laid emphasis on what I thought important and on matters that, to me, were unexpected, unfamiliar, or of unusual interest. For instance, being a specialist in ornithology, I have naturally been more attracted by birds than by rocks or plants. On the other hand for the thirty years since I left college I have lived in California's southwestern corner and at least have had every opportunity of becoming able to make intelligent comparisons.

The picture as a whole leans too strongly to loneliness and desolation. Tucked away here and there in favorable spots is much human life with which we did not come in contact. Those who live there have miserable existences according to our standards, but not when judged by their own. If happiness is based on the ratio of gratified to unattained desire perhaps we should envy them. In any event travellers interested could have discovered more little rancherias than we found. One man may look at Sierra de la Giganta and notice only nakedness, while another would be unaware of the foreground and see nothing but the inhabited hut.

The omissions are as significant as the text. For instance no mention has been made of threats against our persons or property by any of the natives. No unpleasant experiences of that nature are included in the story for the simple reason that there were none. Nor have any ever come to us during ten years of fairly constant travel here. Nor, for the last two decades, has any American whom I know or of whom I have heard been molested by native Mexicans in Lower California or Sonora. Yes, I am well aware of the three aviators. I am also acquainted with a gentleman in Los Angeles County who dares not go to San Diego because it is near the border, and there are thousands of Americans who will not go beyond Tijuana because they are afraid. It is no more than fair for me to ask that the reader, in return for my sincerity, lay aside prejudice, if such he has, and believe with me that any American, man or woman, is safer and less subject to personal unpleasantness in Sonora and Lower California than he would be at home.

The picture contains no references to crime, for we came in contact with none. Felonies and petty thieving alike are rare, for the people are naturally law abiding. I have often laughed over a reply of Señora Leree in San Ignacio. I asked her if certain odds and ends in my car would be safe over night and she answered, with utter unconsciousness, "Perfectly safe, Señor, there are no Americans here." Policing is excellent and justice compensates for its other faults by lightning speed. The few major crimes of which we heard were political.

Native character, as may have been observed, is not a subject for broad generalizations. Statements that all Mexicans are this, or all Mexicans are that, without reserve may be set down as untrue. If such remarks mean anything at all they prove too much. Followed to a logical conclusion—those I have in mind are always derogatory—they would run counter to the fact that Mexico is a civilized nation, poor, perhaps, but functioning. Law and order does exist, property is owned, and there are accumulations of capital, private and public. Mexico, in common with all nations, has citizens of every type. Her relative percentage of those who are honest, clever, and energetic is at least a matter for close figuring.

The subject of government has been touched upon only incidentally and only as it came under our direct observation. One cannot be long in Mexico without becoming aware that official corruption exists; to what extent I am not prepared to say. When you consider the faults of your neighbor's children—well, no government is thoroughly honest and at least Mexico does not approach the magnificent scale on which American officials accept bribes and practice stealing. She is judged harshly partly because her system is unorganized and therefore personal and partly because many items, which we consider graft, locally are looked upon as perquisites of office. In the last analysis a charitable view is that most of the Americans who complain have burned their fingers overplaying business acumen.

Adios, Baja California. Hasta luego, amigo mio.

INDEX

Abalones, 72, 108–9
Abreojos Point, 117
Agave, 36
Agua Caliente, 3, 15–16
Agua Prieta, 62
Almejas Bay, 129, 130
American visitors to the carnival strip of Lower California bordering on California, 3–4, 13 ff.
Ángel de la Guardia, Isla, 353–4
Ángeles Bay, 353, 355, 356, 357
Antelope, 54, 113, 332
Arnes, Padre, 359
Arranco Cabello, 181
Arrowroot, 68
Asia, early navigators' attempts to find a passage to, 230–1
Asunción Islands, 114–15
Auklets, 73, 114, 116; Cassin, disappearance of, from Los Coronados Islands, 25, 26
Avifaunal study, the goal of, 64

Baja California, see Lower California
Balandra Bay, 223, 226
Balboa, 153
Bald eagles, 27, 44
Ballena Bay, 117
Ballena, Isla, 118
Ballenas Channel, 353, 354, 356
Bass, 338
Bats, 164
Behaviorists, present-day school of, 64
Belding plover, 202, 276
Belding rail, 202–3
Bighorn, 54, 332
Bird habits in protection against birds of prey, 44
Bird Island, Scammon's Lagoon, 79–80
Birds, purpose of field work and study of, 63–5; instinct and psychology of their actions, 64–5, 133–5, 245, 340; numbers of, in given locality, dependent on food supply, 105–7, 285–6; purposes

served by collection and study of eggs of, 115–17; select breeding sites close to the one used the year before, 321; division of labor of incubation and housekeeping among sexes, 340
Blackbirds, Brewer, 275
Blanket-fish, or mantas, 249
Bonita, 119
Boobies, 217, 224, 271–2; blue-footed, 244–5, 273, 274; Brewster, 244–5, 273–4, 374
Brain, difference between that of lower animals and of man only one of degree of reasoning power, 346–7
Brandt cormorants, 115, 139–40
Brewer blackbirds, 275
Brewster booby, 244, 245, 273–4, 374
Brewster egrets, 208–9
Brown, George, 61
Buzzards, 277

Cabrillo, 122
Cacti, 36, 60–1, 68, 151, 163, 164
Cactus wrens, 236, 275, 285, 372
Calamajué, 62
Calamujuet, mission of, 359
California, Gulf of, see Gulf of California
Caracara, 132, 320
Cardinals, 210, 233, 320
Cardónes, or giant cacti, 60–1, 130, 163, 164, 197, 236, 320
Cármen Island, 222–8
Carpinteros, 60, 164
Cassin auklets, 25, 26, 73, 114, 116
Cats, ring-tailed, 183, 197, 202
Cavendish, Thomas, 122
Cayo Islet, 208
Cedars, 86
Cedros Island, 85–7
Ceralbo, Isla, 180–1
Chaparral, 83, 145
Chats, 303
Chinese merchants, 188–9
Cholla, 61

397

INDEX

INDEX

INDEX

INDEX

Natural resources, Mexican attitude toward development of, by foreigners, 49–50, 257–8
Nelson shrike, 132
Night hawks, Texas, 372
Nopolo, 209–10

Oaks, 86
Ocotillo, 145
Old Town, Lower California, 3, 14
Onyx, 61
Orioles, hooded, 275; San Lúcas, 308
Ornithology, purpose of field work, 63–5
Osprey, 44, 73, 81, 88, 130–2, 243, 252, 257, 362; nesting habits, 72
Owls, 68, 132; Sanford elf, 163; burrowing, 243
Oystercatchers, 89, 252; black, 44–5, 81; Frazar, 82, 202, 330–1
Oysters, 196

Palmella Point, 169
Palms, 156, 171, 186, 288, 302
Partida, Isla (Espíritu Santo), old volcano on, 182
Partida, Isla (upper Gulf), 348–53; breeding colonies of Least Petrels on, 348–9, 351
Pearls and pearlers in La Paz Bay, 193–7
Pelicans, 26, 71, 88, 223–4, 244, 273, 362
Peña Colorado, the, 56
Permits required for scientific research in Lower California, 9–11
Personnel of the expedition, 6, 24
Petrels, black, 26, 351, 375; Socorro, 26; Least, 348–9, 351, 375
Phainopepla, 320
Phalaropes, 339
Phœbe, San José say, 105; San Lúcas black, 308
Phosphorescence, 328–9
Pine, yellow, 49
Pinocho, native sugar cane product, 175, 191
Pitahaya, 61
Plants, reason of armament of, with spines, 57–8
Plover, 63, 73, 81; Belding, 202, 276
Point Loma, 22
Porpoises, 329
Port San Bartolomé, 101 ff.
Prairie falcons, 362
Prehistoric man, evidences of, on

San Benito Islands, 89–91; at Port San Bartolomé, 105; on Magdalena Bay, 146; on Espíritu Santo Island, 183; in Concepción Bay, 253
Puerto Balandra, 223, 226
Punta Banda, 44, 46, 53
Pyrrhuloxia, 233

Quail, 49, 68, 210, 252, 275, 333; western gambel, 372–3; California, 372–3

Rails, Belding, 202–3; Yuma, 380
Rats, 183, 184, 202, 272
Rattlesnakes, 271, 272, 364
Ravens, 82, 243, 272, 277, 340, 362
Raza, Isla, 336–7, 341 ff.; Heermann gulls on, 341–3, 345; colonies of elegant tern, 343–7
Raza Rock, 348
Redondo Point, 151
Rio Santa Rosalía, 254
Rock wrens, 65, 105, 243
Rogers, Frederick S., archæologist and photographer, 24; remains of primitive man discovered by, 89–91, 105, 183
Rosarito, 3
Rural life in Lower California, 37–8

Sacramento Reef, 74
Sage brush, 36
Sahuaro, or giant cactus, 60–1, 130, 210
Salicornia, 199, 202
Salina Bay, Cármen Island, 222
Sal Si Puedes Channel, 333
Salton Sea, 387
Salvatierra and the establishment of the first missions, 232, 249–50
San Antonio, trout at, 49
San Antonio del Mar, 55, 61
San Bartolomé, Port, 101 ff.; evidences of primitive man at, 102
San Benito Islands, 85, 87–96, 349; evidences of primitive man on, 89–91; elephant seals on, 91–4
San Bruno, 249, 266, 275–6
San Carlos Bay, 329–31
San Diegan Faunal District, the, 35, 57
San Diego Island, 218, 219
San Estéban, Sonora, 334

INDEX